꧁ꕥ꧂

The Beanery

A Village Named Ormsby

꧁ꕥ꧂

James W. Settle, M.D.S.
Oct. 15, 2003

The Beanery

A Village Named Ormsby

An Orphan's Story of Tough Love, Comic Relief,
and Reaching for the American Dream

By James W. Settle, DDS

Robert D. Reed Publishers ❦ Bandon, Oregon

Robert D. Reed Publishers
P.O. Box 1992
Bandon, OR 97411
Phone 541-347-9882 • Fax 541-347-9883
E-mail: 4bobreed@msn.com
Web site: www.rdrpublishers.com

Designed and typeset by Katherine Hyde
Cover designed by Katherine Hyde

ISBN 1-931741-36-0

Library of Congress Control Number: 2003095127

Produced and Printed in the United States of America

These memoirs are dedicated to my loving family, for their continuing demonstration of affection throughout the years.

Special thanks are due to my oldest daughter, Bettye, for many hours spent typing, editing, scanning, printing, and using her paper, ink, and supplies.

Dear President Clinton, and Honorable Hillary Clinton,
I hope you enjoy this book as much as my dad did writing it!
Happy New Year, 2004!
Sincerely,
Bettye R. Pina
Dec 30, 2003

Acknowledgments

When Hillary Clinton wrote *It Takes a Village*, and Newt Gingrich suggested the reintroduction of orphanages as a way to try to solve the problems of inner-city hopelessness for our young children, it struck me that both of these folks, from opposite ends of the political spectrum, may have been right. For my brother and me, it took an orphan village named Ormsby to provide a safe and secure haven during most of our childhood. This home was not only for orphans, but for many young people from extremely poor families, or for those who were misguided or mistreated, or without hope of leading happy and productive lives. We were fortunate that such a village existed for us.

Of all the thousands of young people who were raised and trained at Ormsby Village, it is my belief that no child remained there for as long as I did—from 1919 to 1936. Nor did anyone else who was raised there receive and take advantage of as many opportunities as were afforded me. And yet, after having culminated my training with more than four years of college education, I joined the Navy and left, never to return—never to revisit my childhood sanctuary, to see my many old friends, nor to thank the dedicated teachers and instructors to whom I owed so much.

Many times over the years, I promised myself that I must someday go back and see which teachers were still around, and if they remembered me. Then two years ago, after sixty-two years had passed, I finally went back to the place where I remembered Ormsby Village to be. It was not there. The only trace of it was the old Ormsby Mansion, where Superintendent George Colvin, and later H. V. Bastin, resided. Weeds were growing through its railings and onto its porches. It looked like a haunted house.

I will always be haunted by the fact that I did not return, even once, to thank anybody: not Mr. Bastin, not Anna Brittain Moss, not Margaret (Turley) Norman nor C. E. Norman, my printing and band instructor; not the Kinsers, Pipers, Graysons, Blanchards, Hayneses or Ballards. I didn't even go back to KMI to thank Col. C. B. Richmond for my scholarship to his wonderful school. Nor did I thank the Ormsby Village officials who chose me to receive the scholarship.

Gone are all of the cottages where I spent endless days playing with other boys. Gone are the print shop, the band room, swimming pool, cannery, and even the "bean tank." I wasn't even able to locate the wooded area, nor the creek where I learned to dog-paddle and where I loved to spend my quiet time. Concrete office buildings, parking lots, and streets now cover the football field and all the farmlands.

The old Ormsby House was a small Kentucky mansion, built back in the 1800s. This ancient home symbolized, to me, "My Old Kentucky Home." Not that I lived in it, but I was a wee part of the human landscape surrounding it. And the words of Stephen Foster now have a special place in my heart, as I paraphrase them: "Gone are the days and the places, where my heart was young and gay, in most cases. Gone are my friends, from the string bean fields, away." Most are gone from this earth, but I can still hear their gentle voices and see their faces, as we made the most of our lot and learned to enjoy being among other kids who had similar, or worse, beginnings and longed for a better future.

I am deeply indebted to the people of Louisville and Jefferson County and to the great board of directors of Ormsby Village, which included H. V. Bastin, A. B. Sawyer, Samuel Freedman, Luther Stein, and about six others. These men generously donated their time and energies to manage the home. A few of us older students were allowed to sit in on some of the meetings of the board of directors. Mr. Bastin officiated most of the time. We were allowed to enter discussions, if we were brave enough or really had something to say. We could also make motions and vote.

It is hard for me to imagine what the fate of my family might have been had we not been cared for by this public facility. Newt and Hillary both were right. Ormsby Village gave guidance and assistance to many thousands of young people who were poor and apparently felt they had no future.

⁂

Of the many people who have helped and influenced me in my life, I would especially like to thank the following:

- Leo Rankin, my Navy and Consairway friend, who donated pictures of the Grumman F3F-1 fighter plane from his "Leo Rankin Collection."

- All the band leaders under whose direction I have played: George Gray, C. E. Norman, John Philip Sousa, Edwin Franko Goldman, Captain Charles O'Neill, L. N. Deslauriers, Eddie Wotowa, Bill Hildebrandt, Don Pellcrin, Maestro Bert Viales, Sylvester McElroy, and Colonel John R. Bourgeois.

- Ormsby Village Leaders: Dr. George Colvin, H. V. Bastin, Anna Brittain Moss

- Kentucky Military Institute President: Col. Charles B Richmond

- Consairway Personnel: Richard McMakin, Richard Mitchell, Kerry Coughlin, Johnny Hann, Lloyd Herring, Capt. Lee Weatherhead, Capt. Bill Keating, Flight Engineer Bob Keefer

- Dentistry Associates: Dr. Clinton Gurnee, Dr. William Franklin, Lois Gumper

- University of Louisville Archivist: Dr. William J. Morison

- Watsonville Band Managers: Jack Lundy, Edward Pio

Foreword

It has been my earnest desire and intention, over the last few decades, to start putting down in script, and then in print, a narrative story of my life, as I remember it. This story includes some early disappointments, and my struggle to achieve some degree of accomplishment. I hope the story will be of interest to my descendants. What a treasure it would be, had my ancestors left such an account of each of their lives.

Before I started writing this account, I hadn't begun to conceive how enjoyable it would become to recall, and then to jot down, all the little things that had happened to me: good and bad, funny and sad. As I write, I realize I am not in a give-and-take conversation with anyone. Nor will I be interrupted or contradicted as I relate what happened to me, as well as I can remember it.

Several friends who have read my original manuscript have questioned the inclusion of lists of names I recalled from the orphanage and military. These names, and many more, are dear to my memory, and I hope their inclusion may be of some interest and historical value to the descendants of these individuals, should they ever see them in print.

I am sure some readers may find the inclusion of the elementary typesetting techniques which we used in the old orphanage print shop, as well as the later description of military aircraft engines and the celestial navigation of aircraft, to be of little interest, and I ask their indulgence. Persons with experience in those lines of work might enjoy these portions of my story.

During this endeavor, at the risk of boring potential readers, I have tried to keep to a minimum any vulgar or offensive words or expressions which were in common usage during my early years, usually in the form of jokes, anecdotes, or humorous limericks. I hope my story will have enough socially redeeming qualities to offset my few, feeble attempts to amuse by using benign, borderline-risqué drollery.

As I read what I have written, I am a little embarrassed by the number of "I"s and "me"s in the text. But it is an autobiography, and I *am* writing about myself. To paraphrase Frank Lloyd Wright, "As I read about my past, I can't decide whether to be honestly arrogant or hypocritically humble."

Contents

PART I

The Beanery

Growing Up in Ormsby Village

❧ Four Score and Seven Years ❧

For the last thirty-two years I have been a tuba player in the World-Famous Watsonville Band of Watsonville, California. Whenever we give free concerts or parades in nearby towns, I often bum a ride with fellow tuba player Dr. Guy Welty, an Aptos, California, dentist. I have been retired from dentistry for fifteen years, but we never discuss dentistry because playing music as a hobby gives us a chance to relax and forget about work. Often, when I'm Guy's only passenger on these trips to other towns, I tend to do most of the talking, about myself and all the things that have happened to me during my lifetime. His reaction to my account of the things I have seen and accomplished was that no one could have lived long enough to experience so many careers. When I mentioned to Guy that someone had said, "Everyone should write his memoirs," and that I was considering it, he looked at me and said with a half-grin, "Well, you had better hurry up." I said, "I'm only eighty-seven, so I have plenty of time." Then I realized for the first time that my life span to that date was exactly the same length as the time lapse between the War of Independence and Lincoln's Gettysburg Address.

According to my birth certificate, "four score and seven years ago," about 60 miles north of Hodginville, Kentucky, the birthplace of the Great Emancipator, my forebears brought forth in this state a new baby, conceived in poverty and dedicated to the task of survival and achievement, during an economically unequal period of time prior to World War I. I never met Mr. Lincoln, but I have heard many nice things about him.

❦ Life with My Family ❧

As a person becomes older, he often thinks back to the past and tries to recall the first things he can remember about his life. Before I was born, my parents moved to Louisville, Kentucky, from the Horse Cave-Glasgow area, where my two brothers and two sisters were born. Brother Garnett was born in 1904 at Glasgow, Kentucky; my sister Bettye in 1906, also at Glasgow; my sister Marie in 1908 at Horse Cave, Kentucky; and my brother George in 1911, also at Horse Cave. My father was a mechanic and at one time worked for International Harvester in southern Indiana.

My father died when I was four years old, and I don't remember him. I can just barely remember living in a three-room house on Lee Street in Louisville, Kentucky, with my mother, two brothers, and two sisters, who were all older than I was. I believe this is the house in which I was born on June 28, 1913. Back then, nearly everyone was born at home in his mother's bed. The doctor who delivered me was D. D. Worden, MD. My mother must have thought well of him, because she named me James Worden Settle, instead of James William after my father. Also, I was nicknamed "D. D." Shortly after my birth, our family moved to Brandeis Street, just a few blocks from my birthplace on Lee Street.

My father died on August 31, 1917, four months after America entered World War I. My mother was just thirty-two years old when our father died, and she was left to raise five young children. There was no such thing as Social Security or food stamps in those days, so my mother had to rely on her ability as a seamstress to support the family. My older sister Bettye, who is ninety-four years old as I write this, recalls how our mother would walk to the streetcar line on Preston Street, ride the streetcar down to near the Ohio River, walk to the river, get on a ferry boat, cross to Jeffersonville, Indiana, and walk to the U. S. Army Quartermaster Depot. There she would pick up material that had been cut on machines into pieces for making uniform shirts for the Army in World War I. She would carry as much material as she could back down to the river, cross back to Louisville on the ferry boat, get back on the streetcar to Brandeis Street, and then sit up most of the night sewing the material into shirts, including seams, collars, cuffs, and buttons. Sister Bettye was eleven or twelve years old and remembers helping sew on buttons. Then Mother would deliver the shirts back across the river and get another load of material for more shirts. The round trip from our home on Brandeis Street to the supply depot covered more than fifteen miles of walking and riding the streetcars and ferryboats.

My mother was a small person, somewhat under five feet in height, but apparently energetic and determined. Bettye remembers that she got one dollar per shirt. Mother also took in sewing from people in the neighborhood. Our relatives down in the country used to say of our mother, "She was poor, but always very proud." This was once considered to be the ultimate compliment among the less fortunate.

I can remember walking to the grocery store with my mother. I would always ask for canned corn, and I can still recall its sweet flavor. I can't think of any other food we ate except biscuits and cookies. I remember my mother making cookies that she would shape by hand into Santa Clauses and Christmas trees and put them into a pan on the stove. Another memory is of using a cold chamberpot at night, but we had an outhouse in the back for use in the daytime. As sister Bettye likes to say, "We had three rooms and a path."

I still have a noticeable two-and-a-half-inch dent and two scars on my forehead that were caused when I was playing with my older brother, Garnett. I sort of remember, but have been told many times, about how I was on our front porch, and Garnett was down on the walk in front of the house. He told me that if I dove off the porch, he would catch me. I was about four years old and he was thirteen. He coaxed me to spread my arms and dive, and I did. But he ran out of the way, and I hit my head on the edge of a brick on the walkway. I can't believe he really meant to trick me into getting hurt. Maybe he didn't realize I would do it. My whole life since that day, I have wanted to fly, but I don't believe that was my first effort to do so. I guess my head looked pretty awful and scared everyone. A bandage was put on my head that covered one eye. To make me feel better, Garnett tied a string on each of my arms, pretending I was a horse, and I was running through the house, with him guiding me with the string. Not being able to see well, I crashed into a bedpost and put a vertical gash in the

middle of my forehead. It took a long time for Garnett to live this
down. We laughed about it for many years after, and every time I shave,
I'm reminded of Garnett and how little time we were given to be
together.

I can vaguely remember taking a trip on the old L&N Railroad
down to Horse Cave, about 125 miles south of Louisville, and then
going by horse and buggy to Bear Wallow and Glasgow to visit our
grandparents. Before we left the house someone boarded up the back
windows. I never knew why, and Bettye doesn't remember that. At
times it seems I can still smell the coal smoke from the train engine and
hear the lonely, moaning sobs of the steam whistle as we chugged
south, through the beautiful tree-covered knob-and-gap country and
the farmlands, with cornfields and tobacco patches.

The only one of my grandparents I remember is my maternal grand-
father, Spotsford Redford. He was a rather short man, with what I
recall as a long, white beard. I remember being on the back porch of a
house, watching someone turning a crank, and a rope supported by
pulleys would haul an old oaken bucket full of water to the house. The
water must have come from a cistern or spring behind the house.

In spite of all the hard work required to support and raise five children alone, our mother still managed to take us to Sunday school and
church service at Eastern Parkway Baptist Church. We have a
panoramic picture of the Sunday School class, taken beside this
church. There are about five hundred men, women, and children in the
picture, which was taken in April 1919. The old-fashioned Sunday-go-
to-meeting clothing everyone is wearing has the distinct style of the
early twentieth century. All the women are wearing their favorite
dress-up hats, many quite stylish. The picture was taken about two
years after our father died. We are all in it. Mother was thirty-four
years old at the time, and looked tired, sad, and old for her years. My
sister Marie was eleven; she is standing next to me. I was five, almost
six years old. George, age eight, is sitting on the ground in front.
Bettye, age thirteen, is sitting next to her good friend Ella Showalter.
Garnett, age fifteen, is over to the right.

❧ Separation ❧

S hortly after that picture was taken, Mother was admitted to the Waverly Hills Sanitarium, which housed mostly tuberculosis patients. We think Mother did not have TB when she was taken there, but was very weak from work, worry, and lack of rest.

When Mother was taken away, the five of us children were picked up and taken to a detention home on Walnut Street. On the way there, brother Garnett escaped from the group because he had a paper route to deliver. We didn't see him again for several years. I believe he went to live with distant cousins. Bettye refused to be separated from Mother and was allowed to live at the TB sanitarium until Mother died, in February 1922, at age thirty-six. Marie was taken in by Aunt Jessie (Settle) and Uncle Joe Gatton.

During the first day at the Detention Home, I felt lonely and bewildered. I have a vivid recollection of the cool, naked feeling of my scalp, after having my head clipped bald by hand-powered clippers. A few moments later, my brother George and I were pointing at each other's heads and snickering. All new arrivals at the Detention Home were given a bath, had their hair removed, and were given a clean pair of rompers to wear. Each boy's hair was kept short and was periodically combed with a small, black comb with very fine teeth on each side. After each pass of the comb across the scalp, the comb was laid in a saucer of coal-oil, to wash out any cooties (lice, or *pediculosis capitus*) that may have been harvested.

George and I slept in a small dormitory on the second floor, towards the front of the old building. I remember at meal time going down the stairs, which had a slick, wooden banister on one side. At the bottom of the stairs was our matron, who always seemed to be holding a bundle of spoons in one hand. As each kid reached the bottom step, the matron would tap him on the top of the head with the spoons. This seemed to be her habitual way of counting her charges. I actually looked forward to receiving those friendly little taps, and am reminded of how little else there was to look forward to in this strange, old building. When the matron wasn't around, we often sneaked a slide or two down the slick banister.

George and I stayed at the detention home for about two years. Then we were put in the Jefferson County Parental Home, which was located about ten miles from Louisville on the LaGrange Road between Lyndon and Anchorage at Ormsby Station, on the Interurban Trolley route between Louisville and LaGrange.

At the Parental Home, there were two fairly large buildings for children. George was about eleven years old and was put with the older boys; I was between eight and nine and was put in a building for younger boys and girls. The two buildings were several hundred yards apart. Between these two residences for children, there was a large house that had the appearance of a Southern mansion. It was known as the Ormsby House, bearing the name of the Col. Hamilton Ormsby family, who had owned the property before it was purchased by the state in 1912. The state had purchased the property, including 360 acres of land, as a home-site for dependent children from the area around Jefferson County. There was a school building there, and I recall being in the first grade when I was eight years old, two years older than the other students, but small for my age. I believe I had gone to another school called Fresh Air School in Louisville, maybe while I was at the Detention Home. At any rate, I was ahead of the other first-grade students in reading and arithmetic, and the next year I was put in the third grade. The teacher was a Miss Kendall, and I remember that she had green hair. She was probably putting something on it like henna, which made it look green when the sun shone on it. Also, I recall a boy we called the teacher's pet. Whenever the teacher noticed a bad odor in the classroom, she would have this boy go up and down the rows of seats, sniffing, to find the "barking spider" or "who cut the cheese." We were at this boy's mercy, because nobody wanted to be embarrassed and sent out into the fresh air.

Our mother was in the TB sanitarium for about three years. I remember being taken to the sanitarium and being allowed to look at my mother as she lay in bed. We weren't allowed to get near her or touch her. She was in a ward with several other bedridden patients. Occasionally she would cough and spit in a little cardboard cup.

I was between eight and nine years old when mother died, and I remember being taken with George from the Parental Home to Louisville, to a mortuary house with a coffin in the front room.

Someone lifted me up so I could see my mother's face for a few seconds, and that is all I remember of the funeral. My sister Bettye was fifteen or sixteen years old at the time. She and Mother had been very close during the last years at the sanitarium, and Mother's death was very hard for her to accept. We other four children had been separated from Mother for about three years, but we still felt a great loss, and couldn't really understand why we had lost both parents while we were so young, or why they had been so young when they died.

❧ Louisville Industrial School of Reform ❧

One night at the Parental Home, the building where George and the older boys were living caught fire and burned to the ground. It was in the wee hours of the morning on New Year's Day, 1923. Everyone got out safely, and they came walking through the snow barefoot, with blankets wrapped around themselves, to the building where I was living with the smaller boys and girls.

A short time after the fire, when George and I had been in the Parental Home for about two years, we were all moved to Louisville and placed in the Louisville Industrial School of Reform. This institution was formerly called the Louisville House of Refuge and was truly a reform school. Many years later, I found out why we were moved to this place.

In an article in the *Louisville Courier-Journal*, one of my future teachers, Margaret Turley Norman, presents a little history of the institutions into which we were placed. She writes:

> The concept of a child-care agency for orphaned and dependent children here dates from 1854, when the Louisville House of Refuge, a corporation, was chartered and, late in the 1850's erected a building later known as the Baxter Building on a tract of land donated by the city of Louisville at Third and Shipp Streets, where the Speed Museum now stands. The building was requisitioned as a military hospital during the Civil War and it was not until 1865 that it was considered to be the date of origin of the

institution. Orphaned and dependent children came in great numbers during the following years and other buildings were added, including a chapel, which later became the Playhouse for the University of Louisville. In May 1886 the name changed to the Louisville Industrial School. In 1888 the Louisville Detention Home at 239-43 E Walnut opened to care, temporarily, for dependent, neglected, delinquent, and other wards of Jefferson County. This childcare facility, the Parental Home and School Commission was established in 1912 when the Jefferson County government bought the 400-acre Hamilton Ormsby farm near Lyndon.

On March 3, 1920, the Kentucky Legislature passed a law consolidating the Jefferson County Parental Home and the Louisville Industrial School into a single institution, the Louisville and Jefferson County Children's Home (later known as Ormsby Village), and created a ten member board for it.

Louisville Industrial School (LIS) was a large institution with several three-story red-brick buildings for boys and girls of different ages, and there were shop buildings for training the inmates: print shop, carpenter shop, plumbing, painting, etc. Again, I was separated from George and put with the little boys, in a three-story brick building called the Pettit Building.

This large institution was located at Third and Shipp Streets, about three or four blocks from where I was born on Lee Street. A thick stone wall, twelve to fourteen feet high, with barbed wire on top, surrounded the whole place. We were told we would only be here temporarily—until a new children's home was built at the old Ormsby Station property. It seems that we remained at LIS for a year or more.

Dr. George Colvin was appointed superintendent of the Louisville and Jefferson County Children's Home in 1923. This is the year George and I, together with all the other children in the Parental Home, were moved to LIS. From 1920 on, the "Home" also included the Parental Home at Ormsby Station and the Detention Home on Walnut Street in Louisville. While at LIS, Dr. Colvin replaced the high, imprisoning stone wall with one of a more trusting, friendly height of three or four feet.

LIS had a baseball team, and rumor had it that Babe Ruth had once come there to demonstrate his hitting prowess. We were also told one of the school's pitchers had gained celebrity by striking out "The Babe." Whether this really happened or not, it gave us something to feel good about.

I have many good and bad memories of the Pettit Building. I can recall while there being on my hands and knees, scrubbing the wooden floors of the large rooms. We used individual kneeling boards to slide along as we scrubbed. Each boy would do a strip of floor about three feet wide. We didn't have gloves to wear and our fingernails haven't been that clean since. We scrubbed side by side, and each boy tried to make his strip of floor a lighter color or cleaner than the next strip. We used stiff brushes, about nine inches long, and brown Fels-Naphtha soap. I also remember sitting in the third-floor window and looking out over the stone wall at the Ford Motor Company sign, on a factory across Third Street.

The matron of Pettit Building was a large, strong woman who was very strict. There were twenty to thirty of us smaller boys in this building, and if the matron hadn't been strict, she would have had a rough time trying to maintain discipline. I was between nine and eleven years old and was beginning to outgrow my timidity. I remember having to go out and cut a switch off a willow tree so the matron could give me a few whacks on my backside. I don't know what I had done, but I was probably acting smart or talking too much. We were often told, "Speak when you're spoken to, and come when you're called."

I learned a trick to lessen the sting of the switch. When the switcher tried to hold me out at arm's length to get a better swing at me, I would snuggle up close to her, under her armpit, to reduce her swing, and it really worked. I think it may have made her feel a little more like a mother and less like a matron. Another thing that made spanking less to be feared was to fold a face towel or a couple of washrags and carefully put them in the seat of the pants, so that they couldn't be noticed. This made the punishment painless.

❧ Our New Home ❧

During the time we were at LIS, a new facility was being built on the grounds of the old Parental Home at Ormsby Station. Again, I quote from the article by Margaret Turley Norman.

> On Feb. 9, 1925, the building program at Ormsby Station was close enough to completion that all the children from the old institution at Third and Shipp Streets could be moved to the new facility at Whipps Mill and LaGrange Roads. By then it was fully staffed and operational, but it was not until 1927 that it was given the name Ormsby Village. The legal name was still the Louisville and Jefferson County Children's Home, and remained so until the dissolution of the last board of managers in the 1960's.

The new home was to have the capacity to house 330 boys and girls. We heard that the boys and girls considered extremely delinquent were sent to a place called Greendale, somewhere near Lexington, Kentucky.

The old Ormsby House was the same as I had remembered it from when we were first placed in the Parental Home in 1921. It was a three-story wooden structure that had the appearance of a Southern mansion, with cast-iron railings on the porches, supported by pillars. The house was on a large lawn of several acres of neatly mown blue-grass. Many trees of all types surrounded it: walnut, chestnut, dog-wood, oak, and maple. For me, it was an elegant picture, representing how the past generations of the Ormsby family had lived in Southern comfort. This house became the residence of George Colvin, who was still the superintendent of the institution.

When we were taken from LIS to the new home, we were amazed to see all the new red-brick buildings. There were eleven brick cottages for the boys and girls. The seven cottages for boys were on one side of the lawn area, numbered 2, 4, 6, 8, 10, 12, and 14. There were four girls' cottages, numbered 1, 3, 5, and 7. I was assigned to Cottage 4 and George was in Cottage 6. African-American boys were put in Cottage 14, which was slightly removed from the other cottages. The term

"African-American" wasn't used in 1925, long before most people preferred political correctness in speech. Several years later a new facility, Ridgewood, was built for the colored children, about a mile from the white cottages, and Cottage 14 was then used for the older white teenagers.

Along a street that ran between the two rows of cottages were three long, two-story brick buildings. One contained schoolrooms and a large auditorium with a stage and a balcony, where convocations, concerts, plays, and church services were held. Another of the two-story buildings held living quarters for teachers, secretaries, and other employees, along with a small jail. The other tall brick building contained a large dining room, a kitchen, and administrative and business offices. Near the dining area were a projection room and a large screen, where we were treated to a one-reel silent movie about once a month or on special holidays. The movie was usually a Western with Wm. S. Hart, Hoot Gibson, Buck Jones, or Tom Mix, or sometimes a comedy with Snub Pollard or Fatty Arbuckle. We really enjoyed the movies. They were a highlight of my early years. (My favorite movie channel now is Turner Classic Movies because it often shows the old silents, and occasionally I'll see one that I remember seeing in the home, seventy-five years ago.)

On the back side of the dining room and office-complex building, at the ground level, stood a large carpenter shop, a car repair shop, and a plumbing shop. In back of the teacher's residence building was a brick boiler-room, which supplied steam heat to the hot-water radiators in all the buildings, including the cottages. Behind the school building was a brick-and-glass shop building that contained a print shop, a shoe-repair shop, a band room, and a large cannery.

We were told the home property consisted of 360 acres. Included were several farming areas, a dairy and horse barn, corncribs, and a barn for farm machinery. There was also a thick, wooded area through which Bear Grass Creek ran.

The eleven one-story cottages were exactly alike. Each had a large living room, living quarters for the matron and her family, a shower room, a locker room, a laundry room, and a dormitory containing twenty to thirty beds in three rows.

The children in each cottage had cleaning details, which included mopping or scrubbing floors, washing windows, waxing the living-room floor, washing the walls when necessary, and scouring out the toilet bowls and sinks. Having to do the cleaning made us more careful not to make a mess. Each of us had his own locker, where we kept what few articles of clothing were issued to us. There was absolutely no clutter. Everyone picked up after himself.

Every Saturday we took showers and got a change of clothing. We were furnished one-piece rompers for the younger boys, and overalls and blue shirts for the older ones. At night before bed, we had a toothbrush drill. We would line up with our toothbrushes, and our cottage mother would squeeze out toothpaste on our toothbrushes and watch to be sure we brushed. I remember Pebeco, Ipana, and Colgate brands of toothpaste. I liked the taste of Colgate the best and usually swallowed most of it.

Though George and I were in separate cottages and had different cottage mothers, we saw each other enough that we didn't really feel separated. I felt a great sense of loss in not being with my whole family, but I think I quickly developed a thick skin or a hard shell that helped me get through the early years. We didn't realize it at the time, but being in a place like Ormsby Village turned out to be the best thing that could have happened to George and me.

During the first few years in the home, we were lucky to have the school classrooms within a short walking distance of the cottages. Our schoolteachers were mostly young, well-educated, nice-looking women who were strict about our conduct, but good-natured and fair. They seemed to be very concerned about helping us get a good education. I especially remember Miss Anna Brittain Moss, who later served as the principal of the school for twenty-five years. She was tall and slender, and always had a pleasant demeanor and a great sense of humor. Once when I entered her office for some reason, she looked at me and said, "Well, good morning, glory." Later, when I left, I said, "Good evening, breeze." It caught her by surprise and I thought she would die laughing. She was my favorite teacher.

One of her assignments for the class was to write a short biography of Roger Bacon, the English philosopher. In my report I mentioned that he taught that there should be no conflict between science and religion. I stated that he did scientific experiments and dabbled in alchemy, but he also became a Franciscan monkey. Feeling a little mischievous, I stuck the little "ey" on the end of "monk." I thought I had written a good report, but when I got it back, it had a B on it. Miss Moss had written in red pencil on it, "Your little monkey business cost you an A." But, knowing her, I'm sure she got a chuckle out of it.

Another favorite teacher was Margaret Turley, who taught for many years and also published the school paper, which was printed in the home print shop. She married C. E. Norman, who was the school band director and was also in charge of the print shop.

The school day lasted from eight to five, with lunch period from twelve to one. I don't remember ever having homework to do. There seemed to be plenty of time during the long day in class to read, write, do arithmetic, have spelling bees, memorize poems, and take tests. In the evenings after supper, and on all weekends and holidays, there was plenty of time for playing traditional kids' games, such as jacks and marbles.

The marbles made of stone were called "gritchies." More expensive ones, made of colorful glass, were called "agates." When we competed in marble shooting, we usually played "for keeps," as we tried to add to our individual collections. Before playing for keeps, we would practice for hours on the technique of holding the marble against the bent thumb knuckle with the tip of the forefinger, and then flicking it with the thumbnail as straight and hard as possible.

To compete for keeps meant that each player would place a given number of marbles in the center of a four- or five-foot circle, drawn on the ground or on a section of concrete walkway. Then, with our best agates, we would take turns shooting at the marbles in an attempt to knock them out of the circle. Each kid could keep all the marbles he had knocked out. We carried all our marbles in our pants pockets, and the kid whose pockets proudly bulged out the most was called a "gritchie griever" by the envious losers.

Another favorite game was called "dainty." We would make a dainty by cutting a piece of an old broomstick or mop handle to about five or six inches in length, tapering both ends to a point. Another stick was used as a club or bat. Usually, two to four kids would play at a time. Each player had his own dainty and a club. One at a time, we would lay the dainty on the starting line and use the club to hit down on one of the pointed ends, which would cause it to jump off the ground. Then the player would hit it with the club as far as possible, down the fairway-like stretch of countryside. This game was a sort of "barnyard golf." After the first hit, which was like teeing off, each of us would go find his own dainty, and this time, we could pitch it into the air and hit it as far as possible with the club.

After the tee-off, we were allowed three more hits. The player whose dainty had traveled the shortest total distance was required to pick up his dainty and hop, on one leg, all the way back to the tee-off area. Or if at any time he felt he was fast enough, he could light out and try to outrun the others. If the other players caught up with him, they could whack him on the butt with their sticks—all the way back home.

Another quieter, more restful game was mumble-de-peg. Almost every boy owned a small pocketknife. The game was played by opening the knife with the longest blade fully extended, and the shorter blade at the same end of the knife half-opened, at ninety degrees to the long blade. The knife was placed on the ground with the short blade pointed downward. The knife was then flipped end-over-end into the air, and a number was earned depending on how the knife landed—which blade or blades it landed on, or if it landed upright, on its back. Each player got the same number of tries, and the player with the most points won. There was no prize for the winner, but the loser had to "mumble-de-peg."

A wooden matchstick or other small peg of wood was pounded into the ground by the nonlosers, who took turns pounding on the peg with their knives until it was buried in the dirt. Then the loser, with his hands behind his back, had to blow away the dirt from the end of the peg, or use his chin or lips to help remove enough dirt to allow him to get hold of the peg with his teeth and pull it out. Whenever I lost, I was additionally handicapped by my short upper teeth and jutting mandible.

If the mumble-de-peg loser was unable to remove the peg, or preferred not to try, he was generously offered the alternative of biting a "road apple" in two—which wasn't too bad, if it wasn't a fresh one.

Another after-dark, before-bedtime game we played was called "fly, sheepie, fly." It was a little like hide-and-seek, but it seemed to involve a lot more running, which helped wear us down. After we had washed our hands, feet, neck, and ears, we were ready for a sound sleep in the cottage dormitory.

In the mid-1920s, we would play pitch-and-catch for hours at a time, using makeshift balls that we designed and made from scraps of cloth and rubber bands. No real baseballs or gloves were available. Our football was a tightly rolled bunch of towels, which we tried to shape like a football. This was before a sports program was started for the older boys and girls.

The thing that I remember most vividly about living at Ormsby Village is how we improvised ways to pass the time during the long summers, holidays, and weekends. We couldn't leave the home property, and we didn't have a cent to spend, anyway. There were few, if any, books to read, and we didn't even have a daily newspaper. Kids played together much of the time, but there were many hours and days when each kid had to be his own best friend.

I recall how convenient it was to have large pockets in my rompers or overalls. They not only held my pocketknife and marbles, but I often carried a good supply of hackberries and pieces of sassafras roots, which I could chew, or boil in a can down by the creek in the woods to make sassafras tea. I used to empty the saltshakers from the table in the dining room into my pocket, and use the salt on tomatoes from the farm. Or I could always find some other kid to go with me to the potato field, where we would dig under a potato plant with our hands until we each found one. We would wipe off the dirt on our pants and peel the potato with our teeth, and with a little salt it was delicious. We could also go to the horse-corn crib and pull two or three ears out from between the boards of the crib, shell off the kernels into a gallon tin can, take it to the woods by the creek, and parch it on a small campfire. Then our pockets would be filled with parched corn for a couple of days.

When I was one of the older boys, I had access to the storeroom by the kitchen and the large refrigerators. My pockets always held plenty of dried peaches, apricots, apples, and pears, as well as cornflakes, puffed wheat, or puffed rice. On a birthday or special holiday, we could sneak out a gallon of ice cream. A large amount of food was always kept in the storeroom, so what we took was never missed. It seems we were always nibbling on something, in spite of the fact that we were well fed in the dining room. A dietitian ensured that we had a well-balanced meal. It seems we were fed a lot of canned spinach, cabbage and turnips from the farm, as well as string beans, peas, hull-outs, butter beans, tomatoes that we canned for winter, sauerkraut and weenies, and most of all, dried beans: navy beans, black-eyed peas, and lentils. We ate so many beans that the home was called "The Beanery" and the water tank beside the cannery was called the "bean tank." The home was called "The Beanery" for as long as I can remember.

Our apparent obsession with nibbling was probably normal for young boys with time on their hands. Besides having nothing to read, we had no radio to listen to, and this was long before television was invented. In the mid-1920s, for one dollar, we could buy a crystal set receiver with earphones. By plugging into an electric plug and wiggling a little whisker on a small crystal, we were able to find a spot where we could hear the closest radio station. Sometimes, by moving the whisker around, we could even find a second station. When we were all in bed we could lie there and listen until late into the night.

> And the night shall be filled with music,
> And the cares that infest the day
> Shall fold their tents like the Arabs,
> And as silently steal away.
>
> —*from Longfellow's "The Day is Done"*

One of my favorites on the crystal set, late at night, was "Billy Jones and Ernie Hare, the Interwoven Pair," an advertisement for Interwoven socks, which were popular back in the 1920s. They told jokes and sang songs like, "We call each other Heel and Toe. We're happy-go-lucky wherever we go." As you can see, we were quite easily amused. But in the middle of the night, when we were supposed to be asleep, we kids considered this "electronic marvel" to be a great comfort. Other late-night favorites were Rudy Vallee, The Hoosier Hot Shots, Guy Lombardo, and Fred Waring. We were sometimes allowed to sit on the floor around a real radio in the cottage mother's living room and listen to Amos and Andy as well as Fibber McGee and Molly.

We spent a lot of time down in the woods along Bear Grass Creek. It wasn't long before we had dammed up a suitable spot in the creek and had us a swimming hole about twenty feet across. Many happy hours were spent there during the summer months, learning to dog paddle in our BVD underwear. There were never any adults around, so sometimes, to keep our BVDs dry, we would skinny-dip, which seemed to be more fun. But I worried that a crawdad might nip me in the wrong place. I needn't have worried, because the water was cold and the bait would have been hard to find. There were hundreds of crayfish along the banks of the creek and some grew to be quite large, but we didn't know at the time that their tails were edible, or we surely would have found a way to eat them. I used to eat a lot of little wild cherries from trees in the woods, as well as wild grapes and mulberries.

We used to pick quart jars full of wild blackberries. Someone heard that you could make wine from blackberries. This seemed like a fun thing to try to get away with. We knew we would need a lot of sugar, so several of us emptied part of the dining-room sugar bowls into our pants pockets; we came up with about a pound and a half. We had picked four quart jars of berries. We took about two inches of berries out of each jar and poured the sugar on the berries to the top of each jar. We didn't mix the sugar into the berries; we just let it sit on top. Then we tied a rag over the top of each jar. Each of the cottages had a crawlspace under the floor at the side of the building, which made a perfect place to secretly store our juvenile attempt at making moonshine. Someone decided that our "mash" should be squeezed out in about four months, around Christmas time. We had a lot of laughs among the four of us who were involved in the project as we waited until school was out for Christmas vacation. I crawled under the cottage and located the jars where we had placed them, on a two-by-four ledge above the foundation. The jars were covered with spider webs and very dusty from wind blowing through the air spaces. I got the jars out and took the rag covers off. The berries were covered with mold. I scraped off about an inch, down to the berries. We found a clean rag, squeezed out the mash from the four jars, and got about half a jar of juice. It tasted pretty good and each of us took a couple of sips. We put it back under the cottage and made it last two weeks.

Over the years, many of us long-time residents became very good friends and experienced many good times together. We had lots of advantages that kids in the cities didn't have.

Several of the staff at Ormsby Village had been trained in their trades at the old Louisville Industrial School, where they had spent years as inmates. We admired them for their abilities and considered them to be surrogate parents. It seemed only natural that much of the droll humor of the past should be dribbled down from the LIS alumni to us present villagers. We were told by one of the male supervisors that if, after urination, you shook it more than three times, you could be accused of playing with yourself and could become a nervous wreck, stutter, go blind, or even grow hair on the palm of your hand! When a new boy joined our cottage, it didn't take long before we could exchange jokes with each other. Inevitably, he was told this and would immediately sneak a look at one of his palms. His reaction would also tell us whether he was right- or left-handed, or maybe even ambidextrous.

We learned of things that had happened in the past, concerning both war and peace. We had bad thoughts about Kaiser Bill and his soldiers with spikes on the top of their helmets, but we were proud of the memories of Alvin York, Eddie Rickenbacker, and General Pershing. When we sang "Nearer My God to Thee" in convocation, we thought of the sinking of the Titanic. We were told this was the song the fifteen hundred victims were singing as the ship went down. Though the tragedy took place one year before I was born, it still occupied our thoughts occasionally, along with the saga of Floyd Collins and his fatal entrapment in a Kentucky cave.

I can still recall tales of the feuding Martins (or Hatfields) and McCoys, "the reckless mountain boys." We were also told how the mean "Revenuers" harassed the poor hillbilly "moonshiners." We laughed as we repeated what a young mountain boy supposedly said: "Shoot him high, Pappy, I want his pants."

As I became an older teenager, my thoughts turned to sports activities and the accumulation of the names and records of legendary greats in all the sports. This was long before Babe Ruth was first awarded the obscene salary of ninety thousand dollars per season.

❧ The Staff ❧

George Gray ran the print shop and started the band, which he directed, and he was also the disciplinarian of the older boys.

C. E. Norman later took over the print shop and the band, which he directed until his death about twenty-five years later. Mr. Norman was a terrific cornet player, and it was rumored that he once auditioned for Sousa's band.

Gilder Grayson operated the carpenter's shop, which made some furniture, supplied the cottages with screen doors, and built shelving and other items as needed. Mrs. Grayson, Gilder's wife, was a cottage mother at a small boys' cottage, and their daughter, Wanda, also lived at the home with her parents.

Charles Lehring was one of the supervisors of boys and was our scoutmaster for a while. I still have merit badge cards signed by him. His wife was a cottage mother and their son, Chick, lived with them in their apartment in one of the cottages. Chick was in our scout troop and played trumpet in the Ormsby Village Band. Even though he lived with his parents, he went to school with us, joined in all the home activities, and was considered one of us.

Charley Haynes was the business manager and purchased all the food and other supplies for the home. He also had learned to play the saxophone at LIS and would accompany the band on trips as a musician and chaperone.

When we were transferred from LIS to the new Louisville and Jefferson County Children's Home facility at Ormsby Station, George Colvin was the superintendent. Mr. Colvin was very popular with all the staff, and all of us kids greatly admired him. He was a handsome, well-built man in his late forties or early fifties, prematurely gray and quite distinguished looking. When there were convocations in the school auditorium or chapel, he would give inspiring speeches in which he would tell us of some of his experiences. He could keep us spellbound telling of humorous and sad moments he had endured. Sometimes everyone in the audience had tears in his eyes when he finished talking. Each talk also had a good moral lesson in it. Everyone at the home was sad when Mr. Colvin was selected to be president of the

University of Louisville, which was now located at the old LIS grounds. Some of the old brick buildings of LIS were used by U of L for college classes.

Mr. Colvin's secretary at the home was Margaret Lavin, a very pretty young lady. He took her to U of L with him when he left. Shortly after Mr. Colvin became president of U of L, he suddenly passed away in July 1928. The cause of death was a delayed appendectomy. It was a sad day for all of us at the home who knew him.

I have just learned from the *Encyclopedia of Louisville* that George Colvin had attained celebrity as the captain and quarterback of the famous Centre College football team of 1898. This team, from Centre College in Danville, Kentucky, also produced All-Americans Bo McMillan and Red Roberts, we were told. It was also rumored that this team had beaten Harvard, the erstwhile pigskin powerhouse of the late 1890s. We felt good, and a little proud, to know that little Centre College had been considered to be the best team in the whole country. Probably because of his modesty, we were not aware of Colvin's football fame, or that he had once made an unsuccessful bid to be the Republican candidate for governor of Kentucky, or that he had served as Kentucky's Superintendent of Public Instruction.

H. V. Bastin replaced George Colvin as Superintendent of Ormsby Village. His previous position was as warden of the state penitentiary at Frankfort, Kentucky.

Mr. Bastin and his wife and three children lived in the old Ormsby Mansion, which had been occupied by the Colvins. The Bastins had two sons, Charles and H. V. Jr. The H. V. stood for Henley Vedder, which might explain why he was always called H. V. There was one daughter, Marjorie, who was a large girl and quite pretty. Mrs. Bastin and the children were almost reclusive and had nothing to do with the home, or with anyone living or working there. In the four or five remaining years that I was in the home, I never saw Mrs. Bastin once, even though I passed by the house many times. Their children attended school in Anchorage, up through high school. Anchorage was down the road a ways, and they had a car for private transportation.

Mr. Bastin brought many changes to Ormsby Village, especially in the way disciplinary problems were handled. He used a system of conduct slips to keep a record of each child's behavior. There were good conduct slips and bad conduct slips. These were kept in a file, which was used to determine whether a child should be granted certain privileges, such as being allowed to go visit relatives in the city, or even to have relatives visit the home. It was also considered a privilege to work in the shops, play in the band, or make band trips. Mr. Bastin instituted an incentive program to encourage good behavior. We would be called "Citizens of Ormsby Village." If we had a clean record for three months, we were awarded a Certificate of Honor. I still have a certificate that I have saved from 1927. It states:

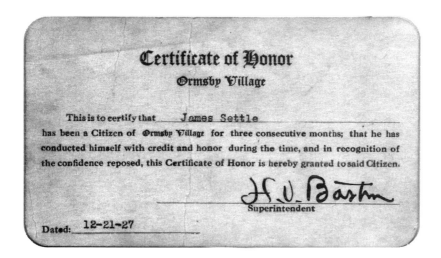

When Mr. Bastin came from the penitentiary, he brought a Mr. Miller with him to assist with delinquency problems. Mr. Miller carried a pistol on his hip, in full view for all to see. He walked with a severe limp, and we were told he had an artificial leg. We used to kid amongst ourselves that he carried the pistol to discourage any kids from running away, knowing that he couldn't catch them on foot. He seemed to be friendly enough with kids like me, who weren't about to get into trouble anyhow. He and his wife and stepson, Richard Colson, lived about a half-mile down the road towards Anchorage, in a house belonging to the village property. Richard was a large, strong young man, very likable and friendly for what we considered an outsider. He was a star fullback at Anchorage High School and often assisted our football coach, Mr. Borders. He taught us how to maneuver when carrying the football, how to spin just before or during a tackle, and lots of other tricks, such as how to hold the ball, how to shift it from one side to the other, and how to avoid fumbling during a tackle.

My brother George hated the new system of conduct slips. He always said that if and when he ever did anything wrong, he wanted to be punished right there and then and have it forgotten, not on his record. I agreed with him there. But with the large increase in the population at the home, I can understand that some sort of system had to be used to keep track of where everyone was coming from and what their problems were.

Brother George was always at odds with Mr. Bastin and couldn't wait to get out of the home. They sent him to Ahren's Trade School in Louisville to take a class in sheet-metal work. He didn't finish high school at the home and was told that if he could get a job away from the home, in the city, they would let him go. The driver of a dry-cleaning truck got acquainted with George and got him a job where he worked.

George was now free, and never had much good to say about Ormsby Village except for his association with George Gray and with his best friend among the boys at the home, Jimmy Cox. Jimmy was a good trumpet player in our band. George played clarinet. Jimmy got acquainted with a Mr. Coogle, a druggist and drugstore owner from Louisville, while the Ormsby Village Band was on a Louisville Board of Trade booster trip. Mr. Coogle offered to take Jimmy in and put him through pharmacy school. He graduated, worked for many years as manager of a store, later bought out Mr. Coogle, and became a well-known Louisville druggist with two stores. He and George remained very close to the end of their lives.

William Blanchard, also called Bill or Pete by other adults, was one of the supervisors of boy's activities and started a Boy Scout troop in 1925. Mrs. Blanchard, his wife, was a cottage mother. When the scout troop was formed, I was twelve years old. Brother George also joined at age fourteen. I was in the Scouts till I was eighteen and advanced to the rank of Eagle Scout. Many of the merit badges were easy to get because of the shops that were available to use any time we asked. Merit badges in printing, music, and bugle-playing I received automatically, because I worked in the print shop and played in the band. I was also the bugler for our Boy Scout troop. Carpentry, plumbing, and swimming were also a cinch. Mr. Blanchard taught us the use of the compass and triangulation in map-making. We learned Morse code and how to signal both with the telegraph key and with a flashlight, and how to make and use a helioscope. Morse code messages could also be sent using a large flag on a pole, which was dipped to the right for a dot and to the left for a dash. This was called "wig wag." Semaphore signaling was done with two smaller flags, one in each hand. Each letter of the alphabet was represented by a different position of the flags. The U.S. Navy has used semaphore signaling extensively for years. We practiced these signaling methods for hours at a time and became quite proficient at them.

Carpenter Gilder Grayson showed us how to use the square, planes, and chisels, how to plane boards flat and square, and how to make dovetail joints with a dovetail saw and hand chisels. This was one of the requirements for the carpenter merit badge. Irby Grayson helped us in the plumbing shop. The plumbing merit badge required measuring, cutting, bending, and threading different sizes of pipe and using joints and unions.

A large new swimming pool was built in 1926 or 1927. It was about 30 feet wide and 65 or 70 feet long. It had a 3-foot diving board and an 8-foot high dive. We were required to use the shallow end of the pool until we qualified for the deep end by diving off the low diving board and swimming at an angle to the shallow end. Because of our previous dog-paddling experience in the swimming hole in the woods, I believe we all qualified for the deep end on the first day the pool opened.

George Kinser became our swimming instructor and later the scoutmaster. Mr. Kinser was a large, heavy-set young man who had experience as a long-distance swimmer and had been an Eagle Scout. His merit badge sash was filled, front and back. He was intelligent and good-natured and became a good friend of the older scouts in the troop. Mrs. Helen Kinser was a cottage mother, and their young daughter was called Baby Helen. I used to carry Baby Helen around on my shoulders; I still have a picture of the two of us together. She seemed like a baby sister to me. When I was in my teens, Mr. Kinser used to let me drive his car, or one of the Model-T Fords belonging to the home, to take him and some of the other boys to town on his business errands. I don't remember having to get a learner's permit or driver's license back then. About 1929 or 1930, Mr. Kinser participated in a wintertime long-distance swim between the U.S. and Canada, up in the Great Lakes area. In preparation, he coated his whole body with a dark grease to keep his body heat in. He did well in the competition until he got bad leg cramps and had to drop out. Also in 1930, he enrolled at U of L in premed, and later graduated from U of L Medical School.

George Gray was supervisor of boys, under George Colvin, when we moved from LIS to the new home. He was comparatively short, with a strong and wiry build, and could run like a jackrabbit. He was able to maintain strict discipline among the two hundred or so boys, about one-third of whom were sent to the home by the courts as delinquent or antisocial. His reputation for being a tough little guy was all it took to make most of us "toe the line." But I recall seeing him demonstrate his unique style of reprimand. If a boy were caught doing an unthinkable thing, such as having a cud of chewing tobacco lumping out his cheek and trying to spit like a big-league baseball player, like Ty Cobb or Tris Speaker, Mr. Gray would approach him and say, "Heah, Simp," or "Heah, Boob." Then he would use the inside of his wrists to hitch up his pants, á la James Cagney, who was not yet in the movies. Then, when he got near to the boy, like a flash, he would give the boy a left-right slap to the sides of the head, followed by a swift kick to the lower part of the body. He was both feared and respected. He was fair, and friendly if he knew you were following the rules. Cottage mothers would seldom need to discipline the older boys. George Gray was readily available if they had a problem with anyone.

Mr. Gray ran the print shop, and I was assigned to work there when I was almost twelve years old. When he started the band, he let my brother George join and started him on the clarinet. A short time later, I was allowed to join, and I started practicing on the E-flat alto horn. We also called the alto horn the "peck-horn," because we usually just pecked out the after-beat notes. The bass horn was the "oom" and the alto horn was the "pah," or "pah pah," depending on whether we were playing two-quarter or three-quarter time. I don't remember ever having a music lesson per se. We were given a horn and a piece of paper with the fingering instructions for use of the valves. We started out learning to play the scales, including the chromatic scales. The more we practiced blowing, the better the sound we made. We learned all the musical nomenclature and phrases as time passed. We could take our horns to the cottages and practice as much as we liked.

During our not infrequent meals of beans and weenies, it was only natural that the kids in the Beanery band would recite, snickering at the old ditty:

> Beans, beans, the musical fruit,
> The more you eat, the more you toot.
> The more you toot, the better you feel.
> Now you're ready for another meal!

When the band was first started at the new home, the practice sessions were held in the living room of one of the cottages. The first pieces that we practiced were quite simple, and George Gray demanded very close attention to our playing in unison and in perfect tempo. He was impatient when we didn't play up to his expectations. He often directed with a bass-drumstick that had a padded ball at one end, which was screwed to the stick with a washer and a round-headed screw. He would walk around between the musicians or behind them, and if someone was playing out of tune or off beat, he would tap them on the top of the head with the drumstick, in time with the music. Sometimes he would throw the drumstick from the front of the band at someone in the back, in the drum section. On one occasion he threw the stick very hard at a drummer, who dodged out of the way. The drumstick hit a wooden ceiling-support post, making a dent about a quarter of an inch deep, which was still there when I left the home. Once, my brother George was sitting near the front of the band when Mr. Gray heard a squeak from his clarinet. He tapped George on the top of his head, and the screw head scratched George's scalp; blood ran down his forehead. George said he hardly felt the tap, but it must have really scared Mr. Gray. From that time on, he treated George like a son. He would let George go to town often, and even gave him spending money.

When George Gray left Ormsby Village, he married Nell Smith, one of the girls at the home. We heard he inherited a ranch near

Lubbock, Texas, from a relative. Years later, I visited them while driving cross-country with my sister Bettye. They had a family and seemed quite happy, and surprised to see us.

❧ Band Trips ❧

C. E. Norman replaced George Gray as the band director and was also in charge of the print shop. He also got his training in music and printing at the LIS. With Mr. Norman as director, the Ormsby Village Band made several trips with the Louisville Board of Trade, on what they called booster trips. I'll never forget the first time I was allowed to go on one of these annual trips. The purpose of these trips was to improve or give business a "boost" throughout the state. The trips lasted about one week and were made during summer vacation. We traveled on a special fancy Pullman sleeper train of the L&N Railroad. It had a coal-burning engine, and its noise and smoky smell reminded me of the time we went down to Horse Cave with our mother, before she became sick. It is hard to describe the pleasure I felt the first time I climbed aboard the train. It was in the late afternoon. We carried on what little luggage we had, put it on our seats, and went directly to the dining car, where dinner was waiting. We sat four at a table, and most everyone ordered prime rib or T-bone steak, mashed potatoes with lots of butter, gravy, peas, and rolls. For dessert, most of the kids ordered chocolate sundaes, which we could hardly eat because we were already stuffed.

When we went back to our Pullman car, the seats that had been there before had been converted into upper and lower berths, or beds, all made up with beautiful sheets, pillowcases, and a light blanket. The smaller kids were assigned to the upper berths, and I was glad, because it was fun climbing up and peeking out through the curtain opening at people walking past below. Climbing down to go to the restroom during the night was an interesting experience. We could go barefooted because the aisle had soft, thick carpeting.

The next morning in the diner, for breakfast, we were told we could order anything we could think of. Most of us kids started off with strawberries and rich cream, which we had every morning thereafter, to the end of the trip. We then could order Kentucky ham or sausage, eggs, fried potatoes, waffles, or anything we wanted—things we hardly ever had at the home. The waiters and porters treated us royally and were very kind and friendly to us, probably because they knew we were enjoying a once- or twice-in-a-lifetime experience that would only last a week. When we returned to the Pullman car, our bunks had been converted back to seats, and we sat and enjoyed the scenery, which was beautiful.

These booster trips were made to different county seats in Kentucky, and once to Peoria, Illinois, just across the Ohio River. On another trip, we went into northern Tennessee. We were a small band, so on the two trips that I remember, Mr. Norman, our director, invited three of his musician friends from the old LIS band to come on the trips, giving the band more volume and a much better quality of music, especially on parade. Their names were Klein, on clarinet, Klotz, on baritone, and Tilford, on bass (tuba). Charley Haynes, the home's business manager, also went along with his saxophone. Mr. Norman on trumpet, together with these four other adults, gave us what we considered an awesome sound.

The first booster trip I made took us to county seats in eastern Kentucky, starting at Ashland, then south through Appalachia, to Paintsville, Pikeville, Hazard, Harlan, Middlesboro, where we visited Cumberland Gap, then to Barberville, and Corbin.

At each county seat we visited, the train stopped at a spot not too far from the city hall or courthouse. The band would form at the front of the group of boosters. Alben Barkley was then a Kentucky Senator and was always on these booster trips, together with the other state senator. I also remember that A. B. Sawyer, head of the governing board at Ormsby Village and also a well-known and much-admired business-man in the Louisville-area farming business, never missed a trip.

Another memorable booster was a Mr. Schopenhorst, who was quite jovial and friendly. The president of Belknap Hardware and many other business notables went on these trips, and we felt honored to be a part of them.

The boosters seemed to enjoy themselves immensely and were always in a good mood. In fact, many of them were "feeling no pain" by the time they lined up behind the band for the parade to the court-house, usually during the hottest part of the day. They each carried a large umbrella with alternating red and white sections and large block lettering spelling out, "THE LOUISVILLE BOARD OF TRADE."

Our drum major would blow his whistle, give a downbeat to the drums, and start us marching down the street, or sometimes a gravel road, toward the courthouse. We usually played Sousa or Karl King marches, and I remember it as a proud moment when I heard the great sound, which was somewhat augmented by the adult musicians among us. I was hooked on playing in a marching band, and I still love it, seventy-five years after I started marching in the Ormsby Village Band. We marched along the streets towards the city hall for the pur-pose of attracting the townspeople to hear welcoming speeches, and always a great speech ad lib by the greatest speechmaker I have ever heard, Senator Alben Barkley.

There were times during the march when the band would stop play-ing to give our lips a rest. Then some of the fun-loving, noisy boosters would start singing their favorite marching song, to the tune of the Iowa State Song. They changed the words, but as I remember, it went:

> We're from Louisville, Loooisville,
> Though the country's dry
> We don't have to cry
> 'Cause we're from Loooieville, Loooieville.
> There's where we moonshine still.

If the singing boosters became too loud or rowdy and were an embarrassment to the group, some of the more sensible and sober boosters like A. B. Sawyer would quiet them down. But for us kids, their antics made the trip more fun and gave us something to laugh about between trips, and a reason to look forward to the next one.

Roy Robinson was one of the older students at the home. He attended Anchorage High School and won several oratorical contests in the county. He was the tuba player in the Ormsby Village Band on my first booster trip. He was a big, friendly, fun-loving kid who enjoyed smoking cigars, when he could get one; but we weren't allowed to smoke, even as older teenagers. On the trip, Roy must have gotten a cigar from one of the boosters, who were very friendly to the band boys. There was an observation car on the train where we could go, sit alone, and watch the scenery go by. The windows were kept open for fresh air. Roy always kept his tuba mouthpiece with him, so he would know where it was and it wouldn't get misplaced. Also, he could put it to his lips and buzz, or blow into it, to improve his embouchure, or lip muscles. Once, several of us were sitting, watching the scenery go by, and Roy was smoking his cigar. He had the cigar in his mouth and was holding his mouthpiece in one hand, and patting it into the other, when Mr. Norman came through the door of the coach, and walked toward Roy. Roy was petrified. He very quickly removed the cigar from his mouth, with his right hand, and threw the mouthpiece out the window with his left hand. He was in double trouble. He was not only caught smoking, but the expensive mouthpiece had to be replaced with a new one, which Mr. Norman had to go find at a music store at the next town. I remember it cost as much as two or three dollars, which was a lot of money in those days.

After the booster trips, it always took a while to settle back down to the harsh reality of being just one of a large group of nondescript, institutionalized orphans seeking somehow to stand out and be recognized. Traveling on the train to all the little towns and being with such a friendly group of people—the porters, waiters, businessmen, politicians, and musicians—and being treated as special made me realize that there was another world outside the Beanery. I believe I realized, though, that life outside the home would not be just a bowl of creamed strawberries, band music, and a plush Pullman berth.

❦ The Print Shop ❦

Having a chance to learn printing and being in the band were advantages I never would have had if I had been reared elsewhere. George Gray ran the print shop as well as the band. I was eleven years old when I started in the print shop, and twelve when I was allowed to start in the band. In the print shop, Mr. Gray started me out as an "ink devil." My job was to clean the ink from type after it had been removed from the press, at night or after a job was complete. I also had to climb on a stepstool and use rags and a solvent to clean ink off the disc and rubber rollers of the small, electric hand-fed press. The press was easier to clean if the ink wasn't allowed to dry overnight. I also kept the floor clean and learned to pick up and store things that weren't being used.

Next, I was given a short demonstration of how to set type, and how to distribute it after it had been used and cleaned. I had to use a wide stepstool when setting or distributing type, because I wasn't very tall at that age. The pieces of type were placed in a "stick," which was a small tray with an adjustable side that allowed the line to be the exact width of the column to be composed. For example, a newspaper column was usually twelve or thirteen ems wide. (An em is the width of the lower-case letter "m" in a given type and size.) An average size of type for newsprint was ten points. (A point is about $1/72$ of an inch.)

At first, it was hard to pick up the small pieces of type and put them in the stick in the right position, with the letter upside-down and facing toward the top of the stick. A nick on one edge of each piece of type helped the setter to place it in the right position. Each letter had its own boxed-in space in the typecase, and it didn't take long to learn the location of each letter, and to compose words into lines to fill the stick. The lead-type words were separated by spacers of different thicknesses, so that a line of type could be made to fit snugly into the stick. Polysyllabic words could be hyphenated to help control the length of the line. Lead slugs the exact width of the line added space between lines (hence the term "leading"). Each piece of type was picked up by the fingers of the right hand, twisted or spun around with the fingers, and placed in the stick. The left hand held the stick, and the left thumb held the type as it was placed in the line.

The capital letters (caps) were in the lower right quadrant of the typecase in straight alphabetical order, except for J and U, which were added to the end of the alphabet at some time in past history.

When the stick was full, with each line of type fitted snugly, the type had to be transferred to a special tray called a galley, where it was made secure and put in a proof-press. Then a copy was printed to check for errors and make changes as necessary. Removing the composed type from the stick was a delicate procedure, where one wrong movement could ruin hours of work. If the composed type wasn't held properly, with pressure on all sides, the whole group of lines could collapse and fall to the floor. Hundreds of pieces of scrambled type, called "pied type," would be scattered underfoot. I've seen this happen, but fortunately, it never happened to me. It's almost considered a calamity. If the face of a piece hits the concrete floor, the soft metal type could be ruined. After each piece of type is examined for damage, it has to be cleaned and redistributed. Pied type takes four or five times as long to distribute as does composed type. Usually the pied type would be set aside and distributed when work was slack.

When the page of type has been composed, proofread, and corrected, it is ready to be put in the press for producing copies. It is locked into a metal frame, or chase, by means of various sizes of wooden blocks and metal wedges, called quoins. These are tightened by putting a key with teeth on it between the two tapered wedges, with the teeth on the inner edges, and turning. Before putting the frame and type in the press, the ink must be applied to the rollers, evenly and in the right consistency. Ink is put on a disc, which rotates a few degrees each time the press goes through a cycle. Two or three rubber rollers pass over the disc and pick up the ink, and it is distributed evenly over the rollers and over the whole surface of the disc. The frame with the type is turned on edge and locked into the press. Now, when the press is started, the rollers pass over the type and spread ink evenly. The paper to be printed on is placed on a bed, against stops that are pinned to the paper padding on the bed. When the blank paper is in place, the press is started. A lever is pulled, and the bed with the blank paper tips over and is pressed against the type. The bed is slightly soft, which allows the face of the type to be pressed against the paper; if the pressure is correct, and the ink is of the right consistency, a nice, clear impression will be made. If there is too much or too little pressure, paper padding can be added, either to the bed or under the type in the frame; or padding can be removed, if pressure is too great. When a good impression is achieved on each try, and the impression is properly positioned on the paper, you are ready to start feeding the press by hand, removing the printed sheet and placing a blank against the guides with each cycle of the press. The speed of the press is controlled with a foot pedal. If the blank sheet of paper is put in crooked or is not put in, the lever that controls the press must be pushed back, so the type won't print on the bed. If it accidentally prints on the bed, the wet ink impression has to be removed by wiping over it with a rag and talcum powder. If all the ink isn't removed from the bed, it will show up on the back of the next few sheets printed.

As mentioned before, C. E. Norman took over both the print shop and the band when George Gray left. Mr. Gray was there for about two years. I printed under Mr. Norman for four years, until I was graduated from high school. This experience helped me get a scholarship, along with three other boys, to the Southern School of Printing in Nashville, Tennessee.

Mr. Norman taught us how to use the large paper cutter to cut reams of paper into letterhead size, or into sizes for book or magazine pages. We printed a lot of letterheads, as well as calling cards, for use by the home. I remember standing for hours at a time on a stepstool, feeding letterheads or calling cards into the press. It was necessary to be very alert. If the paper wasn't placed properly against the guides, one had to be sure to push the lever and not try to grab a paper or card out of the press. One boy got his hand smashed pretty badly by taking a chance or being careless.

When I left the home, I had many fond memories of the hours I had spent in the print shop. Next door to the print shop, and separated from it by a wire see-through partition, was the shoe-repair shop. The shoemaker was a little man with a slight German accent, who greeted me each time I came into the print shop with little German phrases, which I later realized were: *Wie geht es Ihnen* ("How are you?"), *Guten morgen* ("Good morning"), and *Ich danke Ihnen vielmals* ("I thank you very much"). He worked there for the six years that I was assigned to the print shop, and I still miss seeing the friendly little guy. His name was Mr. Brady, but for some reason the kids called him "Dad Bradford." He lived away from the home and parked his nice Pontiac sedan alongside the shop building. I can still see the Indian-head radiator cap at the front of the hood.

❧ Discipline ❧

It is important to mention something more about the subject of discipline at Ormsby Village. I was there for twelve years and have a good remembrance of how the place was run. This was not a dark, dirty, dingy Charles Dickens type of institution, run by sadistic low-lifes who broke the spirits of the little orphans. I knew most all of the older boys in the home, and couldn't distinguish the so-called delinquent ones from the dependents, such as George and me. Almost half of the older boys were sent there by the courts for being unruly or antisocial. They soon learned to fit in with the rest of us. All the smaller boys were considered to be dependents, because they weren't big enough to be very bad. Having so many things to do also helped a lot.

I had many good friends among all the boys in my cottage. Some learned to get along and follow the rules as a result of running into George Gray, the boys' supervisor. They learned early of his reputation, but a few had to be convinced. Mr. Gray never had to use a belt. After he left the home, there were times when I saw evidence that adults had used a belt to strap the palms of some boys—they had swollen wrists and forearms where the end of the belt had overreached the palm. The skin was slightly raised and was dark red and blue in color. I remember seeing the leather straps that were used. They were cut from old, thick pulley belts from farm machinery, and nailed to a wooden handle. I also recall seeing a device called a cat-o'-nine-tails, which was a belt cut into nine strips and fastened to a handle. This was used to flail the seat of the pants, or the bare bottom and legs.

In the twelve years I spent at the home, only two or three times did I see evidence or hear of anyone being whipped. Just the thought of these implements of punishment being available was enough to make us toe the line, and things ran smoothly. "Spare the rod and spoil the child." There were no spoiled children at Ormsby Village while I was there. We learned to get along, work together, and take advantage of the many opportunities given us.

Long before modern psychiatry invented the phrase "obsessive-compulsive behavior," we kids were doing benign little things, such as adjusting our strides to avoid stepping on a crack or a division in the concrete of the sidewalk. We would warn ourselves with, "Step on a crack and break your mother's back." Or if we came upon something dead or rotten, a fresh manure pile, or anything icky, we would spit over our little finger, and say, "Not on my mother's table." These were innocent little superstitious things everyone did, without a second thought. But I would always recall that I no longer had a mother, and would sometimes get a lump in my throat. Having lots of kids around, many with sadder backgrounds than mine, eased the loneliness caused by the loss of my parents and the separation from my older brothers and sisters.

At the age of eight or nine years, I was, understandably, quite timid. I can remember a very large and popular teenager named Marvin Hughes, who was, maybe, fifteen or sixteen years old. He apparently sensed my extreme insecurity and on several occasions would say to me, "Gee, you're ugly." I knew he was trying to see if I would cry. I never did. I just smiled at him, and took comfort in the thought that he was even uglier than I was. I thought of the other kids, both boys and girls, as being members of one big family. Only once or twice during my twelve years as a resident of the Village did I see or know of a fist-fight or scuffle between two boys. I kept in good physical shape by running around the expansive area between the cottages and the woods. I always had the feeling that anyone I couldn't "whup," I could outrun.

Sister Bettye would come out from the city as often as she could, on the old Interurban La Grange Trolley, to Ormsby Village to visit George and me. I got the feeling that she was very close to us at all times, even though she lived over ten miles away; in those days, that seemed like a far distance. She would bring us candy, which was a real treat. There was no candy at the home and we had absolutely no money, anyway. I remember that Bettye once brought me a new red sweater, and once a pair of Union Hardware roller skates for a birthday or Christmas. Almost no one at the home owned a pair of skates, and I don't remember ever seeing a bicycle there. I used those skates to go everywhere, and after a while, I could do some pretty fancy maneuvers on them. I wore them almost to the point that there was no metal left on the wheels. And then I pulled them apart and nailed the two halves of one of them to the ends of a two-foot-long two-by-four. Then I nailed on a three-foot-long upright, put handles on it, and I had a scooter that lasted several months before it finally fell apart.

❧ Scout Camp ❧

One of the big advantages of being in the Boy Scouts was that we got to go to the scout camp for two weeks during the summer break. The Louisville Council of the Boy Scouts of America operated the camp, and they allowed Ormsby Village to send a patrol each summer. The camp was located at Covered Bridge Reservation in Oldham County. It was a great experience away from the home. The food was bland, but wholesome, and activities were well organized. There was a dam across a small river, upstream from where the covered bridge crossed. We had swimming classes and meets, and there were canoes that we could use to practice for the canoeing merit badge, and rowboats to paddle during the balmy summer evenings after supper. There were knot-tying contests and instructions in first aid, bandaging, and artificial respiration. This was fifty years or so before CPR was introduced.

The more adventurous scouts enjoyed an activity called "hunting for the lairs of the hodag." The leaders of the camp were Big Chief Thornton Wilcox, a Louisville physician, and Little Chief Craig. They were both big, husky individuals who were highly ranked in local scouting circles, and were greatly admired by all of us. It was Little Chief Craig who created "lairs of the hodag," which were secret little caves or niches in rocks, or a hole in a large, dead tree trunk. Many of these were located along a big gulch in the woods called Gimme-gash Gully. Finding each lair required getting a slip of paper from Little Chief Craig with instructions for finding the starting point for the first lair. Here, directions were given for using the compass and sighting in a given direction, with a pair of binoculars or a small telescope, to find something like a jutting ledge of rock, a knothole in the trunk of a tree, or the top of a lone sycamore tree across the river. At each of these spots, directions were found for spotting the next hiding place. After finding three of these locations, the next one might say, "You have found Lair #1. Congratulations!" Here, there were also the instructions for finding the starting point for Lair #2. There were several lairs to be found. Going between the different points of each lair required much hiking, climbing, and sometimes swimming. We were lucky if we could find more than one lair in a day. Anyone who found all the lairs was rewarded with an Indian arrowhead stenciled in red enamel on his brown, webbed scout belt.

Another highly prized belt stencil was the White Shark. This was awarded to any scout who, every day during the camp session, would follow an early morning routine of springing out of his bunk at the first note of "Reveille" and rushing down to the assembly area for roll call. Then, after dismissal, he would dash along the riverbank to the swimming hole, remove his shorts, dive naked into the cold water, and swim across the river and back. For each of the two years I was permitted to attend the camp, I was able to earn the White Shark, and proudly wore them on my belt for several years.

My fondest memory of scout camp was going to the little camp store after supper, buying a Bit-O-Honey candy bar, going to the boating dock, getting into a rowboat, pushing out into the quiet stream, and just relaxing, to the sound of frogs, crickets, an occasional cicada, and the trickling sound of the water as it escaped over the dam. Some nights there would be a large campfire, and we would listen to ghost stories, sing scout songs that were new to us at first, and at the last campfire, each patrol would put on a little skit, for which we had prepared during the two-week stay. I have thought of Covered Bridge Reservation many times during the last seventy years, with a feeling of nostalgia and gratitude to the scouting organization for the great memories.

After returning to the Home from Boy Scout Camp at Covered Bridge Reservation and readjusting to the reality of institutional confinement, I would often drift off to sleep at night with pleasant memories of overcoming the challenges of the hunt for the lairs of the hodag along Gimme-Gash Gully. And I'd recall the wholesome camaraderie enjoyed at the campfire gatherings, where we joined with the scouts from the city to sing songs with silly lyrics.

Wali-Ga-Zhu was the name given to the annual jamboree for Boy Scout troops of the Louisville Council, Boy Scouts of America. It was held in the large armory building in downtown Louisville. All of the scout troops in the area would compete for trophies or ribbons. Large audiences would come to watch the individual troops face off in contests of knot-tying, chariot-racing, fire-starting with friction or flint-

and-steel, and first-aid bandaging techniques. These events climaxed in the most popular event—wall-scaling.

For several consecutive years in the early 1930s, our team from Ormsby Village Troop #113 would break the existing speed record for wall-scaling. I was a member of the first record-breaking team. A team of eight scouts was required to scale the vertical side of a nine-foot-high wooden wall, assisting each other in any way possible. Then they would slide down the sloping back side of the wall and run across the finish line. Our team would beat the second-place team from the city by at least ten seconds every year.

Our team was so successful at this wall-scaling that the envious city scouts would sometimes hint that we ought to be good at climbing walls because we were from the reform school. This only caused us to try harder the next year. We often felt the stigma associated with being confined in a charitable institution. We knew we were poor, but with each wall-scaling victory at the city armory, we, like my little mother before me, were very proud of our hard work and perseverance.

❧ Merit Badges ❧

During my late teenage years, I spent considerable time trying to increase my collection of merit badges. Twenty-one were required for earning the Eagle Scout rank. There were five or six that were compulsory. One that wasn't compulsory, but was quite a challenge, was archery. In order to earn a merit badge in archery, we were required to make everything we needed. The scoutmaster, Bill Blanchard, was able to order a bundle of about six yew wood staves from Brazil. We were given a picture and a blueprint, showing the dimensions for trimming the stave to the proper shape. The taper at each end had to be precise, to ensure that the bowstring had sufficient pull to project the arrow a great distance. We were allowed to use the carpenter shop and such tools as the drawknife and the spoke-shave. After sanding the bow smooth, we could paint our name or some design on it, and finish it with several coats of varnish. Next, we made the bowstring out of

waxed linen thread, which we wove or plaited into a strong cord. We
were given dowels for making arrows. There were metal tips to glue
onto one end of each arrow. We used chicken feathers, which we split
down the middle, cut to three inches in length, and glued to three sides
at the back end of the arrow. Then we cut a notch for the bowstring to
fit in. We wrapped the middle part of the bow with heavy cord for the
handgrip, and varnished it. We made a target out of oilcloth and put it
on a bale of hay for shooting practice.

We used to play a game called archery golf. A target was placed on a
tree or fence at each "hole." The targets (holes) were several hundred
yards apart, so a "hole-in-one" was impossible. The number of shots
needed to hit each target was added to get the final score. My bow was
pretty, but never as strong as I thought it should be, so I thought I
could make a stronger one. I found a limb on an Osage orange bush
that looked big enough; but it was only about four feet long when I got
it cut off and removed the branches. I shaped it the way I thought it
should be and put a bowstring on it. It was so stiff I could hardly pull
the string more than a foot away from the bow, but the arrow would go
about half again as far as with my Boy Scout bow. So I usually won at
archery golf. I also got the archery merit badge.

I thought maybe I could use the bow and arrow for hunting rabbits.
There were many cottontail rabbits around the fields and the woods
area. I made a sharp arrowhead by taking the blade of a broken kitchen
knife and cutting it to the right length. Using the grindstone to make a
sharp point, I notched the back end of the blade and tied it to an arrow.
With my Osage orange bow and the sharp arrowhead, I was ready to
hunt. Several of us would go to a field that had a fenced-in corner. We
would spread out and walk toward the corner, and often could get close
enough to a trapped rabbit to get a shot. After many tries, the closest I
ever got to getting a rabbit was once when I found some rabbit fur on
my arrowhead. Thinking back, it's a wonder that one of us didn't get
hit in the excitement. Another time, while hunting alone in the
wooded area, I hit a rabbit. It kept running, and I searched for a long
time and never found my prized arrow. Maybe I was lucky to get rid of
it, but I often wonder what happened to the rabbit.

❧ Lucky Lindy ❧

In 1927, the big event that had us all excited was the solo crossing of the Atlantic Ocean by Charles A. Lindbergh, at age twenty-four or twenty-five. When he returned to the States he made a tour of the country, stopping at some of the larger cities and giving speeches at the airports.

I was fourteen years old at the time of Lindbergh's flight and was in the Boy Scouts. Our scoutmaster arranged to have our troop, in uniform, transported to Bowman Field in Louisville, the day Lindbergh was scheduled to arrive there. We were very excited as we watched the skies and waited for what seemed like hours. Finally, a little speck appeared, and somebody yelled, "There he comes!" The next minute he was circling the field, and he made a smooth, three-point landing. The applause and cheering were earsplitting as he climbed up the steps of the wooden platform that had been constructed for him. There were also many other Boy Scouts there, in uniform, and he seemed to be talking directly to us in particular. The speech was short, but made a big impression on us. It included something like setting a goal for yourself and sticking with it. I sensed that we all wanted to be pilots after that. It was hard to realize that we had actually gotten to go from the home to see Lindbergh.

A year or so after the Lindbergh flight, I had the opportunity to take my first airplane ride. Our scout leader, Mr. Kinser, was driving back from Louisville, and as he passed Lyndon, he noticed at their small airport an old Taylor Craft sitting by the road. A sign near it advertised rides to the public for a special rate of a dollar-fifty a person, or three dollars a couple. Mr. Kinser asked some of the older scouts if they were interested in going up in a plane, and four of us jumped at the chance, but some of us didn't have a dollar-fifty. Mr. Kinser lent us the money. Mr. and Mrs. Kinser took the first flight, and then Charlie Seitz and Butch Sosnin took their turn. They all seemed to be happy to be back on the ground, but apparently enjoyed it.

As "Red" Rafferty and I climbed aboard the old plane, I saw what looked like bailing wire holding something together. The aileron hinges looked a little rusty, but we had seen the others take off and land without a problem, so we just knew it would be safe. The takeoff was a little bumpy, but the flight was actually quite smooth, and I was glad we had invested the money. During the short flight, I was able to see the Kentucky Military Institute barracks building and Ormsby Hall, the administration building, and the Ormsby Village cottages off in the distance. The landing was surprisingly smooth. Our ride was a little longer than the others, for the reason noted below. One of the scouts, "Red" Rafferty, wrote an article for the home's monthly periodical, which I am sure I hand-composed in the print shop:

> Recently, a group composed of Robert Rafferty, Hershel Sosnin, Charles Seitz, Mr. and Mrs. Kinser and James Settle, made a trip to the Lyndon Airport for an airplane ride. The rates were especially low that day: one dollar and fifty cents per person, three dollars per couple. It was the first trip taken in an airplane by any of the group, and each was thrilled in a different way. Robert Rafferty and James Settle were taking their hop when an aviator made a parachute jump, from one of the Lyndon planes. The pilot circled the scene of action, and the boys rode two minutes more than the nine minutes allowed.
>
> One week after the excursion, the plane in which the party rode was condemned as unfit for service. The boys all heartily appreciate the fact that they were not condemned to destruction at the time of their ride.—R. Rafferty.

❧ The OV Bus ❧

Sometime in 1927 or 1928, Ormsby Village got a bus for hauling kids around to events away from the home. I recall a trip to Mammoth Cave with the scout troop. That was a great experience. We also took trips to Lincoln's birthplace and other historical spots. Later, the bus hauled high school students to Anchorage High School, which was closer than schools in Louisville. The football team was transported to games in nearby towns.

I spent many hours on that bus. It was a little strange-looking, and we thought it looked like an antique, compared to other school buses. It was just a tall, perfectly rectangular wooden box, with the engine in a smaller, square metal box on the front. I believe the engine was a White. For seating, there was a long, lightly padded one-foot-wide board running lengthwise on each side. It was about fifteen feet long. A padded board, for the back, ran the full length, under the windows. In the center of the bus, there were two padded boards, for two rows of people, sitting back to back, with a padded backboard between them. All of the backboards were straight up and down, perpendicular to the seat board. Needless to say, nobody got any sleep on the bus.

❧ The KKK ❧

Once, in 1928, the Ormsby Village Band was taken to Shelbyville to march and lead a parade of the Ku Klux Klan. I had heard the name, but didn't know anything about them. Shelbyville was a very small community a few miles east of Ormsby Village. We lined up on the main street, which was more like a wide road. The KKK Grand Wizard, or whatever they called him, was on a beautiful white horse. His flowing, white robe, with what I believe was red embroidery, seemed almost to reach the ground. And he had the familiar, pointed hood with the small eyeholes. The hoods were worn when the members wanted to conceal their identity. The other Klan members had different-colored robes, and it was a colorful sight. The parade was a short one, and I can't recall what marches we played. I don't remember anyone ever discussing that parade, and I have no idea who authorized using a boys' band from a publicly supported home to march for the KKK. There may have been some repercussions, but back then there was still complete segregation of the races, which I never understood, and any one of the officials could have agreed to let the band do the parade.

I remember feeling that I was considered to be "po' white trash," but I only resented the word "trash," because the rest of the phrase was obviously true. Nowadays, I brag to members of the Watsonville Band that I'm the only member who once played under the baton of the

"March King," John Philip Sousa, but I've been hesitant to mention that I'm also the only member who ever played in a band leading a Ku Klux Klan parade.

❧ More on Discipline ❧

When there are 250 to 350 juveniles, both dependent and delinquent, collected into one facility for the purpose of care, training, schooling, or rehabilitation, there is a need for strict discipline, regimentation, and restriction within certain boundaries. Yet during my years at Ormsby Village, I found that, within my confinement, I actually enjoyed more freedom to do more things and go to more places than most kids living in the city, or outside the home, could imagine. Within this huge, unsecured, rural area of Jefferson County, our free time was without any visible supervision, and we could roam through the farmland and barns or down into the woods, to play with the crawdads and minnows in Bear Grass Creek and swing on vines hanging from the sycamore trees. Or we could lie or sit on the ground under a shade tree and watch chicken hawks soar high over the farm area. And I often played with a little "doodle bug" that would burrow into soft, sandy dirt, leaving a smooth little funnel of dirt about an inch across at the top, and reaching a perfect point at the bottom, about an inch deep. When I saw one of these, I knew there was a "doodle bug" down in there, since no other bug, to my knowledge, acted this way or left such a distinctive indication of his whereabouts. To try to get him to come out, I would get down on my hands and knees, put my mouth down near the hole, blow lightly into the funnel, call out in a high voice, "Doodle bug, doodle bug, here doodle bug," and blow again. After about the third blow he would come out, look around, and then dig back in. Then I wondered why I had disturbed him. I was trying to be his friend, but he didn't seem to be interested.

I remember chewing a lot of sour grass (oxalis), which was plentiful in the fields, and I would pick off honeysuckle blooms, pinch off the little hard bulb at the bottom, and slowly pull out a tiny stem with an enlargement on the top, which would pull out a wee drop of sweet nectar. Or I could break off a wide blade of grass, stretch it out between my thumbs, which were pressed together to hold it tight, and then blow against my thumbs, and it would squeak a musical note. This was more fun, and a little more dignified and socially acceptable, than producing the highly suggestive notes we could evoke by putting the left hand under the right armpit and pumping the right arm rapidly against the ribcage.

When I recall that I actually performed all of these inane activities, and many more that I don't dare to admit or can't recall, I realize that each of us had his own quiet, little space where he was free to reflect on past events, and to try to imagine what the future might bring. Thoughts of the lofty stone walls at LIS and of the bars at the Detention Home reminded me of the last verse of a poem by British poet Richard Lovelace.

> *To Althea, from Prison*
>
> Stone walls do not a prison make,
> Nor iron bars a cage;
> Minds innocent and quiet take
> That for a hermitage;
> If I have freedom in my love
> And in my soul am free,
> Angels alone, that soar above,
> Enjoy such liberty.

❦ Village People ❧

Most vivid among my earliest recollections are some of the older children, almost adult, who stood out from all the others. I remember Paul Flanagan, a tall, good-looking young man who had lost his left arm up to the shoulder in an accident in the pump-house, under the large, elevated water tank. He seemed to have adjusted well to the loss. He excelled physically and was an excellent baseball pitcher. I can still visualize his pitching to George Colvin, with George Gray ready to run for Colvin when he hit the ball. I was twelve or thirteen at the time.

From this same time, I remember Zelma Miller, a tall, nice-looking young lady who was being sent on a bus to Louisville Girls High School. When she graduated in 1926, she became a cottage mother. She later married Harold Haynes, who worked at the home. This was in 1928, my first year of high school. The Hayneses left the home and Harold became a lawyer. Zelma returned to the home four or five years later, with two small children, and was a cottage mother for many years.

Some other older teenagers I remember were Marvin Hughes, Russell Griggs, trumpet player Chester Clark and his singing sisters, Ella Mae and (I think) Thelma, who often sang on radio station WHAS. Then there was Fred Marmilott, who had a badly infected right leg that would not heal. There was a deep, wide trench that extended almost from the knee to the ankle. It was always heavily bandaged, but, without the advanced drugs of today, the condition never seemed to improve. Fred was the baseball team pitcher after Paul Flanagan left the home. I could never understand how his right leg could support his entire weight when he leaned back to start his delivery. Fred's younger brother, Charles, was in the Ormsby Village Band for many years, and later with some of us in the National Guard Band.

Sometimes, all the children of one family would be in the home at the same time, scattered among several cottages. I have fond memories of the large Ware family. There were Frances, Ruth, Homer, Freddie, and Jimmy Ware. Then there was the Peters family, consisting of John, Mike, Mary, and Sammy and their first cousins, George and Tony Grady. The Peters family and the Gradys were dark-complexioned, and we were told they were of Syrian ancestry. I can remember visiting a tiny hamburger-hot dog stand built into the corner of a large and very old brick warehouse, on Market or Main Street at Preston or First Street. I believe it was owned by the father of the Gradys. I don't remember ever getting a free hamburger or anything. If I had, I'm sure I would never have forgotten it. I vaguely remember John Peters was a boxer, and I know Mike later owned a print shop in Louisville. Mary Peters graduated from Anchorage High School and later became a nurse at Louisville City Hospital.

I remember a nice family of girls named Simmons. There were

Marie, Henrietta, and little Beulah, who was as cute as a doll. The Metcalfe boys, Orville, Lawrence, and James, were all musical. Orville was solo clarinetist in the band when we went to Flint, Michigan, for the National High School Band Contest. He did a great job performing the solo cadenzas in the "Light Calvary Overture." He, on clarinet, and Lawrence, on the baritone, won local solo contests in competition with musicians from other high schools in the area.

❦ Puppy Love ❦

In the early years (1925–31), Ormsby Village had a strict policy of complete separation of the boys from the girls. The girls' cottages were about one-quarter mile from the boys' cottages. I knew many of the girls' names from being in the same classes at school and in Sunday school. As we matured, so to speak, we older boys would try to guess which boy had his eye on which girl. As I recall, until I was a mid-teenager, I must have believed a girl was just a soft boy. The first girl I was ever interested in was named Marie. She was at least as tall as I, and was a healthy, well-proportioned young lady.

At first, I really thought of her as a sister or cousin. I was fourteen and fifteen years old during this early sort of infatuation. Gradually, the thought of her as one of my relatives changed as we started holding hands, on the sly, when no one was around. At times, if I was lucky, we would end up sitting side-by-side in the auditorium at church service. Each older child in the home had his own soft-backed hymn book. Marie and I had a little secret thing going with the names of some of the hymns. If the title was "Jesus Loves Me," in my book, over the name "Jesus," I would write, in tiny letters, "Marie." Now it said, "Marie Loves Me." In her book she wrote, "Jimmy Loves Me." "What a Friend We Have in Jesus" and many other hymns got the same treatment. We weren't being sacrilegious. It was just an innocent little way of expressing mutual affection on these rare occasions.

Most of the time, while sitting in church during the service, we managed to hold hands, secretly, under one of the hymn books. This must have been our way of attempting to reach out and belong to someone, and it helped pass the sometimes lonely days and months in the home. It gave me something to hope for and to look forward to on weekends. And during the week at mealtimes, I could spot Marie at her assigned chair in the huge dining room, and feel good all over when she returned my smile.

After about two years of what some jealous kid described as our "puppy love," one night Marie was practicing with a group of students for a musical performance, in a second-story classroom next to the balcony of the school auditorium. I knew of the practice session and I was outside the classroom on the balcony, listening to the singing. During a brief recess, Marie came out and saw me, and I held her hand as we talked until she had to return to the practice. We put our heads together and sneaked a quick peck on the lips. I think we both were in a state of shock after this totally unexpected, but welcome, transgression against whatever there was to be transgressed against.

Marie was a favorite of the supervisor of girls at the village. She had noticed Marie and me together. It was her opinion that I was too small and backward or timid to be interested in one of her nice, big girls. I heard a rumor of a little social get-together that the supervisor had arranged in her living quarters. She invited another, larger boy to the event in hopes that Marie would lose interest in me. It didn't work, but I got so jealous about the incident that I did not speak to Marie again for several years. But I believe I secretly thought she was too good for me anyway. She eventually was graduated from Anchorage High School and U of L.

❧ Holidays ❧

During all my years in the orphanage, from the very first years on, I remember how much I looked forward to the school holidays, especially Easter, the Fourth of July, Thanksgiving, and Christmas. At Easter time, we always did the customary dying and decorating of eggs, several hundred of them, which would be hidden on the large, tree-studded lawn area near the Ormsby Mansion, where the superintendent lived with his family. After the Easter religious services, about one hundred or so kids of all ages ran onto the lawn area, and before long each kid had two or three eggs. If someone got too many, he shared with the smaller kids. We always had salt in our pants pockets for the eggs. I liked seeing Easter come, because it meant it would be getting warmer, and soon we could go barefooted till late September. The Fourth of July meant a band concert, in which we always played "Stars and Stripes Forever" and other Sousa marches, and George M. Cohan tunes like "Yankee Doodle Dandy." Then there were barefoot races on the big lawn and watermelon-eating contests. Thanksgiving meant a few days out of school and, of course, turkey and all that goes with it.

Christmas was the holiday I looked forward to most of all. I would get the old copies of the *Courier-Journal* after the cottage mother threw them out. I'd go through them and cut out every picture of Santa Claus I could find in the want ads, and by Christmas time, I would have a huge stack. For Christmas tree decorations, we would make a chain from half-inch loops of red and green paper, alternately looped together, until we had a chain long enough to go around the tree five or six times. Then we strung popcorn onto long strings and draped it around the tree. A few handmade paper ornaments and a star on top finished the tree. We didn't have electric lights, and we didn't dare use candles.

A few days before Christmas, we would go to the stocking bin, where all the long black stockings were kept. These were worn with knickers on special holidays, for church services, or when we went to the city on a visit. I would find the longest stocking in the bin and stretch it to make it longer and fatter. On Christmas Eve night, we would hang the stockings on the metal tubing that formed the foot rail of our beds. Then we would try to stay awake as long as it took for Santa to arrive. We spent what seemed like hours, hoping, listening, and watching the windows, to see if we could hear sleigh bells or get a glimpse of Santa. We never could stay awake all night, and Christmas morning we would always find an apple, an orange, a banana, a handful of hard rock candy, and a handful of mixed nuts, and that was all. Everyone got exactly the same amount. But year after year we went through the same routine of stretching the stocking. We made the goodies last as many days as we could. I can remember even eating the orange peel and the banana peel. That was Christmas. George and I always got a card with money in it from my sister Bettye, and candy and a gift. Most kids got nothing except what was in the stocking. We learned that the main purpose of Christmas was to celebrate the birth of Christ and not to get a bunch of goodies.

During my stay at the home, the cottage mothers were mostly Protestant Christians, but for about two years, I had a Catholic cottage mother. The Protestant cottage mothers had us memorize many Psalms and the Beatitudes and some other Bible verses, as well as all the books of the Bible, Old and New Testaments. The Catholic cottage mother added the Apostle's Creed, Hail Marys, and special emphasis on the Lord's Prayer and the Twenty-Third Psalm. The Presbyterian influence had us singing the Doxology and going to the meetings of the Christian's Endeavor.

❦ Grade School Graduation ❦

It was in June 1928 that I graduated from the eighth grade at Ormsby Village. It was a proud day for the class. We were congratulated by the superintendent, Mr. Bastin, and all the teachers. My sister Bettye was there, and she gave me a five-dollar gold piece. I remember that it was about the size of a dime, and very shiny and pretty. It was like a small fortune back then. I also recall that one of the teachers, Virginia Yont, and her husband wanted to take me as a foster child to work on their small farm. I remember that she was a very pretty young woman and seemed very friendly. I was flattered that they picked me, and a little bit tempted to agree to go with them, to get out of the home. But sister Bettye didn't like the idea, and we didn't know if the couple would continue my education, or if they just wanted a hired hand to work on the ranch. Leaving the home would have taken me from all the friends I had made, and away from the print shop and the band, the swimming pool, and the athletic teams that I had become a part of. Also, I didn't realize that in six months, I would be in the running for a very important scholarship.

As I recall, organized athletics started at Ormsby Village around 1927. Football and basketball teams were formed. There was a new gymnasium that had a boys' and a girls' locker room, a shower room, and wooden bleachers on each side of the court. About fifteen or twenty boys reported for the first basketball practice, and it was a completely new experience for all of us. I was fourteen or fifteen years old and had never seen a basketball. We were allowed to try to dribble and shoot at the basket. I was about 5' 6", so I had to rely a lot on being fast and perfecting my shooting ability. There were enough players at first to form two teams, and we played against each other. The first year of basketball was strictly intramural for both the boys' team and the girls' team. In the late fall of 1928 we got our first experience of playing a team from outside the home.

The Kentucky Military Institute was just about four miles down the road toward Louisville. We had always heard about the great teams of KMI. Their first team played in a league with all the larger high schools in the northern part of the state. The president of KMI needed competition for his third team, and our coach thought it would be good experience for us, so he selected some of us who showed the most promise and formed a sort of team. We practiced for about a week, trying to get a few tricky pass plays perfected. We played the KMI team one Friday night. Everyone at the home attended, because word got around that we were playing KMI, and everyone knew of its reputation. It didn't seem to matter that we were only playing their substitutes. There were about three hundred kids and adults from the home in the gymnasium. The girls had organized a group of cheerleaders just for this one game. We had never had a cheering section before, because we had never had outside competition.

When the game started, the cheering was continuous. Everyone cheered loudly when either team made a basket. Sadly for our team, almost all the baskets were made by KMI. The final score was something like 53 to 15. When it was finally over, the cheerleaders gave the KMI team another cheer for winning. The KMI President, Col. Charles B. Richmond, who was there with the KMI team, was so impressed with the spirit of the Ormsby Village kids that he offered a scholarship to a boy from the home to attend KMI as a student.

When we first heard of the scholarship offer, I thought I might have a chance, because I had good grades in school, and Miss Moss seemed to like me. I was a patrol leader in the Boy Scouts. I was on the basketball team and football team. I was in the band, had worked in the print shop for about three years, and was getting to be a good typesetter and pressman. I had also been in the home longer than any other candidate and was an orphan. The head of each department or activity had a vote. Everyone voted for me except the girls' supervisor, who thought I was too small and too timid to represent the home.

I was glad they chose me, but I didn't know how it would be, mingling with boys from well-to-do homes. I needn't have worried, because I found that many of the KMI cadets seemed to have had some problems at home, or their parents were glad to have them in a boarding school away from home, where they could be supervised and guided in the right direction. This was a fine old institution, with a reputation of turning out many men who would become prominent in business and in the military.

❧ KMI ❧

My scholarship at KMI began in January 1929, the start of my second semester as a freshman. I had finished the first semester at Ormsby Village. Previously, the school program at the home only went through the eighth grade. Older students who were still wards of the home after finishing the eighth grade were taken to Anchorage High School, which was a few miles from Ormsby Village. The Interurban Trolley car also passed between Ormsby Station and Anchorage. There were very few of the high school students and they were trusted to go to Anchorage alone.

On my first day at KMI, during their semester break, I was met by Col. Richmond and Major Charles Hodgin, the headmaster. They fitted me with a uniform, which was of a blue-gray wool material. I noticed in the school catalog that the cost of the uniform was listed as $150 for a paying student.

The uniform consisted of:

1 English-style coat, or blouse	1 regulation sweater
1 pair straight trousers	2 black neckties

2 pairs fatigue breeches	1 black leather belt
3 gray shirts	1 KMI buckle
1 Pershing style cap	2 pairs white duck trousers
1 military overcoat	2 pairs white gloves
1 pair black regulation shoes	White webbing and buckles
1 pair black leather puttees	

All the parts of the uniform were supposed to give service for at least a year, and some of it for a much longer time.

Fixed charges for going to KMI were $800 per school year, which included tuition and admission to lectures, room, board, laundry (twenty-two pieces a week), military instruction and use of military equipment, bugle instruction, and medical care at the school, including services of the school physician and school nurse and the use of the medicines and equipment of the school infirmary—in cases of ordinary illness or injury treated at the school. Also included were athletic coaching, uniforms, equipment, and the use of the grounds and gymnasium.

The total cost of being a military cadet at KMI for one school year was $950. My scholarship included everything except breakfast, supper, and lodging.

Kentucky Military Institute had been established in 1845 and was the oldest private military school in the United States. It was a highly regarded school because of its great scholastic program. It was accredited to Harvard, which, back in the 1920s, was the ultimate goal of many high schools, and it had a fine ROTC program of military training. The school's slogan was "Character Makes the Man." In marching formations called close-order drill, we used the old Springfield .30-caliber rifles from the World War I era. The Professor of Military Science and Tactics (PMS&T) was Capt. Robert W. Norton, U.S. Army, retired. We spent many hours in close-order drill and practicing the manual of arms. During dress parades I was in the marching band playing trumpet, and in my senior year, I was playing BB-flat bass (Sousaphone).

Being a day student at KMI, each day I had to walk about four miles from the home to KMI and, after school, back to the home. The walk was along a little country road. In the wintertime, sometimes the snow got pretty deep. But if I walked on the road in the car tracks, it wasn't too bad. I was very well bundled up in the wool uniform, with a heavy sweater and leather leggings or puttees over the legs of the military-style fatigue breeches. Also furnished was a heavy overcoat that almost reached the ground. I also had a muffler, a wool stocking cap, and gloves.

At the home, each weekday morning of the long winter months, after a quick breakfast of cornmeal mush, oatmeal, or cornflakes in the dining room, I would finish bundling up in my warm, woolen uniform in the Cottage 4 dormitory. Then I was out the Ormsby Station entrance and starting my lonely trudge down LaGrange Pike, past the bare pastures and leafless oaks and maples. If I were lucky, I might see a snowbird or two, or a lone chicken hawk.

On one such cold day, as I approached the KMI gate, I quickened my steps to beat the starting time of my first class, in which I could slowly thaw out. Now each breath produced a steamy cloud, and I was thinking of my English Poetry assignment, which seemed quite timely. I was required to memorize a part of a poem, which I remember to this day:

> The Eve of St. Agnes
> by John Keats
>
> St. Agnes' Eve—Ah, bitter chill it was!
> The owl, for all its feathers, was a-cold.
> The hare limp'd, trembling through the frozen grass,
> And silent was the flock, in woolly fold.

What better way to pass the lonely times than by reciting a beautiful poem that seemed to fit a given moment. The long, cold, soggy winters made the springtimes seem even more glorious.

In the fall and spring months, the weather was mild to warm, and it felt wonderful to be out of the home, walking alone beside the country road. I recall the springtime walks especially. Many varieties of birds began returning to the area, singing and chirping. At first robins, then bluebirds, cardinals, Baltimore orioles, bluejays, sparrows, field larks, woodpeckers, flickers, purple crackles, blackbirds, chicken hawks, brown thrushes, quail, doves, and the tufted titmouse. I just had to investigate the name of this last bird and soon discovered it had nothing to do with rodents or the mammary gland. I would see all these birds and more during the four-mile walk in the country. I made this walk for two and a half years, or five semesters, round-trip, five days a week.

At the beginning of spring, I could almost feel myself growing, as I watched wild violets pushing up out of the ground. It was a feeling of euphoria and exuberance that all young people must feel in the spring-time when they see nature at its best; I couldn't help repeating the words of the poem by Robert Browning:

Pippa's Song

The year's at the spring,
And Day's at the morn;
Morning's at seven;
The Hillside's dew-pearl'd;
The lark's on the wing;
The snail's on the thorn;
God's in His heaven—
All's right with the world!

Many of the early English and American poets, who lived in the rural countryside, have beautifully expressed how they in their youth had felt akin to the earth, with its sod, wildflowers, and trees, and all its living creatures. It gives me great pleasure to read their poems, because they express the same inward feeling of joyous contentment and youthful exuberance that I so often felt in the woods and fields, at the home, and on my daily plodding along the old LaGrange Pike to and from KMI, my other home away from the Home.

Along the sides of the road and in the fields, there was such an abundance of weeds and wildflowers that a Boy Scout merit badge in botany was a cinch for me, because of my wildflower collection.

Each day, at the end of the four-mile walk from Ormsby Village, I would arrive at the main entrance of KMI, which was dignified by a massive arch supported by ivy-covered columns hewn from native limestone. The wrought-iron arch contained large block letters spelling KENTUCKY MILITARY INSTITUTE. The gate was located on the LaGrange Road. The name of the school station on the Louisville and Interurban Street Railway was Military Park. The same trolley cars went past Ormsby Village.

Leading from the front gate was a broad driveway, bordered on either side by maple trees and bluegrass meadows. At the left of the driveway was a lake that was used for swimming events. The inner gate at the campus itself was of large stone pillars, each with a cannonball on top. The walk from the outer gate to the inner gate was about half a mile.

I can clearly recall my feelings as I walked through the inner gate for the first time. I was a little overwhelmed by the grandeur of the stately Southern mansion that served as administration building. This building was Ormsby Hall, so-called because it had been the home of the Honorable Stephen Ormsby, a brilliant statesman of the 1820s and '30s. The mansion had a large portico and high columns across the front. The driveway circled around in front of Ormsby Hall. The campus was covered with many fine old trees and neatly trimmed shrubbery and lawns.

There were two barracks where the cadets lived. Each barracks was 150 feet long, 30 feet wide, and three stories high. They were constructed of iron, concrete, and tile and faced with white cement. All rooms had exposure on two sides and opened directly on wide, railed porches, which extended the full length of the buildings. On each floor there was a large lavatory with all the conveniences, and in the basement there were shower baths and dressing rooms for two hundred boys. In one end of the basement was a government armory for equipment and arms. These barracks buildings were completely fireproof. The rooms were heated by hot water circulating through radiators. A water-heating plant was located in the rear. All porch and stationary railings were of wrought iron. We were told that Ormsby Hall had its original walls, and the massive Corinthian columns had been standing for over one hundred years. (They are still standing seventy-two years later.)

All school classes were held in the Edison Science Building. This building was named for Thomas A. Edison (1837–1931). A bronze tablet perpetuates his message: "To the cadets of the Kentucky Military Institute. You are here to prepare for the battles of life. The victor in this, as in other battles, is the one who thinks best and works hardest and keeps at it all the time."

On the first floor of the Edison Science Building were the classrooms. On the second floor were a chemistry laboratory, a physics laboratory, and two other classrooms. The third floor contained the large assembly hall, or chapel.

As I walked into the administration building, Ormsby Hall, I thought, "I'm still under the long arm of Ormsby." It seemed to me that the family of Stephen Ormsby owned many miles of the countryside in this part of Kentucky.

The headmaster, Major Hodgin, met me, assigned me to a room in the barracks, and gave me my class schedule. As a day student, I was assigned to the one remaining bed and locker. I was able to use the room for studying before classes and before and after lunch.

My roommates were Arthur Irving Cohen, a Jewish kid from Detroit, better known to the cadet corps as Abie; Richard Thomas Wiggington; and a little chubby fellow that everyone called "Little Chief," but I don't recall his name. He was definitely an American Indian, from Oklahoma. We heard he was very rich because oil was discovered on his family's property. He was small and husky, and he and I used to practice wrestling on the rug in the middle of our large room. Abie Cohen was a very nice, friendly kid, and full of fun. I remember he was always quoting corny but humorous one-liners from the Marx Brothers movies, and trying to imitate Groucho by walking around hunched over, flicking a big cigar. He even had the big eyebrows, moustache, and horn-rimmed glasses to go with the act. This was fifty to sixty years before Alan Alda and other would-be Grouchophiles and imitators. All three boys welcomed me to their room in mid-year, and treated me like a brother. We became great friends for the rest of my school years at KMI.

I had no trouble adjusting to the mid-year change to the school program at KMI. I did begin taking Latin, but soon changed to Spanish. My other subjects were English, history, algebra, and chemistry. I was advised that if I took five courses, instead of the usual four, I could finish high school in three years instead of four. However, four years of English were a definite requirement of graduation. The principal of the

Ormsby Village School and Miss Moss, my favorite teacher at the Home, arranged for me to take the third year of English during the summer at Ormsby Village. This allowed me to graduate at the age of eighteen instead of nineteen, helping me to make up the time I had lost before first grade at age eight. Miss Moss took the time to design a special concentrated course in English literature. I'll never forget her dedication to teaching the children at the home. She later became principal of Ormsby Village School, a post she held until her retirement many years later.

I thoroughly enjoyed the military training at KMI. I had been marching in the Ormsby Village Band for about three years, so I knew how to march in formation and keep in step. The close-order drilling at KMI was done with rifles, and it wasn't long before I could do the manual of arms as well as the other cadets. During drilling formations, we drilled as squads, practicing right-face, left-face, about-face, forward-march, to-the-rear-march, right-flank, left-flank, and halt. The movements were a little more complicated when we were carrying rifles.

There were enough squads of eight cadets each to form two companies. We usually drilled in the same positions each day, next to the same cadets, and there was always a feeling of camaraderie among the cadets of the same squad. We did a little clowning around when the squad leader or one of the officers wasn't watching. Sometimes, when the companies were all lined up at attention in close formation, we would try to do little things or make little funny remarks without moving our lips, with the hope of getting some cadet to shake with laughter and get reprimanded by one of the very dignified cadet officers up front. One thing I became famous for was being able to bend my right leg backward at the knee and twist it very quickly to the right, kicking the cadet to my right in the seat of the pants, which caused him to move noticeably and be fussed at. I could do this without any noticeable movement on my part. Several cadets tried to get even with me, but it backfired on them because they moved more than I did. The cadets that I spent the most time with seemed so much like the boys at the home that it was hard for me to distinguish between them, especially in the childish clowning around and droll joke-telling.

On one cold, clear Monday morning, after several days of steady snowfall, a smooth layer of snow blanketed the country road and the surrounding fields. In my haste to leave the home and start my hike to KMI, I had neglected to use the toilet at my cottage. From experience I had learned I could easily make it to KMI before I needed to take a leak, if I did so before starting the walk.

This particular morning, after I had covered about three miles of the trip, the urge to go was becoming unbearable. As I approached the front entrance to the military school, I noticed an embankment of earth by the roadside that presented a flat, smooth surface of snow.

In the home, when we kids played outside in the wintertime, we took considerable pride in being able to write our names in the snow with a steady stream of steaming pee-pee.

Now, with very little traffic on the icy pike that morning, I decided to relieve my discomfort by inscribing my autograph on the blackboard-shaped area of flat snow near the arched entrance gate. The temperature must have been near zero degrees, so I decided not to remove my warm, heavy, woolen gloves. This caused some delay in the preparations and I worried that a passing car might interrupt my attempt at comic relief.

I had learned by experience, back at the home, that I never had the capacity to write my whole name, even in script. But, by shortening my name to Jim Settle, I was now able to finish the name, and even have enough left over to dot the "i" and cross the "t"s.

When I arrived at the barracks, Abie Cohen informed me that the day's schedule was running a little late. The bugler couldn't sound the 6 A.M. reveille because some clown had pooped in his bugle. This caused a big stink in more ways than one. No cadet dared to admit doing it, and the whole cadet corps was punished by having to walk off penalty tours around the "bull ring." Because I was a day-student, I was excused. This event was chuckled about for months and remembered for years, especially if a bugler, anytime, anywhere, hit a sour note.

Whenever we had time to kill, either at the Beanery or at KMI, we seemed to spend it trying to amuse ourselves or each other by seeing who could be the most comical, or who could get the biggest laughs with his collection of one-liners. On my daily walk from Ormsby Village to KMI, oftentimes it seemed as if I were walking from one "funny farm" to another. But good humor kept our spirits up during what could have been a very sad and dreary childhood. The boys at both places seemed, consciously or unconsciously, to use humor as a shield against sadness and depression, á la "Laugh, clown, laugh." When things seemed to be getting too serious and stressful, it seemed that our minds were telling us to lighten up and laugh it off: "All things happen for a reason."

After the age of six, I had been thrown in with large groups of kids for most of my early life. I spent twelve years in a children's home with two to three hundred children, including two and a half years in a military school with two hundred boys. Thus I believe I was exposed early on to every imaginable form of humorous expression, whether it be a word, a pun, a limerick, an alliteration, a simile, or a gesture, and whether it referred to man, beast, or both. Being confined with this many people with spare time on our hands and a sense of humor in our minds helped me to accumulate a repertoire of what I considered funny one-liners that I used to help people lighten up when they seemed worried about something, or maybe just bored. It seemed to work, and I didn't get backhanded too often.

❦ Band Competitions ❧

In the spring of 1930, there was a Kentucky State High School Concert Band Contest at Lexington, and the Ormsby Village Band competed for the first time. We were a small and inexperienced band and had to compete with much larger bands. All the bands were required to play the same piece of music before a group of judges. The contest number was an overture by Franz von Suppé called "Morning, Noon and Night in Vienna." It was a difficult piece of music for us, considering the short length of time some of us had been in the band. We didn't win any awards, but we must have sounded good enough to impress our director, Mr. Norman, and other officials at the home, because they somehow arranged for us to make a trip to the National High School Band Contest in Flint, Michigan. This competition was divided into three classes, according to the number of musicians in the band, or what quality of music they had played in past competitions. Our band consisted of sixteen musicians, including three drummers.

We were much smaller than any other band there, and several members were still in grade school. We weren't loud, but after practicing many hours together, we thought we sounded pretty good. We were assigned to class C because no one had ever heard of the strange-looking group of kids from a Kentucky orphanage. Our uniform was quite plain in style, and didn't fit some of us very well. If we had worn a uniform as striking as the KMI dress uniform, we might have attracted a little more attention.

The piece of music that class C bands were all required to perform was the "Light Calvary Overture" by F. von Suppé. I had switched from trumpet to baritone, because the smaller trumpet mouthpiece cut into my upper lip. My two front teeth were slightly rotated, and the edges touched my lip right where the mouthpiece applied pressure. After a short while, the director asked me to change to trombone because he needed two trombones in the front row of the marching band, which was scheduled to parade after the concert band competition. I had been on trombone for only about two months before the competition.

Class A bands all played Beethoven's "Egmont Overture." Some of these class A bands had 125 to 150 musicians. We were amazed by the huge volume of all of the class A bands. We sat and listened to the rendition of "Egmont Overture" by ten or fifteen bands. They all sounded wonderful to me. I didn't understand how any judge could pick a winner. The intonation and balance were better than anything I had ever heard. Of course, I hadn't heard much, if any, classical music in the home. The only radio programs we got to listen to consisted of comedy shows on Saturday nights, in the cottage mother's sitting room, sitting on the floor; or the Hoosier Hot Shots on the crystal set, late at night. I can remember quite clearly how I got goose bumps and the hair stood up on the back of my neck during some of the more intense passages of the Beethoven overture. Beethoven became, and still remains, my favorite symphony composer.

Our Ormsby Village Class C Band didn't win any medals playing "Light Calvary Overture," but we got a little plaque acknowledging our participation. The day after the competition, there was a gigantic parade down the main street of Flint. Huge crowds watched the parade. The little band from Ormsby Village was the last band in the parade, and the crowd filled in behind us and followed the parade to the giant stadium, where the massed bands formed on the field and faced a ceremonial stage. There were about thirty-five hundred musicians. This was called the "largest massed band ever." The gigantic stadium was packed with spectators, who were treated to a concert of great marches played by this massive band, under the batons of John Philip Sousa, Edwin Franco Goldman, and Capt. Charles O'Neill. It was a thrill I have never forgotten.

Each of these musical giants directed the massed band playing some of his own marches. Sousa directed his own "Stars and Stripes Forever" to end the concert. The applause was loud and prolonged. Sousa died two years later, in 1932. I saved the newspaper picture of the massed bands in the stadium, and also one showing the Ormsby Village Band, sixteen strong, bringing up the rear of the parade, with huge crowds filling in behind us. In the picture, I am playing trombone in the first row.

That was seventy years ago, but it doesn't seem that long. During the train trip back to the home from Flint, "Egmont Overture's" dominant theme kept playing in my head. It still does!

❧ KMI Band ❧

During my first months at KMI, besides doing close-order drill with a rifle, I also would practice marching with the marching band, playing trumpet. We would parade around the large open area that was used for athletic activities. Dress parades were held once or twice each semester on certain Sundays, when visitors, including relatives of cadets, would observe the two companies of cadets and the junior school company. White duck trousers were worn in the warm months, and with the white webbed belting crossed at the chest and on the back and a big brass buckle at the crossing in front, the uniforms were a striking sight to see. I had never seen a military dress parade before.

The band would lead the formation onto the parade area and past the reviewing stand. Then we would stand at one side, from where we could observe the precision drilling. The march that we always played was the old standby, "Our Director March." All school bands were familiar with this march. We had also played it in the Ormsby Village Band, and I'm sure we played it on the Board of Trade booster trips as well. During practice for the dress parades, I used to hear some of the cadet corps in little isolated groups singing in unison, but not very loudly, and I thought that maybe the school song was sung to the music of "Our Director March." Then I found out from my roommate, Abie Cohen, what they were really singing. The trio of the march is a nice melody to which they sang these words:

> For we're a bunch of b_____s,
> From KMI
> We're the riders of the night
> We would rather,
> We would rather _____ than fight.

By singing quietly and out of hearing of the more serious cadet officers, they were able to have a little fun, and it was something to giggle about. I'm sure the more mature senior cadet officers had once giggled to the same tune, but they seemed to maintain their dignity, and during dress parade they were quite impressive in their Sam Browne belts, sashes, and glittering sabers. I thought the band looked impressive too, and sounded great, and I was proud of my shiny little trumpet.

❧ Another Summer Is Near ❧

As soon as it got warm enough in spring, we were allowed to take our shoes off and go barefoot until late September. This cut down on the cost of supplying shoes to the children, and it also made the little shoe repairman, Dad Bradford, happy, because the shoes would last longer before they needed new heels and soles. I could almost hear him saying, "*Danke schön.*" Going barefoot somehow gave us a feeling of freedom as we first walked on the large, sodded lawn up by the Ormsby mansion house. It tickled a little the first few days. There was a small lawn at the front of each cottage, but there was not much room to run. To get to the big lawn required walking on a hot tar-and-gravel roadway. At first, our feet were very tender, and we had to walk as lightly as we could. The gravel felt very sharp, and sometimes, if we stepped on a soft spot, the hot tar would get on our soles, and sometimes between the toes. Also, sometimes we would pick up a glob of tar and try to get rid of all the gravel in it. Then we had something else to chew on. In a week or so, our soles would be so tough that we got brave enough to step on honeybees, but occasionally, if we were careless, one would get us on the soft instep. Then we would wonder, "Whose idea was this, anyway?"

In the hot and humid summer months during the school vacation, regular church services were held, and everyone was required to attend. We often sang, "Count your blessings. Name them one by one. Count your many blessings, see what God has done." As I recount the many blessings which I received from Ormsby Village, what stands out most are the great teachers, such as Anna Brittain Moss and Margaret (Turley) Norman. Their requirement that we must commit to memory certain poems or prose from early English or American poets, with the intent that they should uplift our spirits and help us think of our youth as a joyful, carefree time of life, certainly worked for me.

> On many a carefree summer's day,
> When my shoes and stockings were put away,
> The legs of my overalls rolled to the knee,
> John Greenleaf Whittier often spoke to me.

> *The Barefoot Boy*
> by John Greenleaf Whittier

> Blessings on thee, little man,
> Barefoot boy with cheek of tan,
> With thy turned-up pantaloons,
> And thy merry whistled tunes;
> With thy red lip, redder still
> Kissed by strawberries on the hill;
> With the sunshine on thy face,
> Through thy torn brim's jaunty grace;
> From my heart I give thee joy,—
> I was once a barefoot boy!

During these warm months, I was allowed to spend many happy hours at the swimming pool of the home. My swimming suit was the old-fashioned style: a one-piece, dark blue suit with a Junior, and later a Senior Red Cross Lifesaving emblem on the front area, near the top. Being a lifeguard meant that I could spend many hours of the day at the pool. I used to practice holding my breath as long as possible without passing out. This enabled me to win the underwater swim-for-distance contest. To help us get a good tan, we got olive oil from the storeroom and completely covered our bodies with a thick layer, which seemed to prevent our getting sunburned, and, we thought, improved our tan.

During the summer vacation, I divided my time between the print shop and the swimming pool. When the weather was extremely hot and humid, often we were allowed to use the pool from one hour after supper until just before dark. Sometimes, I even sneaked back in at midnight, with others.

❧ A Real Football ❧

There was no football program at Ormsby Village until the fall of 1928, when I was fifteen years old. That's when we got to practice with a real football, instead of our makeshift one consisting of a couple of worn-out rompers, which we fashioned into a tightly bound, cylindrical roll. It served the purpose. We also got football uniforms with shoulder pads, pants padded lightly in the thigh area, a jersey, cleated shoes, and a leather helmet that was lightly padded and wouldn't have given much protection. None of the school uniforms in those days was very protective.

The "flying block" back then was still legal. I was the quarterback, and in one game, I was running interference for a halfback and threw myself sideways at a would-be tackler. He bent his knees slightly; I hit my right lower ribs against one of his knees and had to leave the game. The coach taped me up, almost from my armpit to my hip. The following week, I did very light practice and signal calling, but still walked to KMI and back, four miles each way, for the whole week. At first, I walked with a severe starboard list, but as the days passed, I gradually began to straighten up, and by Saturday, I was able to play a full game against a visiting team.

We had so few players on the team that the first team played both offense and defense against the other teams. As the quarterback on offense, I became the safetyman on defense. I was short and weighed about 140 pounds, so I had to be fast to survive.

Our coach was a Mr. Borders. I believe he said he was from a small college called Transylvania College, near Lexington. He impressed us with his knowledge of football. To get us in shape, he had us push a wooden sled that had two-by-eights for runners and was wide enough for six of us to push. Leaning against padded uprights, we pushed it slowly along in the sod or dirt by the athletic field. And, of course, the coach planted his two-hundred-pound frame in a seat on top, so he could see if any one of us wasn't doing his share of the pushing. The sled was built by the home's carpenter, Gilder Grayson. (He also built the ten-foot-high and eight-foot-wide wooden wall that was used by the Boy Scouts to practice for the wall-scaling competition at the Scout Jamboree, or Wali-Ga-Zhu, in the Armory building in Louisville.)

Another way to help get us into shape was to have us do laps around the large athletic field. After each practice session, the coach had us line up at a starting point and do a hundred-yard dash to see who was the fastest runner on the team. Every race was won by one of our half-backs, named James Hamlett, who would beat me by a foot or two. No matter how hard I tried, or how well I trained, he would always beat me by the same amount. He was a little larger than I and had longer legs. I often wondered if he only ran just fast enough to be first. I'll never know.

In one of our away games, I called my own signal for an end run and ran towards the sideline, and as I went out of bounds, one of my feet tripped over the chain that stretched the ten yards between the downs markers. I fell and hit the back of my head against the ground. I got up and seemed to be all right, but when I tried to think of what the next play should be and what numbers to call, I couldn't even remember where I was, or why.

On the way back to the village on the home's old bus, my memory began coming back, and by the time I got to the home, I seemed to be back to normal. The substitute quarterback must have done great, because we won the game. Back in those days, we never huddled to plan which play to run and what numbers to call. We memorized our plays and knew what number went with each play. Each backfield player had a number, and by using only double-digit numbers, and an easily changeable formula for scrambling them to confuse the other team, we didn't need to huddle. The quarterback decided all plays for the whole game. There was no coaching from the sidelines.

In the fall of 1930, Ormsby Village won all the ten football games it played except the last game. We were beaten badly by Pleasureville, a bigger and more experienced team. The score was 24–0. But the game I remember most, and the most fondly, was the one against the KMI third team. One of the players on the team was Vic Mature, the future movie star. I kept my helmet on the whole game to avoid being recognized by some of my KMI classmates. We beat them 12–0, and I just happened to make both touchdowns. But I also missed both extra points by attempting to score them with a drop-kick, which was the most used method back then of scoring the point after touchdown. At KMI, I never mentioned to anyone that I had played against their team, and no one there knew about it until it appeared in the little statement next to my graduation picture in the KMI yearbook for 1931.

Another future actor who attended KMI while I was there was Jim Backus. I had seen him and knew his name, but being a day student, I didn't get too well acquainted with many of the cadets, except those in the band, my roommates, and some of the students in my classes.

Victor Mature was in my freshman class, and I have the KMI 1929–30 catalog, which has a freshman class picture including him at age fifteen and me at sixteen. He was just a big, friendly, sometimes mischievous kid who seemed to be forever walking off penalty tours in the "bull-ring," in the early morning hours when I arrived after walking from Ormsby Village. My sister Bettye and her husband, Elliott, knew of him and his family. Elliot and Bettye owned the Limerick Market, a grocery store and meat counter at Seventh and St. Catherine Streets in Louisville. The Matures had a cart or wagon with, I believe, a knife-sharpening business that would come by the store.

❦ KMI and the Village—My Two Worlds ❧

By being a day student at KMI and a ward of Ormsby Village, I had all the advantages of both worlds. I was able to mingle among boys from some of the finest old families—mostly of Kentucky, but from many other states and countries as well—who made up the cadet corps at KMI. And in my other world, down the road a piece at the "Beanery," I had all the great kids I had spent most of my life with, day and night, year after year, many of whom were approaching high school graduation, just as I was. Ormsby Village had slowly grown up, along with its older children, into a four-year high school. Some of the students who were graduated from Anchorage High School by 1930 and 1931 were Roy Robinson, Frances Ware, Marie Hourigan, Hershel Sosnin, and Merrill Gyles. Superintendent Bastin's children, Charles, Marjorie, and H. V. Jr., were also graduated from Anchorage. In 1932, the last Ormsby students to be graduated from Anchorage were Mary Peters, Claudine Cundiff, Sue McFerron, and Florence Ridney.

Although I was a student at KMI, most of my time was spent at the Village. All my involvement with athletic teams, including football, basketball, and swimming, was at the home. I still spent most of my time in the print shop, hand-composing and printing calling cards and letterheads, and the home was just beginning to print the first school publication. During planting and harvesting seasons, when extra hands were needed, we were given assignments to help plant or harvest crops, or work in the cannery.

Having been exposed to both institutions during my late teen years, in comparing KMI and Ormsby Village I find many similarities and a few differences. During the years I was associated with KMI, I never heard of any major disciplinary problems. Minor infractions of rules or disruptive childish pranks would result in penalty tours of the bull-ring, in full uniform and with rifle at "right shoulder, arms." Corporal punishment was never necessary, or even considered as an option. The mere threat of a probation or expulsion from this revered institution was enough to discourage any serious infractions. But at Ormsby Village, whereas the threat of probation might have been effective, the threat of expulsion would have been seen as more of a promise, and would, no doubt, only have encouraged more belligerence.

Both schools taught their students to be studious, hardworking, and respectful of others. KMI's slogan was "Character Makes the Man." At Ormsby Village, good character was emphasized through training in the Boy Scouts and Girl Scouts organizations and, by example, from the words and the behavior of the supervisors. Both institutions held regular ecumenical religious services and both practiced giving thanks before each meal.

On both campuses, the boys were discouraged from bragging or acting cocky when they received an award or excelled in some school project or athletic competition. We were all taught to study and work hard to prepare for whatever opportunities might become available in the future. But if any kid indicated by his actions that he felt a little superior to some of the others in his company or cottage, he would be reminded that we were all one family, thrown together by happenstance, and we should help each other in any way possible. If one of us acted "uppity" or "stand-offish," he would be accused of thinking that the aroma of his fecal droppings was not unpleasant, but was reminded that he was betrayed by his foul flatulence. (This is a translation of the original, earthier wording of the chastisement.)

At the end of each school day at KMI, I would put my books in the locker in my room, unless a final exam was coming up, say good-bye to Abie Cohen or whoever might be there, and head out the front gate and down the road back to the Beanery, four miles away. When I reached my cottage, I would go to my locker, and get out of my uniform and into my overalls and denim shirt. I would neatly fold and hang my uniform garments in my locker, and occasionally, I would wash the collar, cuffs, and armpits of the flannel shirt, if its appearance or smell indicated this was necessary. About once a week, I was allowed to borrow an iron from the cottage mother to iron my shirt or press the crease back into my pants and jacket. The full-time students at KMI lived on the campus in barracks the entire school year. Their tuition included their laundry and cleaning for a specified number of articles. I was my own laundry man and cleaner, and I think I succeeded in looking as neat and clean as most of the other students. I tried to blend in and not be viewed as "that little orphan waif from the reform school down LaGrange Road." The uniform was made from material of the highest quality and I was able to make it last for the entire two and a half years without any replacements, although parts of it were not new when it was issued to me. I wore it only when absolutely necessary. I never wore it at the home except when walking to and from KMI.

During the warm months, after changing into my playclothes, I was free to go lie under a shade tree and watch the chicken hawks soar over the distant farmlands, or I could go find another doodle bug to pester. On Saturdays or during the summer months, I was free to go to the print shop, say "*Wie gehts*" through the wire partition to Dad Bradford in his shoe-shop, and see his smile as he stitched on a new sole or pounded a heel. I could sweep up the print shop, clean the press, set or distribute type, or run off a few envelopes or calling cards. Or I could put on my swimming suit, grease down in olive oil, and play lifeguard at the pool. Still later, I might go buzz a few notes through the big Conn recording BB-flat tuba. I look back in amazement at the freedom I enjoyed in this fenceless place of refuge in the countryside. During the school year, I was privileged to walk down the road every morning to a well-structured and disciplined confinement and be with my other friends from different parts of the world. They were from another end of the social spectrum, but in no way were they better or worse than the older boys at the home, nor did they ever pretend to be. I loved them all.

❧ Instrumental Competitions ❧

The KMI Marching Band offered me a different type of military marching experience, and also a lot of fun. At the same time, the Ormsby Village Band not only played marches, but also gave concerts that included all types of music. We played popular music, operettas, and classical overtures. During my senior year of high school, I had changed from trombone to E-flat tuba, and in a short time was told by the Village bandleader, Mr. Norman, that maybe I should enter the high school tuba solo contest for schools in the Louisville area. Other band members also would enter the contest, on trombone, French horn, baritone, and cornet. The tuba solo contest number was called "Storm King." The E-flat tuba had the same fingering as the B-flat cornet and the baritone, in treble clef. This, plus the fact that the E-flat tuba mouthpiece wasn't much bigger than the baritone or trombone mouthpiece, gave me the advantage of being able to adapt quickly to the larger instrument, and to articulate the fast runs and any double- and triple-tongue passages in the composition. There were only two other students entered in the tuba competition, and I won. Two of the other Ormsby Village entrants also won first place. We were accompanied on the piano by one of the teachers from the home, and we had lots of time to practice together. I always had my music on a stand, which I took on stage with me; no one told me not to, and besides, I didn't feel as self-conscious if I played while looking at the music.

The winners of the county competition were allowed to enter the state competition. We heard in advance that there would be stiff competition at the state level, and I was so worried about not winning that, when I would kneel by my bed at night to say my prayers, I would pray that I would win the tuba solo competition. It didn't seem to bother me at the time that by praying that I would win, I was praying that someone else would lose. When I went out onto the stage carrying my stand and music, and looked at the hundreds of people in the audience, I felt clumsy and helpless. When the piano finished the introduction and it was time for me to blow, my mouth was so dry that the first two or three notes didn't materialize. By the time I got into the solo, I realized that I didn't have a chance of winning, but I relaxed and played the rest of the solo the best I had ever done it. I didn't get any ribbons, and besides, I was informed that a soloist in these contests never takes his music with him, but should have it memorized. No one at the home knew this because this was the first year anyone had ever entered the contest. Anyway, I switched to BB-flat tuba for dress parades at KMI, and that has been my instrument ever since.

❧ KMI Graduation ❧

Having made up one year of English at Ormsby Village in summer school, under the guidance of Miss Moss, the principal, I was able to graduate from KMI in the class of 1931. Graduation day was warm and sunny, and there was a large crowd of cadets' relatives and friends from around the county. My sister Bettye and brother George were there.

We cadets were dressed in the summer dress uniform of white ducks and blue-gray coat. The graduation ceremonies were conducted on the portico and front lawn of the old Ormsby Hall, the Southern mansion with the big white columns which was now used as the administration building. With the audience set up on the lawn in front of the building, the Hall made an impressive background for the ceremonies.

Kentucky Governor Flem D. Sampson presented the diplomas after he had addressed the cadets. As our names were announced, we would walk up to the front of the student body and salute the governor as he presented our diplomas. When he handed me my diploma and congratulated me, I was walking on air all the way back to my seat. Bettye took snapshots of the ceremonies, and I still have the pictures, including one of George, Bettye, and me. I was holding my diploma and wearing the KMI uniform for the last time. The 1931 yearbook was a very nicely bound hardcover book called *Saber*. Around the letters KMI in the seal, in block letters is the slogan, "Character Makes the Man."

I always had the feeling that Colonel Charles B. Richmond and Major Charles E. Hodgin were great young men who were wonderful examples for the cadet corps to look up to. Together with the rest of the faculty, they ran a school that was second to none, and their scholastic standards were the envy of other high schools in the area. Their use of strict military discipline gave many students the guidance they needed and craved. I am proud to be a graduate of KMI, the Kentucky Military Institute, and I will be forever grateful to the memory of Col. Richmond for the gift of a wonderful experience and excellent schooling. The year after my graduation, Col. Richmond offered KMI scholarships to five more Ormsby Village boys simultaneously, and specified that they should be good students and musicians to play in the KMI

Band. Bettye gave me a beautiful class ring, with a large ruby and all the KMI lettering, and the date 1931 and my initials inside. I know it was quite expensive and I will always treasure it. I wore it until much of the lettering was worn almost smooth. I still have it, and once in a while I put it on my little finger and think of her.

PART II

Flexing My Wings

Venturing into the World

❦ Printing School ❧

After my graduation from KMI, I started to wonder if I was going to have to start looking for a job as a printer, or what. In 1931, the depression was at its worst. It is hard to describe the poverty that existed, especially in the cities. Since 1929, when the stock market crashed, practically everyone who had been employed before was now laid off. Many tried to sell apples or pencils on street corners. It would have been impossible to get a job from a company that had laid off all their experienced employees.

Fortunately, Ormsby Village came to my rescue. I was lucky enough to be given a scholarship to the Southern School of Printing in Nashville, Tennessee. Along with three of my buddies who were students at the Village, I would be living in Nashville for the next six months. The four of us were driven down to Nashville and taken to a private home at 1912 Adelicia Avenue. This was a very nice two-story home belonging to a Mr. and Mrs. Stevens. They were a delightful middle-aged couple who had no children, or never mentioned it if they did have any, but who treated us four orphans as if we were their family. We heard that Ormsby Village paid thirty dollars a month for each of us. This included a large bedroom for the four of us, two meals and a packed lunch each day at school, plus weekend meals and laundry.

The Southern School of Printing was run by the Southern Master Printers Federation, a non-union organization. The school produced printers who were qualified as typesetters and pressmen. Their specialty was linotype machine operators. At the beginning of our course at the school, all typesetters spent about a month in hand composition. This was something that we were all fairly skilled at, since we had been doing it for several years at Ormsby Village. After the month, one of our group, Orville Metcalfe, was assigned to the press department because he wanted to be a pressman. Homer Ware, Robert (Red) Rafferty, and I wanted to be linotype operators, so we would spend the next five months studying the machine, learning how to operate the keyboard, and how to adjust it and make repairs or replace parts as needed.

An American inventor born in Germany named Ottmar Mergenthaler (1854–99) invented the linotype machine in 1884. The *New York Tribune* first used it in 1886. It is a magnificent machine consisting of thousands of parts, and the intricacy of its many coordinated movements is amazing to watch. We were required to learn the names of all the parts, and of all the adjustments and allowable clearances necessary for perfect operation. Then we would spend every day, five days a week, at the keyboard, setting columns of lead slugs of type. The slugs were molded of hot lead and ejected into a galley which, when full, could be taken to a proof-press, where a proof could be made and proofread for errors. If one letter was wrong or missing, or a word was misspelled or hyphenated in the wrong place, the whole line, and any other lines affected by the error, wound have to be reset and recast. This is why extreme accuracy was expected before we could start thinking about how fast we could make the machine operate.

In typesetting on a linotype machine, as the lettered keys are pressed to form words, the machine assembles brass matrices into a line, casts a slug, and then distributes the matrices back into their proper slots, waiting in line for the next time their key is pressed. After the slugs of type had been used for printing an article or whatever, they were cleaned of any ink on the lettered edge and returned to the machine for remelting in the hot lead pot, which stands behind and to the left of the keyboard. The lead used to cast the slugs had to be at precisely the correct temperature. If it was too cold, the casting would be incomplete. If it was too hot, it would leave too many little fingers, or fins, along the top, or lettered edge of the slug. If it was extremely hot, the cast slug would not cool down and solidify enough to allow the long, flat plunger to eject it from the bright, polished steel mold. Once the temperature of the lead was properly set and tested, it seemed to do a perfect job all day during continuous operation of the machine.

The keyboard of the linotype machine is completely different from that of a typewriter. I had never had the use of a typewriter, so I wasn't at all confused by the arrangement of keys on the linotype. By graduation time, my keyboard operation was fast enough to "keep the elevator hung" at thirteen ems, the width of a newspaper column in the *Nashville Banner* at that time.

Everyone at the printing school dreamed of getting a job at the *Banner* on linotype. We had been told that a graduate of the printing school had been hired during a strike at the *Banner* a few years earlier, and he was now making fifty dollars a week on the linotype machine. In 1931, at the bottom of the worst depression this country has ever seen, that was a fortune. This former student was driving a Stutz Bearcat and sporting a Derby hat and spats when he was spotted by one of the students.

Each day at the printing school we were given ten words to take home and learn to spell and to hyphenate in the proper places. The next morning, to begin the day, we went into a classroom, and the words were called out. We had to write them down on paper, with hyphens separating them in all the proper places. After six months of this procedure, we were extremely careful about hyphenation during typesetting.

Nowadays, when I read the newspapers, I am appalled at the complete lack of any indication that anyone is proofreading to correct errors in hyphenation and spelling, not to mention split infinitives and precariously dangling participles. Ending a sentence with a preposition is done by almost everyone now, so I presume it is now acceptable. Our own Channel 8 brags about bringing us "News You Can Count On," but I suppose that sounds more cool than "News on Which You Can Count."

Saturdays and Sundays the school was closed. We spent some of our free time studying for the exams we were periodically given covering the operation, mechanical repair, and adjustments of the linotype machine. We had no means of transportation, and no money for riding the streetcars or buses, so we walked a lot. At what seemed to be two or three miles from the boarding house was Centennial Park, which wasn't too far from Vanderbilt University. This park was our favorite place to visit. I remember a large reproduction of the ancient Greek Parthenon, where we would spend many hours strolling around the stately Doric columns. This was a nice, quiet, peaceful place where it was possible to forget the linotype keyboard.

The head instructor at the Southern School of Printing was J. E. Mickel, but the instructor who spent the most time with the students was the very friendly and helpful L. N. Deslauriers. I can still see him plainly in my mind's eye, leaning over a galley of type that had been hand-composed, a cigarette at the corner of his mouth, dangling half-stuck to his lower lip, and the smoke curling up into his face, making his eyes water. He couldn't remove the cigarette because both hands were too busy. The use of both hands is necessary for transferring a stick full of composed type from the stick to the chase, or frame, to prepare for printing.

Mr. Deslauriers was very nice to us four orphans, and when he learned that we all played in the Ormsby Village Band, he informed us that he was the director of the Vanderbilt University Band and would like to have us play with his band at the football games that fall. Vanderbilt was a member of the Southeastern Conference of the NCAA and played against Kentucky, Tennessee, Alabama, Georgia, Georgia Tech, and others. We were lucky enough to get to go and play at three of the home games. After this wonderful experience, we got along with Mr. Deslauriers even better. We had no spending money, so he even picked us up at the boarding home, drove us to the Vanderbilt stadium, provided us with instruments, and then delivered us back to our house after the game. He couldn't locate a tuba for me, so I played trumpet.

While I was in Nashville attending the printing school, I received a penny postcard from my brother George. He said he was on a hobo trip in the South and would try to get to Nashville to visit me. George and our older brother, Garnett, would take hobo trips across the country on freight trains, usually riding the rods under the freight boxcars, if they couldn't find an empty boxcar with an unlocked door. They would go from town to town, looking for work or offering to work for food. This was considered a more exciting way to live than just sitting and doing nothing.

George never did show up in Nashville. He later informed me he had been caught by a freight-yard dick and spent a few days in a chain gang in Georgia. This was in 1931, not long after the stock market crash, and before FDR and his benevolent make-work social programs slowly began helping idle workers earn enough to survive.

After six months, as we approached the completion of the linotype training course, I was chosen to be interviewed by the owner of a weekly newspaper in a small Tennessee town. The head instructor at the school, Mr. Mickel, advised me not to accept a salary of less than $23.50 a week. The man came to the school, and I met him in Mr. Mickel's office. He seemed friendly enough and told me that my job would be to set all type for the newspaper on a linotype machine, and prepare it for the press. In my spare time, I would go out to the businesses in the countryside and try to sell advertising space in the paper. He asked what salary I was expecting to receive, and when I told him $23.50 a week, he was quiet for a moment. Then he said, "Is that about the size of it?" I didn't know if he was referring to the expected salary or what, but I nodded my head to indicate a yes. Then we stood and shook hands, and he left. We never heard from the man again, and I wondered if I had asked for too much money, but Mr. Mickel said no. This one interview was the closest I ever came to getting a job in printing.

After getting our certificate of graduation from the Southern School of Printing, we four printers were returned to Ormsby Village, where we spent Christmas. We were all worried about not being able to find employment in the printing industry. The depression was at its lowest point and there was no possibility of finding any kind of work. I was the only one of us four printing-school graduates who had finished high school. The other three boys would stay at Ormsby Village to finish high school, since no jobs were available in the printing industry. I lucked out again when Mr. Bastin, the superintendent, told me that he needed someone to be part-time supervisor of delinquent boys at the Detention Home in Louisville. It seemed a shame that I wouldn't be able to pursue a career in printing, after all the training I'd had—about six years, in fact.

Mr. Bastin's offer was too good to refuse. He also told me that if I took the job, I could enroll at the University of Louisville full-time, and work at the Detention Home in the evenings and on weekends. I would receive room and board, plus ten dollars per month. This would allow me to pay the small tuition at U of L and buy second-hand books cheap.

The Detention Home was at 243 E. Walnut Street, and was a part of Ormsby Village. It was a place to detain all boys and girls who were being processed through the court system, until the courts determined where to send them. The extremely delinquent and unruly boys were sent to a place called Greendale, the State Reform School, near Lexington. The orphans, other dependents, and some delinquents were sent to Ormsby Village. Between one-third and one-half of the Ormsby Village children were delinquent, in the era of the late 1920s. They never remained delinquent for very long, under the strict but fair discipline of the Village; they soon blended in with the dependents, until none of us knew anything about anyone else's past, or cared. I got along well with everyone. There were few, if any, foster homes back then, so any children who were not sent back to their own homes either went to Ormsby Village or Greendale.

After school expenses, the ten-dollar-per-month stipend would leave me with enough money, after two or three paydays, to buy a pair of white duck trousers, a long-sleeved white shirt, and a new pair of Thom McAn shoes. These were good quality shoes, and I considered them almost a luxury at $3.45 a pair, but with resoling and new heels, they should last me through four years at U of L. By not squandering my pay on other luxuries, such as riding the streetcar to school, in a few months I was able to buy a pair of two-toned white and brown shoes. These, with my white ducks and white shirt, the sleeves rolled up in a tight roll above the elbows, put me right in style with other affluent young men in the downtown smoky industrial area between Market Street and the river.

❧ The Louisville Detention Home ❧

The Louisville Detention Home was first opened in 1888. It had formerly been the home of the Ballard family. It was a three-story brick building with a full basement. In the basement at the rear of the building was a large coal-burning furnace and boiler room, which supplied steam heat to iron radiators in all the rooms of the large building. The front of the older part of the building, on the first floor, contained the admittance office, plus a bedroom and small kitchen for the use of the head supervisor. There was also a large hallway, and to the right there were offices for social workers. A smaller hallway led back to a large kitchen, and further back was the dining room. The second floor of the older front section of the building contained a dormitory and two other large bedrooms for dependent girls. There were quarters for three matrons and a medical examination room. The front third floor was mostly vacant, but there was a small bedroom and a bathroom that I would occupy much later.

The back section of this establishment seems to have been added on to the much older front portion. It was built more like a brick jailhouse. All three floors of this back section had heavy iron bars on all the windows. The first floor was for younger dependent boys. The second floor was for older delinquent girls, and the third floor held the older delinquent boys. The bottom floor was just one large room with bunk-type beds at one side, and a large play area took up the rest of the room. There was also a big bathroom with two toilets, four washbasins, and four showerheads.

The second and third floors of the prison-type back section of this building were exactly alike. Each had one big, bare room with no furniture of any kind that could be destroyed, burnt, or made into clubs or weapons. Each had bathroom facilities, including showers. At one end of the rooms on each floor were three cell-blocks, each containing two double-decker bunks and an iron gatelike door made of one-half-inch steel bars spaced about four inches apart. This was the only door to each cell, so inmates could be seen from the big open area at any time. This rear end of the building was simply a well-built prison. Around the yard on each side of the lock-up section of the building was a ten-foot wall to prevent escape during exercise periods outside in the yard area.

My job was to supervise the older delinquent boys in the evening hours and on weekends. I didn't actually lock any of the cellblocks unless a boy was known to be belligerent or escape-prone. If anyone tried to escape, it was my job to chase him. In over four years, there was only one attempted escape while I was on duty. It was a boy I had trusted to go to the kitchen to bum a snack. I was on the front porch when I saw him run past the building, headed down the street toward town. I couldn't believe it was really he. I instinctively lit out after him, and after about three blocks he saw I was gaining on him, so he stopped, and we walked slowly back to the home. He was embarrassed and apologetic, and I really think he intended to sneak back in later and not be missed.

When I first started the job at the Detention Home, I was quickly reminded that this was the same place to which all of my brothers and sisters and I were brought in 1919, when our mother was taken away from us and put in the sanitarium, after she became too ill to take care of us. As I now walked again through the old building, it seemed I could remember once sitting in a window high up in the building at night, with my legs hanging out through the bars and my hands gripping the bars like a monkey, while looking at the Colgate-Palmolive sign and clock lit up across the Ohio River, and listening to the steam calliope of the Belle of Louisville or the Delta Queen stern paddle-wheeler. I recall it as a lonesome time, and yet I had a feeling of warmth and security behind the protective bars. We all survived, and here I was, back in the same place twelve years later, and it seemed that nothing had changed. The first night there after my return, I went up and looked out through the same bars, and there it was, the Colgate-Palmolive clock, exactly the same.

The Detention Home was about a mile from the Fox Theater, where I used to watch some of the oldies from the balcony. The theater was on Fourth Street, near Broadway and the fancy Brown Hotel. Back seventy years ago in downtown Louisville, the streets seemed so very wide, especially Broadway. Maybe that was because I had spent so much time walking down little one-lane roads out in the country. When I returned to Louisville in 1961 on a visit, I couldn't believe how these same streets had become so narrow that double lanes of traffic almost had to squeeze past each other.

Getting settled in at the Detention Home wasn't difficult. Everyone was nice to me and seemed pleased to have me around. Each of the supervisors ran his own department, and our boss was Mr. Bastin, who lived out at Ormsby Village. Mrs. Minnie Reimers had her quarters near the front door and worked in the admittance office. She was available day and night to receive whomever the courts sent to be confined there. She would notify the proper supervisor, who would come down and take the person to the proper room or cell. Mrs. Ruth was supervisor of dependent girls. Mrs. Mitchell had the dependent boys. I don't recall who was in charge of delinquent girls.

❧ Two Good Friends ❧

The cook was a wonderful person named Mrs. Bertha Hester. She was hardworking and very generous to me. She would always have a snack waiting for me after school, such as a bowl of homemade soup or a ham or tuna sandwich. She always seemed to be glad to see me, and we often talked about my schooling. She told me that she was putting a daughter through college at a university in Tennessee. It was an all-black university, very highly regarded for its scholastic excellence. Bertha insisted on washing and ironing my white shirts and white duck trousers. The kitchen had a big cast-iron stove. It seemed that most of the time there was a ten-gallon can of boiling clothing on top of the stove. Bertha would occasionally use a stick to punch the clothing up and down in the boiling soapy water. She had an ironing board down in the basement where she did the ironing. She would never take any money from me for all the nice things she did. The white clothing was difficult to get clean because it picked up a lot of soot from the factories' coal-burning furnaces. Shirt collars would get especially bad. This is why they had to be boiled. Scrubbing them on a washboard would have been too hard on the knuckles.

After I was at this job for about a year or so, Bertha got help in the kitchen. Another cook was hired. Mrs. Mary Mundy was a little older than Bertha and she, too, was very kind to me.

The three of us, Bertha, Mary Mundy, and I, spent many hours in the kitchen. This was a happy, relaxing time for me as we compared notes on our lives and activities and joked and kidded each other. When I returned from U of L each day of the week, I would have a snack, then I would sit at a small wooden table at one side of the stove. I would sometimes do homework, but mostly, we just told stories and kidded each other. Sometimes we would call each other funny names. When Mary Mundy would get a little upset, she would sputter when she talked, and I would call her "Mush-Mouth." Then she would come after me with the laundry-stirring stick and I would get outta there, and we would all double up with laughter. At another time I might say, "Mary Mundy, born on Tuesday," and she would shake her head, look up at the ceiling, and say, "Pray, Church," followed by, "He don't know we're livin'." They would both kid me about eating all the time, and I would say, "My name is Jimmy, I'll take all you gimme."

The cooks both lived away from the Detention Home. They would leave by the side door and walk down the sidewalk, on their way home or to a streetcar. Mary Mundy would usually carry a brown paper bag filled with clothing or something. Sometimes I would be on the second-floor porch, which was just over the front entrance, when Mary Mundy would walk past below, outside the fence. When she got just past the front of the building, I would often holler, in a loud, gruff voice, "Mary Mundy, whatcha gottin nat bag?" She would stop, turn, and shake a fist at me, jabber something, and then chuckle and smile, and I'd know she wasn't mad at me. I've always remembered those two good people.

❦ My First Car ❦

My friend, Merrill Gyles, was connected with the home almost as long as I. I remember his being in the Detention Home while George and I were there in 1919 and 1920, and he was at the Parental Home, the LIS, and Ormsby Village, until his graduation from Anchorage High School. Then he lived with a grandmother or aunt in the west end of Louisville, down near the river. Merrill attended U of L while I was a student there, and I can remember he walked all the way from his grandmother's house to U of L, and back home. This route was even farther than the one I had to walk. Often, on his way home from U of L, he would drop in at the Detention Home for a snack, and would sit in the kitchen and study or cut up with Bertha Hester and Mary Mundy, the cooks. When Merrill left to go home, he would have his deep overcoat pockets stuffed with anything edible he could find, such as a sandwich, or whatever dried fruit he could find in the pantry. These were extremely hard times in the city, and good old Bertha and Mary Mundy would just grin and chuckle as Merrill headed down

Walnut to the west end and his grandmother's house. I was very fortunate to have this Detention Home job, where there was always plenty to eat, a nice warm cot to sleep on, and endless hours to spend with my friends in the kitchen.

Merrill and I found an old Reo Roadster that someone said we could buy for twenty dollars, so we saved our pennies for a while, put in ten dollars each, and actually became the owners of our first car. In Ormsby Village we didn't even have a bicycle, and I still can't ride one. The Reo Convertible Roadster was red, with black fenders. It had red leather seats, including a rumble seat. We could tell that, in its prime, it had been quite stylish. In bad weather, the canvas top could be pulled forward and clamped to the top of the windshield. The canvas side-curtains contained windows of a type of flexible celluloid which we called isinglass—a forerunner to clear plastic.

The Reo was a rugged little machine. You would have needeed a sledgehammer to put a dent in its quarter-inch-thick fenders. It was very difficult to crank-start the engine, but we were in pretty good shape and could get it started after a few tries. We had to save our money to buy enough gas to go, maybe, out to the Beanery, to show off a little. This was a trip of ten miles each way. It was fun driving out LaGrange Road in the country, with the top down and the warm breeze blowing our hair back. We could almost get it up to forty miles an hour. It even had a cut-out, which was a four-inch section of the exhaust pipe, just forward of the firewall and windshield. When you pulled on a toggle on the dashboard, a wire connection to the cut-out section of exhaust pipe would lift it up and the engine would roar loudly when we stepped on the accelerator. In reality it was just a control hole in the exhaust system. We had a ball using it out in the countryside and at the Beanery, where the kids got a kick out of it too.

We kept the Reo in the alley behind the Detention Home, and I could check on it by looking out and down through the bars of the third-floor cell windows. Winter sneaked up on me one night, and the next morning, when I looked out the window, everything was covered with snow. I hadn't put the top up on the Reo and it was filled with snow.

We never used the car for driving to school because we couldn't afford to buy gas. And the tires were always smooth, so it was difficult when it was icy. Whenever too much fabric was visible on a tire, we would go to the dump, find one that still had a little rubber on it, and buy it for twenty-five to fifty cents, depending on how old the sidewall looked. We seldom had a tire with any tread left.

I never saw Merrill—whom, for some reason, I had nicknamed "Old Motes"—after he was graduated from U of L, but we did exchange Christmas cards until his death at age eighty-five.

❦ The University of Louisville ❦

The University of Louisville was located at Third and Shipp Streets. For me, this would mean a walk of at least five miles each way, to and from the Detention Home. When I walked out to register, I went down Walnut and zigzagged across the downtown area. I remember passing an old brick building that had a sign over the door saying, "Dental College," or something similar, and I wondered if I could become a dentist or an MD. Someone informed me that the cost would be too much for me.

Third Street was the street I usually traveled when I walked out to U of L. There were fairly nice homes on the route, mostly two-story brick houses with full basements and attics. I remember seeing, occasionally, some of the better homes on sale for around three thousand to thirty-five hundred dollars. That was almost a fortune in 1932, during the big Depression. Near U of L, I passed by the home of the doctor who delivered me back in 1913. A little sign in the front yard read, "D. D. Worden, M.D." A little closer to U of L, I came to Lee Street, where I was born in a small two-story four-plex. Then, when I got to Third and Shipp, there was a high statue of someone and, next to it, the U of L campus.

The old fourteen-foot-high stone wall of the Louisville Industrial School had shrunk to a much less restrictive three-foot-high wall. There were some new buildings, but what I saw, mostly, were the same old red brick buildings that I remembered from ten years earlier. I especially noticed the old Pettit Building, where, as a nine- or ten-year-old, I used to scrub the wooden floors on my knees, with a big brush and a bar of Fels-Naphtha soap. It seemed that on that first day of college, in my mind, I had relived much of my earlier life.

As a graduate of KMI, I had no problem enrolling at U of L to pursue a bachelor's degree in Liberal Arts, with a major in English. I assumed that, with my job experience in printing and a college education, maybe I could get a job as a reporter or as a printer with the *Courier-Journal* or some other newspaper. With my ten-dollars-a-month salary from the Detention Home job, I was able to pay the tuition or registration fee at U of L. Studying dentistry, medicine, or any other scientific course was out of the question, because I wouldn't be able to afford the laboratory fees and books required. I don't remember having an advisor at any time; I was on my own now, and assumed that I should major in journalism. U of L was very small at that time, and didn't have a journalism school. In fact, as I remember, there was just one course, called History of Journalism. So I decided to major in English. Other courses I took in my freshman year were French, Economics, the Western World, and Music (Band and Symphony Orchestra).

While working at the Detention Home and going to U of L, I was able to visit my sister Bettye, who was now married to Elliott V. Ashcraft. They lived in Highland Park, a southern section of Louisville. I also was able to see my brother George occasionally. He was married to Evelyn Philpott, whose family lived in Highland Park.

George joined the 138th Field Artillery, Kentucky National Guard. He was a member of the band, playing clarinet. Shortly afterwards, I also joined the National Guard Band playing tuba (Sousaphone). It was a concert and marching band. The conductor was a Lt. William Hildebrandt. There were several ex-Ormsby Village Band members in this band—my brother George, Glendon "Babe" Sewell, Elmer "Bottsie" Sewell, two Armour brothers, Charles Marmillott, and Robert Phipps.

The National Guard Band met once a month, for about a three-hour practice session, and occasionally a concert in a park. A part of the scheduled time was spent putting on our uniforms. These must have been straight out of World War I surplus. I wonder if, somehow, I could have been wearing one of the shirts put together by my mother for the troops in that war. The uniform was of a khaki wool material and included the long-sleeved shirt, fatigue pants that laced at the bottom, brown, high-topped boots that laced almost to the knees, a black tie, and a wide-brimmed hat with a chin strap. The uniform felt nice in the winter months, but was hot and itchy in the summer. I have a picture of this band from 1933, which I believe was taken at Camp Knox.

In the National Guard we got paid once a month. We also reported for practice or a performance once a month. The rate of pay was one dollar a day. There were no withholding taxes in those days, so we got a check for one dollar each month, if we didn't miss a practice.

Each summer, the National Guard encamped at Camp Knox, later named Fort Knox. This period of concentrated training lasted for two weeks. The band members could practice individually as much as they wished, and then we would rehearse together for about two hours. If the troops fell in for inspection or had a dress rehearsal, the band would play the National Anthem and lead the parade with marches. The officers and some of the troops rode well-trained horses that didn't seem too alarmed by the band music. Some of the big guns or field pieces also were horse-drawn. It was a relaxing two weeks. We spent much of our spare time in the large swimming pool, or relaxing and reading. This was my vacation from the Detention Home. The best part about going to Camp Knox was that it was a paid vacation. For the two weeks, we received fourteen dollars, a small fortune in the early 1930s.

Some of my most pleasant memories of U of L were of the hours I spent in the band room, both with the band and with the symphony orchestra. Eddie Wotowa was our director, and a Mr. Marsian, who was also a professor in the music department. Mr. Wotowa was from Nebraska and had gone to Indiana University. I believe he wrote one of their school songs, and also taught music there. He later taught music at Male High School in Louisville. He was at U of L when I enrolled, and was very active in teaching and directing the band and orchestra. He was a well-liked and admired person.

Roy Robinson, who had played tuba in the Ormsby Village Band, played stringed bass violin and tuba at U of L, and also played dance gigs around Louisville on the stringed bass. Dottie Drillett was a piano student who seemed to spend a lot of time around the music department. Later, Dorothy and her husband Bo, for Bohannon, became lifelong friends of my sister Bettye and her husband, Elliott. Sixty years after the days at U of L, I learned from Dot that she had a crush on Roy Robinson. Roy was mentioned earlier in these memoirs as the tuba-playing kid who mistakenly threw his mouthpiece out the train window and held onto his forbidden cigar, while on a booster trip with the Ormsby Village Band.

The U of L Band played at home football games, and we formed a "Hungry Five" German Band to play at basketball games. I played the BB-flat tuba.

In my sophomore year, I went out for football. Before the first game, during a practice, I was carrying the ball and tripped on an uneven piece of sod. While my foot was twisted, a huge tackle fell on my ankle, and ended my football-playing days. (Johnny Unitas would star here thirty-plus years later.) I was on U of L's wrestling team, which had just been formed. Hershel (Butch) Sosnin, an Ormsby Village alumnus, was a big football star and outstanding wrestler, later becoming a pro wrestler for a short time.

In the early and middle 1930s, during the Great Depression, some members of the U of L student body were attracted to socialism as an answer to the country's economic problems. I remember one such student who was called "Socialist Bill." He seemed to be a very bright student and was popular on campus. As I recall, he and his group were instrumental in inviting the perennial Socialist candidate for president of the United States, Norman Thomas, to speak to the U of L student body. Everyone was anxious to hear what he would say, and there was a large turnout of students and faculty. When I entered the auditorium, I noticed several men wearing American Legion caps standing at intervals around the back of the audience. At the time I wondered why they were there. Norman Thomas gave an excellent speech and didn't seem to be any more socialistic than Franklin Roosevelt; by today's standards, Thomas would be considered a middle-of-the-road conservative. Socialist Bill eventually married my old friend Marie, around the time of their graduation from U of L. She was my first girlfriend at Ormsby Village, when she was sweet sixteen and my village queen.

One of the requirements for a Liberal Arts Degree was the completion of a specific number of units in the English Department. One required course was called "The Novel." The course involved the reading and discussion of several novels by English authors. The novels assigned were Thomas Hardy's *Tess of the D'Urbervilles*, *A Tale of Two Cities*, by Charles Dickens, and the three-inch-thick *Vanity Fair*, by William Makepeace Thackeray. This novel course began with the delightful Tess, with whom I became immediately infatuated. As I read the novel, I felt as if I were actually living back in the English countryside, where my ancestors once lived. I spent so much time on this novel that I wasn't keeping up with the class schedule. I was an extremely slow reader, which I attributed to my many years of typesetting and proofreading, where I scanned each word and sentence for transposed letters, misspelled words, improper hyphenation, and split infinitives. It didn't matter that I was reading works of the masters of the English language, because they didn't do the typesetting for the books. This was an ingrained habit that I was unable to break, and still haven't. It could almost be considered as an obsessive-compulsive disorder, which demanded that I should not leave one sentence or paragraph and go to the next until I was convinced that I completely understood everything the author meant to convey. By the time I had finished dissecting the Hardy novel and had crept through *The Tale of Two Cities*, the rest of the class was almost finished with *Vanity Fair*.

When I was called on in class to give my opinion on something I was supposed to have read, I just sat there and said nothing, and the professor would write something down and call on another student. This student would elaborate fluently on the social significance of a passage in the book, and I would sink lower down in my seat, feeling like some poor soul who had just farted and wished he was someplace else. Rather than taking an F in the course, I dropped it, and would be required to repeat it the following year. I promised myself right then that "when I repeat the course, I will be a more Hardy reader and, what the Dickens, I Will Makepeace with Thackeray, and maybe even allow Becky Sharp to replace Tess in my youthful fantasies." Alas, three different books of equal length were substituted for required digestion in the new novel course.

Having already spent four years at U of L and still needing several units, including the "The Novel," to graduate, I lost interest in continuing this routine of working for peanuts and walking the ten-mile round trip between the Detention Home and U of L. Also, the

Depression seemed to guarantee that I wouldn't get a decent job if I did graduate. I could have applied for the Flying Cadet program of the U.S. Army after two years of college; I don't recall why I didn't. I heard that the U.S. Navy also was accepting applications, and I applied, passed the physical exam, and enlisted for a four-year hitch.

Leaving the U of L campus and the Detention Home meant I was leaving my stone walls and iron bars forever. My college education was made possible by the job at the Detention Home, which was a city branch of Ormsby Village. My keeping this job depended on my attendance at U of L. When I joined the Navy, it meant that I was finally leaving behind, after sixteen years of association with Ormsby Village, the feeling of complete security that I had learned to accept and enjoy. I felt "free at last," but a little uneasy about how I would do on my own.

It brought to mind Lord Byron's poem, "The Prisoner of Chillon":

> These heavy walls to me had grown
> A hermitage—and all my own.
> My very chains and I grew friends,
> So much a long communion tends
> To make us what we are: —even I
> Regained my freedom with a sigh.

Family Tree of James Worden Settle

Paternal grand-parents, John William Settle (1840–1914) and Alpha Walton Settle (1850–1896)

Maternal grandparents, Spotsford Samuel Redford and Addie Carter Redford

Father, James William Settle (1883–1917)   *Mother, Fannie Redford Settle (1885–1922)*

Uncle and aunt, Spotsford and May Redford

Brother, William Garnett Settle (1904–1979)

Sister, Bettye Settle Ashcraft (1906–)

Sister, Alpha Marie Settle Wells (1908–1996)

Brother, George Marshall Settle (1911–1993)

James Worden Settle (1913–)

Ormsby Village

Dr. George Colvin, Superintendent, Louisville and Jefferson County Children's Home 1923–26
President, University of Louisville 1926–28

DEDICATED TO THE
LOVING MEMORY
OF
DOCTOR GEORGE COLVIN
WHO DIED JULY TWENTY-SECOND
NINETEEN HUNDRED TWENTY-EIGHT

James returns to the old Ormsby House in 1998. The only remainder of Ormsby Village, it was the home of Superintendents George Colvin and H. V. Bastin.

Early 1925: George Settle, Jimmy Cox, James Settle. Three orphans transferred from Louisville Industrial Facility to the new Louisville and Jefferson County Children's Home at Ormsby Station. Cottage Eight is in the background.

Young residents of the Louisville and Jefferson County Children's Home play near a cottage in 1927, the first year the facility was called Ormsby Village.

H. V. Bastin, Superintendent 1926–1953

Louis Piper, school principal

Miss Anna Brittain Moss, my favorite teacher

Band of the Louisville and Jefferson County Children's Home, 1925. Photo taken in front of new cottage at Ormsby Station near Anchorage, Kentucky.

Ormsby Village Band, 1928. James Settle on trumpet, seated fourth from right.

Ormsby Village Band plays for the Louisville Board of Trade extension tour, 1928. State capitol, Frankfort, Kentucky. Top row: C. E. Norman, director; Roy Robinson, Charles Haynes, Homer Ware. Middle row: Marian, Robert Rafferty, George Settle, John Wyck, Chick Lebring, Jim Settle, Gilbert Scales. Bottom row: Elmer Sewell, John Kennon, Clifford Webb, Glendon Sewell, Earl Schell, Albert Ebertshauser, Marion Webb.

Ormsby Village band, 1929, above; 1930, below

Ormsby Village Girl Scouts, 1928–29

Ormsby Village School faculty, 1928–29

Ormsby Village printshop. Above: Boy in center stands on box while hand-feeding the press.

Left: Hand-composing type from type cases in backgound. Cutting paper in foreground.

EIGHTH ANNUAL

WALI-GA-ZHU

JEFFERSON COUNTY ARMORY

Troop 113 - Ormsby Village - Winners of Achievement Air Meet

Ormsby Village Boy Scouts

Scouts Settle and Lindsay with flag

NATIONAL COUNCIL
BOY SCOUTS OF AMERICA
CHARTERED BY CONGRESS
JUNE 1916.

200 FIFTH AVE., NEW YORK CITY
THIS IS TO CERTIFY THAT UPON RECOM-
MENDATION OF THE LOCAL SCOUT AUTHORITIES

James Settle

IS REGISTERED FOR THE YEAR ENDING

November 1926

AS A MEMBER OF THE CHARTERED TROOP AS INDICATED
ON THE REVERSE SIDE OF THIS CERTIFICATE AND IS EN-
TITLED TO WEAR THE OFFICIAL UNIFORM AND INSIGNIA
OF THE BOY SCOUTS OF AMERICA ACCORDING TO HIS
RANK SO LONG AS HE MAINTAINS HIS REGISTRATION AND
GOOD STANDING IN SAID TROOP WITH THE UNDER-
STANDING THAT AS A SCOUT HE WILL FAITHFULLY OB-
SERVE THE SCOUT OATH AND LAW AND DO A GOOD
TURN DAILY AND EFFICIENTLY CARRY OUT THE
SCOUT PROGRAM SO AS TO "BE PREPARED" TO MEET
ANY EMERGENCY.

HONORARY PRESIDENT   PRESIDENT

HONORARY VICE PRESIDENT

HONORARY VICE PRESIDENT   NATIONAL SCOUT COMMISSIONER

HONORARY VICE PRESIDENT   CHIEF SCOUT EXECUTIVE

3300923
NOT TRANSFERABLE
COPYRIGHTED BY BOY SCOUTS OF AMERICA, 1916

"BE PREPARED"

"DO A GOOD TURN DAILY"

NATIONAL COUNCIL
BOY SCOUTS OF AMERICA
CHARTERED BY CONGRESS
JUNE 1916.

2 PARK AVE., NEW YORK CITY
THIS IS TO CERTIFY THAT UPON RECOM-
MENDATION OF THE LOCAL SCOUT AUTHORITIES

James Settle

IS REGISTERED FOR THE YEAR ENDING

Nov. 1929

AS A MEMBER OF THE CHARTERED TROOP AS INDICATED
ON THE REVERSE SIDE OF THIS CERTIFICATE AND IS EN-
TITLED TO WEAR THE OFFICIAL UNIFORM AND INSIGNIA
OF THE BOY SCOUTS OF AMERICA ACCORDING TO HIS
RANK SO LONG AS HE MAINTAINS HIS REGISTRATION AND
GOOD STANDING IN SAID TROOP WITH THE UNDER-
STANDING THAT AS A SCOUT HE WILL FAITHFULLY OB-
SERVE THE SCOUT OATH AND LAW AND DO A GOOD
TURN DAILY AND EFFICIENTLY CARRY OUT THE
SCOUT PROGRAM SO AS TO "BE PREPARED" TO MEET
ANY EMERGENCY.

HONORARY PRESIDENT   PRESIDENT

HONORARY VICE PRESIDENT

HONORARY VICE PRESIDENT   NATIONAL SCOUT COMMISSIONER

HONORARY VICE PRESIDENT   CHIEF SCOUT EXECUTIVE

4997920
NOT TRANSFERABLE
COPYRIGHTED BY BOY SCOUTS OF AMERICA, 1916

LOYALTY   SERVICE
PATRIOTISM

"BE PREPARED"

"DO A GOOD TURN DAILY"

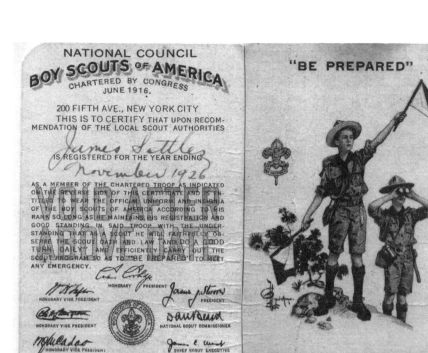

The American National Red Cross

JAMES SETTLE

IS HEREBY ENROLLED AS A
Senior Member
OF THE
Red Cross Life Saving Service
HAVING PASSED THE PRESCRIBED TESTS AT

ANCHORAGE, KENTUCKY.

NOV 14, 1930

DIRECTOR, FIRST AID AND LIFE SAVING

Boy Scout Troop 113 at wall scaling

Kentucky Military Institute

Approach to KMI inner gate in 1929

James and wife Shirley at remains of inner gate in 2000

KMI outer gate—a welcome sight at the end of my daily hike from Ormsby Village

Barracks No. 1. My room was on the ground floor.

1928
KENTUCKY MILITARY INSTITUTE

1928 SCHOLARSHIP FROM Col. C.B. RICHMOND

MAJ. HODGIN

SAMUEL B. MARSHALL

DAVIS E. MARSHALL

JOHN ELMO PACE

LEWIS H. GREGG

WILLIAM P. GROSECLOSE

E. HAGAN RICHMOND

HUGO QUAID

ROBERT W. NORTON PM SGT

WM. C. TWITTY

HENRY M. ELLIOTT

LLEWELLYN CHAMBERS

ROBERT KEENE

JAMES B. MOODY

REUBEN ELLISON

KMI 1928 freshman class. Jim Settle is seated second from left. Victor Mature is on the back row, far left.

KMI band, 1928. Jim Settle, trumpet

JOSEPH FRANCIS RODERICK
"Rody"

Boston, Massachusetts

1930-31—Private, Company "A"; Henry Watterson Club of Journalism; Wrestling Team; Glee Club; Golf Candidate.

"Respected by all men; loved by all women"—now, you know Joe. Just why this Bostonian lad left the culture and refinement of New England to seek his education in the South, no one knows; but he did, and it is with regret that we bid him goodbye.

CLYDE RAYMOND SALMONS
Hartford, Connecticut

1929-30—Private, Band; Orchestra.
1930-31—Sergeant, Band; Non-Commissioned Officers' Club; Orchestra; Journalism Club.

"Sally" is another New Englander who has inherited the fine qualities of his noble ancestors. In the class room and on the campus he models his life after Calvin Coolidge, but when he plays his "sax", one recognizes another Rudy Vallee. *Bon Voyage*, old man, and may all the good things in life come your way.

JAMES SETTLE
Anchorage, Kentucky

1928-29—Private, Band; Literary Society.
1929-30—Private, Band.
1930-31—Corporal, Band; Non-commissioned Officers' Club.

Gentleness *plus* hard work *plus* determination *equals* "Jimmy", and, of course, you can't beat this kind of a combination. "Jimmy" is Ormby Village's representative on the K. M. I. campus, and because of his modesty, it was not learned until a few days ago that he produced both of the touchdowns against our Third Team when they visited Ormsby Village last fall.

From the KMI yearbook, "The Saber," 1931

𝕾enior 𝕮lass 𝕽oll

OFFICERS

JOE QUILLIN DOUGHERTY ....*President*

ALTON JAMES ELINE, JR. ....*Vice-President*

HENRY CARMEN MCCOWN ....*Secretary*

WILLIAM CALVIN TILLMAN ....*Treasurer*

OYD ELVERT BANKS ....*Sergeant-at-Arms*

SENIOR CLASS

Eugene William Austin
Charles Stafford Baals
Harper Anthony Barrett
George James Chelekis
Edward Barton Coffey, Jr.
Arthur Irving Cohen
Edgar George Davis, Jr.
William Alexander Fisher
Craig Perry Froman
George William Gillespie
John Jacob Hailston
Walter Berndt Hannah
Robert Charles Heckman
Leon Elias Hirsch, Jr.
Charles Edward Houston, Jr.
Harry Harless Hughes
Edward Gilmore Kelly
Philip David Kelly
William Arthur Kirkendale
Kenneth Adolph Kruhm
Leo Loeb, Jr.

James Guthrie Long
Filadelfo Luarca, Jr.
David Manly
Rex Martin
Earl Hillman Memory
Charles William Nold, Jr.
Frederick Leander Pickett
Joseph Francis Roderick
Clyde Raymond Salmons
James Settle
Clarence Lee Sievers
Horace Hamilton Smallridge
Ben Frazier Taylor
James Woodrow Thompson
Charles Mitchener Wilkin
Gordon Will
Miles Frederick Woody
James Oscar Young
Oly Leo Spence
Elmo LaVerne Hartman

MAJOR JOHN ELMO PACE, *Faculty Adviser.*

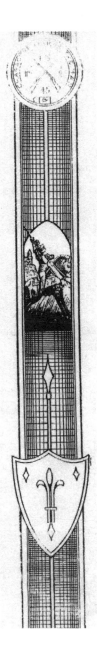

From the KMI yearbook, "The Saber," 1931

Ormsby Village football team, 1930

First team, above; second team, below

James Settle, quarterback

James with sister Bettye and brother George at KMI graduation, 1931

Best friend Charlie Seitz

Sea Scout Seitz at pool, Cottage 8 in background

Albert "Scout" Howe

*Jim Settle, Fred Ware, and
"Billy-Bo" Piper, 1929*

*Above: George Settle at Scout Camp,
Covered Bridge Reservation, 1928*

Left: "Baby Helen" Kinser, 1930

Right: Jim Settle with Baby Helen

*Left: Jim Settle with Wesley
Bratcher, 1929*

*Right: Earl Smith and Jim
Settle, 1929*

Above: Jim Settle

Below: Jim Settle and Orville Metcalfe

Left: C. E. Norman, Director of Ormsby Village Band

Right: Placecard for homecoming dinner

ORVILLE METCALFE   JAMES SETTLE   HOMER WARE   ROBERT RAFFERTY

A Four-leaf Clover from Louisville

James Settle, Orville Metcalfe, Homer Ware and Robert Rafferty are four boys now at the school, having received scholarships from the Open Shop Printers Association. They arrived in Nashville, June 23, after a long one hundred ninety-five mile automobile ride. Their former residence was at Ormsby Village, situated on the LaGrange road.

They are now boarding in the vicinity of the school and are attending school regularly. A few comments upon each of the boys will make you better acquainted with them.

JAMES SETTLE has proven himself a most capable boy. Past records also show him to be a prominent leader in academic and vocational activities. He is an all-round athlete and played quarter-back on the Ormsby Village football team. He plays bass horn in the Ormsby Village band.

HOMER WARE left school at the eleventh grade. He is an all-round athlete; baseball, however, being his favorite sport. Homer does most anything he puts his hand to with success. He has been at Ormsby for about ten years.

ORVILLE METCALFE, nicknamed, (Heavy) by all associates, is most popular wherever he goes. He makes friends easily and greets every one with a boisterous "Hello." He plays clarinet in the Ormsby Village band; entering the state musical contest for the past two years and winning second place both times.

ROBERT RAFFERTY (Red) has been at the Ormsby Village school ten years. He has an abundance of nicknames, but is commonly called "Red" by almost everyone. He plays trombone in the Ormsby Village band; and toots a "mean" harmonica when away from the band.

FOOTBALL

Oct. 6, 1934.
U. of L. -- Georgetown

No.	U. of L. Name	Position	No.	Georgetown Name	Position
61	Doll, Kenney	H.	11	Stephenson, Bill	E.
60	Lamar, Harmon	E.	12	Clark, Bill	G.
59	Harman, H.	G.	13	Grossman, Al	E.
58	Threlkeld, Bill--Capt.	C.	14	Turner, Bob	H.
57	Davis, Harry	H.	15	Shallers, Lloyd	G.
56	Montgomery, Bob	H.	16	Powell, Gene	H.
55	Ryan, Bill	H.	17	Johnson, Joe	H.
54	Eiling, John	G.	20	Eison, Bob	H.
53	Long, Harry	E.	21	Robinson, Ed	E.
52	Loew, Melzar	F.	22	Day, Ed --Capt.	F.
51	Carwell, Ivan	H.	23	Fuller, Bob	G.
50	Finger, Fritz	T.	24	Day, Bill	C.
43	Archer, Ira	H.	25	Edney, V. J.	H.
42	Pirkey, Everett	T.	26	Balof, Wm.	G.
41	Banks, Fred	T.	27	Green, Tom	H.
40	Ryan, George	G.	28	Miller, Earl	C.
39	Sosnin, Herschel	T.	29	Tudor, Loftus	T.
38	Strull, Asher	E.	30	Roberts, Julian	T.
36	Forsee, Tyre	H.	32	Patrick, Joe	Q.
32	Rouse, Bert	E.	33	Morgan, Gene	G.
31	Edelen, Marshall	H.	34	Shields, Lewis	H.
30	Craig, H.	G.			
29	Weber, Mike	E.			
24	Settle, James	H.			
22	Sehlinger, Geo.	G.			
34	McGee, Sam	T.			
20	Wagner, Henry	E.			

PROBABLE LINE-UPS

53	LONG	L. E.	STEPHENSON	11
39	SOSNIN	L. T.	TUDOR	29
54	EILING	L. G.	SHALLERS	15
58	THRELKELD, Capt.	C.	MILLER	28
59	HARMAN	R. G.	CLARK	12
50	FINGER	R. T.	ROBERTS	30
60	LAMAR	R. E.	GROSSMAN	13
61	DOLL	Q. B.	PATRICK	32
51	CARWELL	H. B.	JOHNSON	17
43	ARCHER	H. B.	GREEN	27
52	LOWE	F. B.	DAY, Capt.	22

Coach Ben Cregor
Mascot "Cardinal"

Coach "Bob" Evans
Mascot "Tiger"

HOME GAMES
Nov.   3   Centre
Nov. 24   Union

Louisville National Guard Band
Fort Knox, 1933

PART III

The Old Salt

Serving in the Navy

❧ Boot Training ❧

It was in May 1936 that I joined the U.S. Navy. Because of my ROTC training at KMI, I was put in charge of the recruits from the area around Louisville on the trip to the naval training station at Norfolk, Virginia. Boot training lasted for three months. We were assigned to one of the many barracks buildings. There were about forty apprentice seamen in each of the barracks. The sleeping portion of the building was just one long, rectangular room that was bare except for four rows of large iron posts, one row on each side of the room and two rows running down the middle, with a long shelf suspended between them. We soon learned that these posts were for tying our hammocks to, about five feet above the floor—oops, I mean the deck. And the walls became bulkheads, and the ceiling, the overhead.

As apprentice seamen, we would receive eighteen dollars per month, plus all parts of the basic uniform. There were two white un-dress middies and one white dress middy, which was embellished with thin, blue piping running along the edge of the collar and two stars on the back of the collar. There were two pairs of un-dress white trousers, not bell-bottomed, and two white hats. For colder climates or seasons, there were two pairs of un-dress navy-blue trousers with a button-up flap in the front, two un-dress middies of navy-blue wool, and one dress-blue middy, which had white piping and two white stars on the collar. A navy-blue neckerchief was worn with both dress middies. There were two pairs of dress-blue trousers.

We received a white hammock, a thin mattress with mattress cover, a thin wool blanket, and a thin pillow with pillowcase. We also received a sea-bag, which would hold all clothing, winter and summer, including a pea coat and a blue flat hat to go with the dress-blue uniform. We also received a bucket, scrub-brush, and saltwater soap for scrubbing clothing, hammock, mattress cover, and sea-bag. It was unbelievable that everything we owned, including an average-sized bucket, would fit into one sea-bag, if it were stowed properly.

Other clothing items issued were white and blue socks, black shoes, and "skivvies," which were white boxer undershorts and short-sleeved undershirts. We soon learned that the term "skivvy sleeve" had many humorous connotations. For example, anything that projected or hung loosely from an aperture could be described as hanging out like a skivvy sleeve. And the comical flat hat was the butt of many crude jokes. This portion of the narrative, concerning things nautical and sometimes naughty, would be incomplete, and I would be remiss, if I didn't recall one example. If a sailor wanted to confirm with emphasis some statement or recent happening, rather than saying, "Cross my heart and hope to die," he more likely would say, "Well, I hope to s— in your flat hat!"

Our platoon leader or boot-training chief was Chief Gunner's Mate J. Zoilkiewiecz, which everyone pronounced Zockovitch. He was an old salt from World War I days who tried to act tough, but we had him figured out as a softy underneath. He had a high rating among the other platoon leaders for having the most precise formations during dress parades. The drilling came easily for me because of my time at KMI and in the National Guard. We also had regular calisthenics, which we did in rhythm with music by a Navy band stationed on base. I briefly considered going to a Navy music school, but I really preferred a career in aviation, if the chance came up.

Boot training consisted mostly of calisthenics, marching in formation, learning nautical nomenclature, and how to recognize all types of naval vessels and what armament each carried. We also learned something about naval history, the principal sea battles and some of the famous naval personnel.

Once or twice, there was a sea-bag inspection of all our clothing articles and uniforms. We were required to stencil our names on an inside seam of all uniform parts and hats, as well as on underclothing, hammock, mattress, mattress cover, ditty-bag, and even our bucket and scrub brush. Any clothing not being worn was rolled up and stored in the sea-bag. Special care was used in rolling each article of clothing.

Middies and trousers were turned inside out, and each was folded to make a long rectangle about ten inches wide, the stenciled name visible at one end. Then the item was tightly rolled into a cylindrical roll, which was about ten inches long and three inches in diameter. The stenciled name was visible on a seam on the outside of the roll. The rolls of each article of clothing would be almost uniform in size.

For the big sea-bag inspection, we would each spread our hammock out flat on the deck, under our sleeping space, with the mattress and cover on it. All the clothing articles were neatly lined up in rows on the mattress, with the stencils all perfectly lined up. Underwear and socks were also placed to show the stencils, as were the white hats, flat hats, pea coats, and even the comical regulation swimming drawers, which no one ever wore except maybe for a laugh. They were unflattering, droopy, made of thin black jersey and held on by a black pucker string. The sea-bag inspection was a fairly formal affair for which we wore dress-white uniforms, with white hats and white canvas hook-and-eye lace-up leggings. Each hammock was supplied with a hemp line, one-half-inch in diameter, which was used to tie the hammock into a tight roll when it was not strung up for use. Each hammock had this line coiled neatly and placed at one end of the laid-out sea-bag display. The whole platoon stood at attention at the other end. High-ranking naval officers would inspect us and our displays, and comment on the neatness, or lack thereof.

I gained many good friends during boot training. Ira Newbill was from Newport News, just across the bay from the training station. He was an amateur boxer and used to spar with Tom Sharkey, another boxer in the platoon. Tom may have been related to the famous heavyweights, Jack and Tom Sharkey, of the Jack Dempsey era. Newbill used to kid me about my slightly jutting chin. His nickname for me was "Bullgator." After he left the base at the end of boot camp, I received several letters from him, and they were all addressed to J. Bullgator Settle. I still miss him. I used to hand-wrestle with Tom Sharkey and always beat him. He was a great boxer, but I was more muscular in the arms and had done some wrestling. Bill Brennenstuhl and I became great friends. He was from Louisville too, and when we went on leave after boot training, he invited me and another friend, Joe Gantz, to his home for the two-week leave period. His mother, father, and sister greeted us with a warm welcome, and we all had a wonderful two weeks, just eating delicious food and going to Fontaine Ferry Park down by the Ohio River.

My sister Bettye came to the Brennenstuhls' to visit me and meet everyone. She became a good friend of the Brennenstuhl family, and visited or corresponded with them for years thereafter. Nine years after I last saw Bill, he was to become a much-decorated chief machinist's mate on the aircraft carrier U.S.S. *Bunker Hill*, when Japanese suicide bombers off Okinawa damaged it in 1945.

❦ Machinist Mate School ❦

We were advanced to seaman second class after finishing basic training. Our pay was now thirty-six dollars per month. Just before boot camp ended, I was notified that I was accepted into the machinist mate school. After our two weeks' leave, we were assigned to barracks, which were different from the boot camp barracks. Instead of hammocks, we had low, iron cots. We used the same mattress, cover, and pillow as before. We also had a large locker and didn't have to live out of a sea-bag anymore. I never slept in a hammock again.

Machinist mate school involved working around oily and greasy machinery, so we were issued dungaree shirts, pants, and jacket. Also, because it was approaching cold weather, we received a long raincoat and navy-blue wool stocking cap. Each morning after breakfast in the mess hall, usually of creamed ground beef on toast, chipped beef on toast, or maybe beans with catsup or scrambled eggs, we would form in front of the barracks in a column of twos, dressed in our dungarees, and walk to the machinist's school's large machine shop. Here there were three rows of metal lathes, a row of shapers, several milling machines, and two large grinders. Most of our time was spent on the lathe. The cutting tool or bit of the lathe had to be ground to the proper cutting-edge angle, with a gouge-shaped cutting edge, for cutting small or large straight rods or shafts and then sanding and polishing them. We were assigned projects to manufacture to exact sizes. We learned to cut threads on different-sized rods or bolts, with a varying number of threads per inch, and varying pitch of the threads. The finished threaded project would have to fit perfectly into the threads of the corresponding nut or threaded hole. Some time was spent on the shaper, which used the same cutting tool as the lathe. The shaper would cut square or rectangular flat pieces of metal used on a project to the exact thickness required.

Many hours were spent making Babbitt bearings and scraping the soft Babbitt-metal to fit a mandrel, which was the exact size of the shaft, on machinery that was being fitted with new bearings. The bearings are split into two halves. Prussian-blue paste was applied to the mandrel, which was then rotated in each half of the bearing. The blue color marks the high spots, or where the mandrel is touching the Babbitt. High spots are scraped off, and the process is repeated until the whole bearing shows an even coating of blue.

We were given written examinations covering a textbook we used. Grades were given on these tests, as well as on machine-shop projects, and on a notebook which each of us was required to keep. The term of the machinist mate school was six months.

In January 1937, at about the midpoint of the machinist mate school course, there was a terrible flood that involved most of the Mississippi River Valley and, closer to home, the Ohio River Valley. Over three-fourths of Louisville was flooded. My sister Bettye and her husband Elliott were safely above the floodwater in Highland Park, but everyone's job was put on hold until the mess was cleaned up. Many years later, when Foster Brooks became a celebrity by imitating a comical stuttering drunk, we were reminded that he first gained celebrity status by broadcasting the Louisville Flood from the top of a telephone pole. This was before television so that, in Virginia, we weren't really aware of the amount of damage caused by the flood. The next time I returned to Louisville, everything looked exactly as it had before I left.

❧ Aviation Machinist Mate School—1937 ❧

The four top students in our class at the machinist mate school were given the option of enrolling in the aviation machinist mate school, which was located at the same naval training base, near Norfolk, Virginia. The four students picked were William Minton, Robert B. Miles, Ora Erskine Gaines, and myself, James Worden Settle.

When classes started at the aviation mechanics school, I felt that I was finally where I belonged, in aviation. The four of us who got into this class by going through machinist mate school were the only sailors with the rank of seaman second class and pay of thirty-six dollars per month. The rest of the class of twenty students was chosen from the fleet ships and other bases. They were all seamen first class and their pay was fifty-four dollars per month. All of the students were in their early twenties. I was twenty-four years old.

We soon learned all the terms related to flying and all types of aircraft: heavier-than-air (land or seaplanes), lighter-than-air (free-flight or dirigible), and autogyros as well as helicopters. We also learned that the aircraft carriers in use at that time were the U.S.S. *Langley*, which was a converted collier, and the U.S.S. *Lexington*, *Saratoga*, and *Ranger*. The early carriers were named after famous battles that were fought early in U.S. history. The battleships were named for states, cruisers for cities, destroyers for famous people, and submarines for sea creatures, for example, *Cuttlefish* or *Nautilus*.

In the shops at the aviation mechanics school there were several old military biplanes or parts of planes. They all had fabric-covered wings, control surfaces, and fuselage. We were required to take the bare aluminum frame of a wing and cover it with mercerized cotton fabric, which we stitched to the wing ribs. Then we used a heavy fabric tape to cover the stitches that ran from the leading edge to the trailing edge of the wing. We then covered the fabric with dope (methyl methacrylate). Several layers of dope were used. The dope could be tinted to match the fuselage. Each layer of dope applied seemed to draw the fabric tighter until, when it was thumped with a finger, it would sound like a drum. Another project was to make repairs of torn fabric on some part of a plane. The tear would be stitched closed; then fabric tape was used to cover the stitches, and several layers of dope were applied.

In the shop there were also several radial engines. I remember an old nine-cylinder Wright Cyclone engine and a fairly new fourteen-cylinder Pratt & Whitney Twin Wasp Jr. engine. We learned the names of all the parts of the engines and how to disassemble and reassemble them. The older engines didn't have pressure lubrication, so we had to learn all the parts that would need to be oiled. We learned to pack rocker-boxes with grease. We heard that sometimes in Alaska, it got so cold that the rocker-box grease had to be cut with scissors to pack the rocker-boxes, and then a fire was built under the engine to melt the grease and thin the engine oil before the engine could be started. We learned to grind valves and valve-seats, replace piston rings, sandblast sparkplugs, and repair and install magnetos, starters, and generators. Nearly all studs, bolts, and nuts were specially designed for receiving safety-wire, which was installed by using pliers and diagonal side-cutters (dikes).

Toward the end of the six-month course, we were allowed to take an examination for the third class aviation machinist's mate (AMM 3/c) rating. Whatever grade we received on that test was entered into our records. When a seaman is being considered for advancement in rank, the grade on the exam is one factor, and length of service is another. Most everyone in our class was advanced to AMM 3/c. The four of us from machinist school made the advancement, thus skipping over the seaman first class rating. The pay for third class petty officer was sixty dollars per month. Before we left the school, we also were allowed to take the examinations for second class, first class, and chief aviation machinist's mate ratings, and have our grades on these tests placed in our records for future advancement. A minimum of one year had to be spent in each rating before we would be eligible for the next advancement. Another obstacle to future advancement was our being in competition with old-timers, who automatically received a bonus of ten points added to their exam score for every four-year hitch they had put in. Each hash mark on the sleeve meant a four-year hitch. Three hash marks meant thirty points would be added to the score.

Several of the students with the highest scores in the school were told that they could apply for flight training at Pensacola Naval Air Station. After completion of training, they would be noncommissioned aviation pilots. I was offered the choice, but decided I would rather be an officer and fly in the Army, rather than fly off carriers out at sea. I don't know why I made that choice. Robert B. Miles took this flight training and got his wings, and later a commission. I heard later that he was one of the pilots shot out of the air at the Battle of Midway. I heard that he was one of the pilots in Torpedo Squadron Six on the U.S.S. *Hornet*, flying a Douglas TBD Devastator. This was the squadron that lost all its planes and personnel, except one pilot, Ens. George Gay. I have often wondered what might have been my fate if I had taken flight training at that time.

After finishing AMM school and getting advanced to AMM 3/c, we were given thirty days' leave and received new assignments. I was to be in Fighter Squadron Three, attached to the aircraft carrier U.S.S. *Saratoga*.

I decided to spend my leave on a bus and train trip to Washington, D.C., and to New York City. I had never been anywhere since the Ormsby Village Band went to Flint, Michigan. It was late in the year 1937, and I had to wear my dress-blues, pea coat, and white hat. While sightseeing in Washington, D.C., I met a young man who was wearing a Navy midshipman's uniform. I told him that I had just finished the aviation machinist school at Norfolk, and he confided in me that he had just flunked out of the U.S. Naval Academy at Annapolis, Maryland, and was sightseeing before returning home. His name was Thorlen. We were good company for each other and had a fun time walking up the stone steps of the Washington Monument, all the way to the top. Then to the Smithsonian and all the other Washington sights. For lodging, we stayed at the YMCA there, and also in New York. In 1937, prices were still very low, and my sixty-dollar paycheck went a long way. There was no income tax or any other tax to pay, so I got to spend the whole sixty dollars.

In New York, we walked across the Brooklyn Bridge, went up in the Statue of Liberty and the Empire State Building, and went to Radio City Music Hall to see the Rockettes, and to two or three burlesque shows. Thorlen tried to act dignified at times, and by the end of our leave I was calling him Lord Thorlen, and he was calling me Admiral Settle. I learned a short time later that there was, indeed, an Admiral Settle in the Navy. I wanted to visit Louisville for part of my leave, so I left Lord Thorlen in New York and took the bus south. After a nice visit with sister Bettye and Elliott, I headed west on the Greyhound, made one layover in Texas, and then on to San Diego.

❧ Fighter Squadron Three ❧

When I arrived in San Diego, I rode the ferry across the bay to North Island. After reporting in, I was directed to the Fighter Squadron Three (Fightron Three) Barracks. On Monday, I walked down to the Fightron Three hangar and met the squadron commander, Lt. Commander Cooper, and then Chief Petty Officer Shea, who was the leading chief in charge of enlisted personnel. As soon as I reported in, I was taken out on the flight line, where I first saw the little Grumman fighters of the squadron. They looked to me like short, fat bumblebees, shining bright silver in the San Diego sun. I was led to the back section of the formation of parked planes, and there was 3-F-18, the last plane in the squadron, which was to be my assignment for the next two years. I was to be the plane captain of this plane and would have one or two assistants, as needed.

All of the single, enlisted personnel of the squadrons based at North Island were quartered in two-story barracks at one end of the base. The administration building, mess hall, and gymnasium were nearby. The large runway area and the plane hangars were several blocks from the barracks. We were served typical Navy chow at the mess hall, much the same as at the mess hall at the Norfolk training station. I learned to like the navy beans with ketchup, and even the creamed, chipped beef on toast. The last-mentioned delicacy was universally known by another name that wouldn't look good in print. The beans with catsup for breakfast must have been an invention of the Navy. It's a wonder that they didn't think of it at Ormsby Village—the Beanery. A majority of the sailors went on leave on weekends to San Diego, which had a lot of bars, or to Tijuana, which had more bars and cheap trinkets for sale. Or they could go to the beach by the hotel on Coronado Island.

The fighter planes of VF-3, Fighter Squadron Three, were Grumman single-seated biplanes, with the Pratt & Whitney fourteen-cylinder Twin Wasp Jr. engine. All of the aircraft of the Navy were assigned letters and numbers to identify the intended function of the plane, the model number and manufacturer, and the series number of that model. Our fighters were given the identification F3F-1, which meant fighter plane, model #3, by Grumman (F), and the final 1 meant it was the first in a series of that model. Another set of letters and numbers was stenciled on both sides of each plane, indicating the carrier to which the plane was attached, the intended function of the plane, and the plane's position in the squadron. For example, my plane was 3-F-18. The 3 meant it was attached to the U.S.S. *Saratoga*, the F meant fighter, and the 18 meant it was the last plane in an eighteen-plane squadron. The F3F-1 Grumman fighters in our squadron had our mascot—a black "Felix the Cat" running and holding a round black bomb in his outstretched hands—stenciled on both sides of the plane, just in front of the cockpit.

The *Saratoga's* identification number was CV-3. The *Lexington* was CV-2. The *Langley* was CV-1, and the *Ranger* was CV-4. The *Wasp*, *Hornet*, and *Enterprise* were still under construction in 1937, I believe. During the time that I was attached to the *Saratoga*, on sea maneuvers, each aircraft carrier carried four squadrons of planes. Each squadron had a different function. Besides the fighter squadron, there was a torpedo squadron, a scout-bomber for dive-bombing, and a scout-bomber used principally for scouting. Besides our F3F-1 fighters, there were Douglas TBD-1 torpedo bombers, called Devastators, that were lost in great numbers in the Battle of Midway. They were very slow and obsolete, and were used when there was no chance to give them fighter protection. As I mentioned before, my friend from aviation machinist school, Bob Miles, was one of the pilots lost in these planes. The planes on the *Saratoga* designated as dive-bombers were Douglas SBDs, and the scouting planes were Curtis SBCs. Each of the four squadrons had eighteen planes, for a total of seventy-two. During peacetime, it wasn't necessary to haul any spare planes to the carrier, but we usually took a spare engine and other parts, just in case.

During long periods between trips or maneuvers, the aircraft carriers were at their home base in the San Pedro–Long Beach area. All of the squadrons were stationed at the naval air base at North Island, San Diego. Just across the inlet was Point Loma, an elevated peninsula and well-known landmark welcomed by sailors when first sighted at the end of a lengthy cruise. From North Island, each squadron had its own schedule of flying in formation locally, out to sea or up the coast. I believe there was an area where they could practice the spot-landing to help them prepare for carrier landings. Occasionally, we would have night duty when the squadron was doing formation flying. We would use flashlights to guide the pilot, after landing, to his proper parking position. Then we would chock the wheels and tie the plane down for the night.

The Grumman F3F-1 fighter plane was a single-seat biplane. The fuselage looked short and chunky from the side view, but a top view of it, from the cockpit, showed it to be quite streamlined. The fuselage had an aluminum framework covered with sturdy aluminum skin, which was a semi-glossy silver color. The tail, or empennage, consisted of an aluminum-covered vertical fin and an adjustable aluminum-covered horizontal stabilizer. The leading edge of the vertical fin was offset a few degrees to the right of the center line of the fuselage, to help correct for the left-twisting torque produced by the right-handed rotation of the propeller. The rudder and elevator were of aluminum framework covered with doped fabric. The wings were constructed of aluminum framework, including an aluminum-covered leading edge, and the whole wing was covered with doped fabric. The ailerons were also covered with fabric. There were aluminum trim tabs on the rudder, elevator, and ailerons.

The Pratt & Whitney fourteen-cylinder Twin Wasp Jr. engine was covered with a two-piece aluminum cowling. The cowling was easy to remove by loosening two turnbuckles on each side, and then separating the two halves.

This plane used a two-bladed Hamilton standard adjustable propeller. The pitch of the propeller and the engine RPM were controlled by engine oil pressure, which could be released into a cylinder on the hub of the propeller. The cylinder was connected to two counter-weights, which, in turn, caused the propeller blades to change their pitch. Oil pressure pushed the cylinder forward, moving the propeller blades to a low pitch, or low angle at which the blades bit into the air. The low pitch and less resistance allowed the engine to run at a high RPM. Moving a control next to the throttle controlled the oil pressure to the propeller and the engine and propeller RPM.

❧ Plane Captain ❧

The plane captain is responsible for maintaining his plane in the best condition possible. It is also his job to keep the plane spotlessly clean and waxed. We would compete to see who could have the best-looking plane in the squadron. Each plane captain had another mechanic assigned to help service and do repairs or adjustments on his plane. He was designated the second mechanic or "second mech."

When the planes landed after a flight, each plane captain would meet his plane near the parking area and run along with one hand on the left wing tip, guiding it past the parked planes to its usual parking spot. The pilot would report any malfunctions of the engine or any other problems. Almost always there was some oil seepage from the engine which would spot the windshield and front end of the fuselage, aft of the engine cowling. This leakage was usually from around the pushrod-housing packing nuts.

If the engine ran rough or missed at any time, it almost always meant fouled sparkplugs, and that the engine was burning oil. The fourteen-cylinder engine had two sparkplugs in each cylinder, for a total of twenty-eight plugs. As the hours of running built up on an engine, the piston rings would become worn and allow too much oil on the cylinder walls. And if the bottom oil-scraper rings got fouled up and didn't scrape the oil off the cylinder walls, it would burn in the combustion chamber, and black smoke would pour out of the exhaust pipe. On radial engines, the cylinders nearest to the bottom of the engine are upside down and have their cylinder heads, with two spark-plugs each, at the bottom. Any excess oil remaining on the cylinder walls gravitates down into the sparkplug points. As the time on the engine built up, it was common practice, before starting the engine, to remove at least the two plugs in the bottom cylinder to let the oil drain out of the cylinder. Then the plugs were cleaned and replaced. Before starting the engine, the prop had to be pulled through by hand several times with the throttle open, to make sure nothing interfered with the engine rotation.

Most of the engine maintenance consisted of checking for oil leaks, broken or loose safety-wire, and proper bonding across neoprene hose connections, which prevented possible sparks from static electricity or other current source.

Almost all of the oil leakage that I encountered came from the pushrod-housing packing nuts. The Pratt & Whitney engine was advanced enough to have pressure lubrication to most engine parts. Older engines depended on splash lubrication and the packing of heavy grease into the rocker-boxes. In the newer engines, oil under pressure reached the rocker-boxes through the hollow pushrods, oiling the rocker-arms and eliminating rocker-box packing. This oil returned to the crankcase through the aluminum housing which loosely surrounded the pushrod. This housing had a flange at each end, and was secured to the rocker-box at one end, and the crankcase at the other end, by two packing nuts. The packing nuts were actually little sleeves about three-quarters of an inch tall, which had inside threads at one end and notches in the other end. They were called pushrod-housing packing nuts because a semisoft, waxy, feltlike packing was used to prevent oil seepage. The two nuts were slipped onto the housing unit with the threaded end of the nuts facing the end of the housing. Then the pushrod was inserted into the housing, one end of the pushrod was inserted into the engine against the cam, the rocker-arm was depressed to provide the necessary clearance, and then the pushrod contacted its bearing surface against the rocker-arm. The oil hole in the pushrod matched the hole in the rocker-arm. Now the packing nuts were screwed tight, using a spanner wrench. If insufficient packing was used, or if the nuts weren't tight enough, leakage would occur. When an engine becomes hot, the oil becomes water-thin, and oil seepage is a constant problem. The packing nuts were held tight and prevented from loosening by safety-wire. On the fourteen-cylinder engine there were twenty-eight pushrod housings and fifty-six packing nuts. Needless to say, I have never forgotten the hours I spent on one end of a spanner wrench or removing, replacing, twisting, and trimming safety-wire.

In 1938 the economy was still depressed, and the military services didn't have a lot of money to spend for new parts or accessories, even though the prices were very low. For example, after an engine had been in service for a given number of hours, we would remove the spark-plugs, disassemble them, clean and sandblast them, and adjust the gap between the electrodes. When the electrodes became too worn to adjust the gap small enough, then we could request a new set of plugs, which cost maybe fifty cents a piece. Magnetos, generators, starters, fuel pumps, and oil pumps were all rebuilt, if possible. Nowadays, it's cheaper to buy a new one than to repair the old.

The accessory compartment between the engine and the firewall was narrow, and replacing one of the accessories without removing the engine was a cramped operation. The digital dexterity and tactile sensitivity that I had developed during my typesetting days in the Ormsby Village print shop and the Southern School of Printing enabled me to hold a nut, a washer, and a lock-washer in one hand, reach behind the engine, locate the studs with my fingertips, then place the washer, lock-washer and nut on the stud and screw the nut finger-tight. After all the nuts were tightened with a ratchet wrench, cotter-keys or safety-wire prevented their loosening.

After replacing sparkplugs or an accessory, the engine was started and tested for proper operation. The F3F-1 used a hand-cranked starter to start the engine. When the planes were ashore, the plane captain would have a second mech, or anyone available, to operate a crank, which would rotate the starter faster and faster until the proper inertia was attained. While the starter is being cranked, the mechanic or pilot in the cockpit has primed the engine, has the throttle cracked, and holds his toes on the brakes. With the starter turning at full speed, the cranker removes the crank and stands away from the propeller, while the mechanic in the cockpit pulls the starter toggle to engage the turning starter to the end of the crankshaft. If properly primed, the engine should start before the starter loses its inertia. If not, the process is repeated.

Proper priming of the engine saves much work and time in getting the engine started. The primer injects a squirt of gasoline into the throat of the carburetor or intake manifold. The squirt is actually vaporized or atomized and is immediately available to the sparkplugs. If the proper amount of prime is used, the engine should start almost immediately. When a plane captain has started the same engine many, many times, he learns the exact amount of prime necessary for that particular engine.

All aircraft engines of the dual-ignition, internal-combustion type use a dual-ignition system. Each cylinder has two sparkplugs, and each engine has two magnetos, which generate the spark that fires the sparkplugs. I believe the left magneto supplied the rear plugs and the right mag, the front plugs. After the engine is started and gets warmed up, the condition of the sparkplugs is checked by switching off one magneto and noticing any drop in RPM. Then, you switch back to both mags, and then switch the other mag off and notice any drop in RPM, then switch back to both mags. The mags are checked with the engine running at cruising speed. A predetermined drop in RPM is allowed. If the drop in RPM is too great, sometimes it can be corrected by running up the engine to a much higher RPM to allow burning off of any oil or carbon that may have built up on the plugs. If this doesn't correct the excess drop, the plane is grounded until the bad plug or plugs, or maybe bad ignition wire, is replaced. Dual ignition makes flying twice as safe, because if one plug or bank of plugs or one magneto fails, the engine will still function well enough to get the plane safely down on the ground.

We plane captains tried to build a reputation for maintaining a plane that was not only nice-looking but mechanically efficient, and especially, we strove to have an engine that would start easily. This gave the pilot confidence in the mechanic and made him feel safer, especially when flying over water for long distances.

❧ Maneuvers on the U.S.S. Saratoga ❧

In April 1938, a few months after my assignment to Fighting Squadron Three, the fleet went on maneuvers in the Pacific. This was my first experience aboard a naval vessel. Fightron Three was one of the squadrons attached to the U.S.S. *Saratoga*. Transferring the squadrons from North Island to the carrier was an extensive and intricate operation. All of the squadron personnel and equipment from North Island that couldn't be flown to the carrier aboard the squadron planes were loaded onto barges, or lighters, as they were called, and these were towed out through the channel by tugboats. We were towed out past the tip of Point Loma to the *Saratoga*, which was anchored a short distance offshore in an area designated Coronado Roads. The channel wasn't deep enough for the large carrier to pass through without the danger of being grounded. On both the carriers *Saratoga* and *Lexington*, their draft was too great to risk navigating the waterway between North Island and the Point Loma peninsula. This is what we were told at the time.

On the first day of the cruise, the carriers would cruise down the coast from San Pedro to the San Diego area and anchor. The planes were on the flight-line at North Island, all ready for the pilots to fly them to the carrier. It must have taken at least an hour for the lighter to reach the ship. Even from a distance, the *Saratoga* looked fairly large, but when we came alongside, to me it was a magnificent sight, and a little intimidating. The flight deck seemed to be at least forty or fifty feet above the water line. We climbed up an iron stairway to the quarterdeck area, paused and turned to salute the flag, and stepped aboard, where each sailor saluted the Officer of the Day and requested permission to come aboard. This was my first experience in boarding a naval vessel. I had been in the Navy for over a year and a half and I was finally going to sea. I thought that now, finally, I would be able to call myself "an old salt." Later, when I did so in front of some sailor with a bunch of hash marks, he said, "Get some time in, Mack. I've peed more salt water than you've seen." Only he didn't say "peed."

Cranes were used to lift the heavy equipment, tools, all sea-bags and personal items from the lighter to the carrier. When all the loading was complete, the carrier weighed anchor and headed out to sea. Now the squadron commanders at North Island were alerted to prepare to take off. The carrier was headed into the wind and the carrier operations officer signaled the planes to start to land. The commander of Fighting Squadron Three landed first, in 3-F-1. The pilots tried to make a three-point landing. The landing hook hung down lower than the tail wheel and caught on one of the three arresting cables which are stretched athwartships across the flight deck. Lt. Commander Cooper was our squadron commander and made what I thought was a near-perfect landing. I was amazed at the efficiency of the arresting cables, and the ingenuity of the mechanism that allowed the cable to appear to stretch like a rubber band as the plane slowed and quickly stopped rolling. Toward the edge of the flight deck, at each end of the cable, the cable is permitted to extend by rolling off of vertically positioned rotating drums, which use hydraulic pressure to ease the planes' momentum.

One by one the fighter planes landed, in numerical order. Finally 3-F-18 landed, and I was relieved. Plane handlers were part of the ship's company, and they positioned the fighters as far forward as possible, toward the bow, to allow all airborne planes to have room to land and to taxi. After the last plane had landed, all planes were pushed aft and respotted, after being topped off with gas. To use all available space on the flight deck, the planes were fitted close together, with each wing-tip near the fuselage of the adjacent plane. This was necessary on the older carriers because it would require at least one-fourth of the length of the flight deck bow to be completely clear in order for the first fighter to have enough distance for a takeoff run. However, the planes needed to be positioned so that all propellers would be clear when engines are started again. After the planes have been spotted for the night, the wheels are chocked, and lines are used to secure the wings and the tail to hold-down areas on the deck. Then the oil is checked and topped off if needed. For the night, the cockpit, hatch cover, and entire engine area of each plane were protected with a tarp. Then the aluminum propellers were given a coat of grease to prevent salt water from etching or pitting the surface. Sometimes with rough seas and wind, salt-water spray would reach the planes, especially those parked near the edge of the deck.

The enlisted men of our squadron were quartered on one of the lower decks, in what was called the torpedo compressor room. We had three-decker bunks and slept on our thin mattresses and mattress covers, which had our names stenciled in black ink on the edge. Our hammock was stowed on the bunk under the mattress. For cover, we had our thin wool Navy blanket. Evening chow was at about 1800 hours (6 P.M.), and there was time to take a shower or explore the ship and locate such things as the ship's store, library, etc. The large hangar-deck had two elevators that could be used to lower planes from the flight deck for repair or engine change. Some planes could be kept on the hangar-deck if more space was needed on the flight deck.

After a long, busy day transferring to the carrier, I believe I was in my bunk by 2100 hours (9 P.M.) and I think lights-out and Taps were at 2200 hours. Then the boatswain's whistle would sound over the intercom, and he would command, in a deep voice, something like, "Now hear this. Turn in your hammocks, keep silence about the decks. The smoking lamp is out." It was easy to sleep with the gentle rolling of the huge carrier. During maneuvers, there was practically no seasickness, even in rough seas. The ship's center of gravity was below the waterline, and this minimized the amount of roll. Also, our bunks were almost right at sea level.

Ship's company officers and squadron pilots had quarters in the forward part of the carrier. There were Marine enlisted men aboard who mostly just stood guard at the passages to the officers' quarters, waiting for orders. They were always dressed impeccably in their dress uniforms, and looked very stern and businesslike. The ship's company sailors jokingly referred to the Marines as "seagoing bellhops." The ship's company called the squadron personnel "airedales." In turn, we called them "deck-apes."

Reveille was at 0600 hours, which gave us time to get up, wash, and shave before breakfast at 0700 hours. Breakfast was usually beans with ketchup mixed in, chipped beef on toast, or sometimes scrambled eggs.

If flight operations were planned for the day, we would climb up the gangway ladder to the flight deck and prepare the planes for flight. This involved removing the tarp from the engine and the cockpit sliding hatch cover, wiping the grease off the propeller, removing tie-down lines, and preparing the engine for start and warm-up. At a given, pre-set time, all four squadrons would prepare to start engines. Some of the other squadrons had engines that were equipped with electric wind-up starters, and others had starters that were cranked with shotgun-shell type of inertia. My 3-F-18 had a crank starter, but starting the engine on board the carrier was a one-man operation. To limit the number of sailors on the flight deck during starting of all engines, each plane captain was solely responsible for getting the engine running. Because of this practice, the danger of someone stepping into a propeller was greatly reduced, but the pressure on the plane captain was enormous.

The operations officer, on the bridge in the superstructure, would command over the loudspeaker, "Stand by to start engines." The starter crank would be in place and ready for cranking. The plane captain, in the cockpit, would prime the engine, crack the throttle a bit, then crawl quickly out of the cockpit over the wing to the crank location and frantically start cranking, to get the starter turning at the proper momentum before the operations officer ordered, "Start engines."

The sound of shotgun-shell starters popping off and the roar of their engines starting immediately increased the urgency and the pressure on the one-man crank-and-start plane captain. During the seconds of time it took to start the engines in the other squadrons, we plane captains in the fighter squadron had to remove the crank from the spinning starter, stow it between the landing gear wheel and the wheel chock, then climb over the wing, jump into the cockpit, hold our toes on the brakes, pull the starter toggle, and hope the momentum of the spinning starter was still sufficient to make the engine take hold and start. After having started this engine many times on North Island, I was always one of the first in the squadron to get his engine started. Usually, one or two of the other engines had to be cranked more than once. On one occasion, several cruises later, I had a problem. I had to climb out of the cockpit and recrank three times, while every other engine on the flight deck was running. I could see the operations personnel on the bridge looking down at me, and I was mortified to think that this was happening to me, after two years in the squadron. After the third crank, when I was about ready to pass out, someone was finally sent to crank for me, and after a couple of coughs, the engine started. This happened to me only once. I kept myself in pretty good shape, but on the fourth try, I could hardly lift myself out of the cockpit, and was thankful for the help.

I will bring you back to my first experience with starting all our engines together on the *Saratoga*. Everyone got his engine started on the first try and we ran them long enough to warm up and check the magnetos. Then all engines were stopped. Everything was now relatively quiet until the bullhorn commanded, "Pilots, man your planes." Plane captains stood by their planes while the pilots and other flight crewmembers, such as gunners, observers, and so forth, swarmed out and quickly found their way through the bunched-up planes to locate their own.

The squadron of Douglas TBD-1s were the torpedo bombers. They had been the last squadron to land on the carrier and were spotted at the stern of the flight deck. In addition to the pilot, the TBDs carried an observer and a rear gunner. The next two squadrons, forward of the

TBDs, were the Douglas SBD scout-bombers and the Curtiss SBC scout-observation squadron. The planes of these two squadrons each had two cockpits. Besides the pilot, they each carried an observer-gunner. Our fighter squadron's F3F-1s, spotted closest to the bow, were single-seaters, for one pilot.

The armament of these fighter planes was one .30-caliber and one .50-caliber machine-gun, each mounted near the top of the fuselage, between the engine cowling and the cockpit. The machine guns were synchronized to fire through the turning propeller without hitting it. The fighters were also fitted with bomb-racks, and they sometimes practiced dive-bombing in the ocean area off North Island. The fighter pilots also participated in target practice, firing the machine-guns at a long sleeve which was towed by a slow-moving observation plane. There was an ammunition box in each side of the fuselage, one for .30-caliber and one for .50-caliber rounds. I recall seeing the belts of ammunition in the ammo boxes, and I noticed that some of the points of the bullets were painted a bright red. I was informed by another plane captain that his were green and that this was the way it was determined which pilot hit the target the most times. This was peace-time, and no one suspected that in a few months they would be shoot-ing at other planes and pilots and bombing their carriers.

Returning to my first experience on the flight deck on the *Saratoga*, since the engines of all the planes were already warmed up, the pilots, with their flight jackets, helmets, and goggles, climbed into the cock-pits, where the plane captains usually held the shoulder straps of the parachute and slipped them over the pilots' shoulders. This was just a courtesy, but it helped speed up the preparations for takeoff. The pre-fitted parachute stayed in the cockpit, making a cushion for the seat and back, and was snapped on before takeoff. When all the pilots had manned their planes, the loudspeaker growled, "Stand by to start engines." The plane captains of our squadron started cranking the starters. A few seconds later came the order: "Start engines." The warmed-up engines started immediately. The crank was removed and stowed in the wheel-well of the landing gear.

The pilots revved up the engines and again checked the mags. Wheel chocks were removed from 3-F-1, which was in the center of the deck and ready for takeoff. Lt. Com. Cooper closed the cockpit sliding hatch and started revving up his engine, with his toes on the brakes, while watching a signalman who was making a rapid, rotating motion with a flag. The flagman also watched the bridge for the signal to take off. The pilot gave a thumbs-up if he was pleased with the sound of the engine. The flagman pointed the flag toward the bow, the pilot released the brakes, and the plane started rapidly. The carrier was headed into the wind, and when you added the speed of the wind to the speed of the carrier, the distance needed for lift-off was usually around one hundred feet or less for the fighters. The TBDs needed more distance for taking off, and there was more deck available after the other squadrons had become airborne.

When all four squadrons, seventy-two planes in all, were airborne, the flight deck was kept clear for any possible emergency landings. Oil spots were wiped up, and the mechanics could pass the time away reading, sunbathing, or catching up on scuttlebutt. The planes were completely out of sight, and I never knew the nature of their activity. We were told they would be gone for one and a half to two hours. I usually passed the time catnapping because the early reveilles and the balmy breeze on the flight deck made me drowsy. Also, the exciting activities during the takeoffs and landings were very exhausting.

After about an hour and a half, we began to notice groups of planes approaching from a distance. The carrier was headed into the wind, and soon the first fighter approached the fan-tail. A flagman signaled from a position on the port side, aft on the flight deck. He signaled with what looked like two oversized ping-pong paddles, one in each hand. They were held straight out from the body if the plane was at the correct approach altitude. If the plane was too low, the paddles were lowered, and if too high, they were raised above the horizontal. When the plane had almost reached the flight deck, the signalman moved the right paddle across his front, which meant throttle back the engine and land. If the plane was in an attitude from which it couldn't possibly land safely, the signalman waved it off, and it had to go around the pattern again. If the plane was waved off, it had to bank to the left to be clear of the ship, in case the engine failed or didn't respond quickly enough to the full-throttle setting. The superstructure was on the starboard side of the flight deck. In case a plane had to ditch into the ocean, two destroyers, one on each side of the ship, were assigned to follow each carrier during flight operations.

The first fighter plane landed, and then all the other planes landed without any major problems. The fighters were pushed to the bow, as usual, but this time we were told they would remain there and be tied down for the next few days, while we joined the rest of the Pacific Fleet on a cruise to Hawaii. This was exciting news, especially to those of us who had never been at sea before.

It took four days for the *Saratoga* to reach Hawaii. There wasn't much for the squadron personnel to do, once our planes were properly tied down and any oil seepage wiped off the engine to prevent it from dripping onto the deck. Once again, the propeller was covered with a layer of thick grease to protect it from saltwater spray. The tie-downs that secured the wings to the deck were left a little slack, to allow for shrinkage if they became wet from rain or sea-spray from over the bow.

It was a relaxing cruise, with plenty of time to sunbathe, read, or just watch the whitecaps go by and wonder where the porpoises and whales were. Many nights, before time to turn in, I would sit and watch for the lights of other ships of the fleet, especially blinking lights. Signalmen would often use Morse code to relay orders or other information, using a large light with a movable shutter covering the lens, which could signal dots and dashes. I had learned Morse code as one of the requirements for the signaling merit badge when I was a Boy Scout at Ormsby Village. I hadn't used it for almost eight years and had to practice a while before I could begin to make sense of the signaling-light messages. It was a lot of fun trying and helped pass the time. Once or twice, I saw messages being sent with the two semaphore flags, and I had better luck remembering that code and understanding the words. A lot of my spare time was spent walking around the edge of the flight deck. The *Saratoga* and the *Lexington* were sister ships, and each was over nine hundred feet long, which was equal to the length of three football fields.

As I recall, the weather was calm for most of the trip, and each day became a little balmier as we got closer to the Islands. We sighted the big island, Hawaii, first, with its two volcanic peaks: Mauna Loa and the slightly higher Mauna Kea. Mauna Loa is an active volcano.

Mauna Kea has long been dormant. I was surprised when I first learned that it is about 116 feet higher than Mauna Loa, and is the world's highest island mountain at 13,796 feet. Hawaii was on our port side as we headed toward Maui. We got a good look at Mauna Kea, but we were too far away to see much else. After another two hours or so, we dropped anchor at Lahaina Roads, Maui. It was late afternoon, and we were told there would be liberty boats leaving the ship the next morning.

At about 9 A.M., after breakfast, we boarded motor launches that took us to the dock at the town of Lahaina. This was the area of the first white settlement in the Hawaiian Islands. It was also the pineapple and sugarcane center of the islands. When we were there, it was a town of about three thousand people or less. It is located on the western side of Maui, in a fairly sheltered area of the island. I remember some cocoa palm trees, ferns, and lots of bougainvillea vines with bright-colored flowers. The beauty of the islands and the balmy breezes made me feel that I could, with very little effort, get attached to this place. We walked around with the rest of the swarm of sailors on shore-leave to get the feeling of walking on solid ground, and later went to a pub for a glass of beer or two. I don't remember going to the beach here. We had been told we were going to reanchor at Waikiki Beach later, so we just bought a hot dog and walked back to the dock, to wait for the liberty boat and return to the carrier. I have some photos of the fleet anchored at Lahaina Roads which show two or three carriers and many other vessels. I would have taken many more pictures if I had known how important they would be to me later on. I suppose that when a person is young, he is only concerned with the present, and not with what his desires might be sixty-five years later.

The next morning we weighed anchor and cruised the short distance to Oahu. We anchored well outside Pearl Harbor and were given liberty again. We couldn't wait to get our swimming trunks on and go swimming at Waikiki Beach. The beach was pretty, with a clear view of Diamond Head, the extinct crater which is the principal landmark of Oahu. There were just two visible hotels here at Waikiki in 1937: the faded pink Royal Hawaiian and the off-white Moana. Slightly hidden by the Royal Hawaiian was the old Halekalani, a residential-type building. There were no buildings between the Royal Hawaiian and the Moana. There was a place near the Moana called the Outrigger where they rented surfboards, outrigger canoes, and other equipment. There was also a place where we could change into swimming suits. The beach area between the Moana and Diamond Head was completely undeveloped and gave a beautiful view of the tropical growth and of Diamond Head. The beach in the vicinity of the hotels wasn't nearly as wide or sandy as the beaches where we used to swim near the training station at Norfolk, such as Ocean View or Virginia Beach. Also, parts of the shallow water had to be avoided because of sharp coral, which cut our feet. We all had our pictures taken with Diamond Head in the background, but no one wore the regulation trunks that had been issued at the training station. We would have been laughed off the island. They looked as if someone had taken a pair of black long-johns and cut them off at the waist and just above the knees. They were a loose, droopy fit and, when wet, showed every nook, crater, and volcanic peak.

I have just discovered an old air-mail letter that I wrote to sister Bettye from Oahu on April 20, 1938. It tells of my being out of work for three weeks because my 3-F-18 was put out of commission, but it had been replaced with a new plane, which we had made ready to fly. It also tells of my receiving "flight skins" (explained below) and being treated to a four-hour sightseeing flight over the whole Hawaiian chain of islands in a Navy PBY patrol plane. The letter also states that Fighter Squadron Three was replacing Fighter Squadron Four on the U.S.S. *Ranger* for the remainder of these Pacific maneuvers.

On the last day of our leave, the liberty boats dropped us off in the Pearl Harbor area, and several of us took a tour around Oahu. We drove past Diamond Head, which didn't look too much like a crater from the roadside. I remember the beach in the Kanehoe Bay area, and also the beautiful, panoramic view of the Pali from a roadside overlook point. And of course, we had to stop at one spot along the beach and watch the "Blow Hole" shoot up a squirt of water with each wave.

When we returned to the *Ranger* that evening, we were tired, and we turned in early. The next morning, we weighed anchor and headed back to San Diego. The U.S.S. *Ranger* CV-4 was slightly newer and somewhat smaller than the U.S.S. *Saratoga* CV-3. It seemed to slide through the water a little easier, but maybe its smaller bulk made it just seem to be faster. I remember there was some seasickness, even among the old salts, and we were told the ship rolled excessively because its center of gravity was slightly above the water line. We also noticed that when the *Ranger* suddenly changed its course, it listed much more than the *Saratoga*. These unfamiliar gyrations gave me a sick feeling in my stomach which I had never felt on the *Saratoga*. When we got near the California coast, we were informed the squadrons would take off and do practice landings one or more times before the maneuvers were over. We wiped the planes down, removed their tie-downs, respotted them in takeoff position, warmed all engines, crank-started for the pilots, and the whole takeoff and landing procedure was repeated. By this time we were getting anxious to get back ashore. Unlike the *Saratoga* and *Lexington*, the *Ranger* could be docked near North Island, which made unloading a simpler operation. More than 500 aircraft and 160 naval vessels took part in these 1938 Pacific maneuvers, said to be the most extensive in naval history.

I learned from the other plane captains of a little smuggling operation they had pulled off on previous maneuvers. At the end of gunnery exercises and target practice, the two ammunition boxes in the fighter fuselage were now empty, so it was a perfect place to put cartons of sea-store cigarettes, which we could buy for forty-five cents a carton. I bought ten cartons and stored them in the plane. The planes flew from the carrier to the hangars at North Island. We were required to go through customs for inspection and declare anything bought in sea-stores. We were allowed to bring in one carton of cigarettes each. They cost a little more at the store on the base, so we were very popular with our enlisted friends in the squadron who smoked, when we went to the hangar and unloaded our booty into a shopping bag. No one ever squealed on us because we shared the cigarettes with anyone, for a small profit. We also could afford to supply moochers who never bought cigarettes. There were some sailors who seemed to be broke soon after payday and couldn't even afford to buy cigarettes, and they seemed to be chain smokers. I discouraged them from bumming from me by carrying a sack of Bull Durham, with cigarette papers, for rolling your own. It worked.

Back at North Island, we got into the routine of going to the hangar every morning and afternoon. The pilots flew the planes almost every day, and we were kept busy keeping the engines running smoothly and cleaning and polishing the fuselage. After a given number of hours, the engine had to be changed for a new or reconditioned one. A very close friend of mine worked in the engineering crew of the squadron. He was Johnny Hann, and he was from Cleveland. He and I were promoted to AMM 2/c (aviation machinist's mate second class) at about the same time. Having been at the rank of third class petty officer for the required one year, I was eligible for second class, took the exam, beat out some old-timers, and was promoted. The pay was now seventy-two dollars a month.

A system was in practice whereby the higher-rated mechanics, and other non-flying personnel of fighter squadrons whose planes had only one seat, were allowed to earn extra pay periodically by flying as observers or gunners in the squadrons of scout-bombers or torpedo planes. To receive flight-pay we were required to fly for four hours in a month. The pay amounted to one-half of the base pay, added to the regular salary. When I was third class, I used to get flight-pay every six months, but as second class petty officer, I would be eligible every two or three months, depending on how much pay was allocated to the whole squadron. This special flight bonus to fighter-plane mechanics was nicknamed "flight skins." It was an attempt to equalize the pay of all rated mechanics. Often everyone in our squadron who was eligible to fly for flight-pay was taken with a group of as many as ten or twelve mechanics down to the estuary and put on one PBY observation seaplane. We were then flown around the San Diego–Point Loma area for four hours to satisfy the month's requirement. Then, after landing, we would get on a bus and ride back down to the hangar. As a third class petty officer, I had received flight skins during the Hawaiian cruise.

The engineering crew to which Johnny Hann was assigned spent most of its time in the large squadron hangar, where their primary job was to receive new or reconditioned engines and prepare them for installation on the planes scheduled for an engine change. They were also responsible for the removal of the old engine and installation of the new one. When my 3-F-18 got a new engine, and the engineering crew had completed the installation, I was responsible for any needed adjustments to the oil or fuel pressure and for running up the engine to check the magnetos and the adjustable propeller operation. Usually there was very little oil seepage on the replacement engines. The engineering crew members prided themselves on being very thorough and dependable.

❧ U.S.S. Lexington—Fleet Problem XX ❧

Fighting Squadron Two was attached to the U.S.S. *Lexington*. They were designated VF-2. Their hangar on North Island was adjacent to our VF-3 hangar, and a common wall separated them. I had friends in VF-2. One of their plane captains, Joe Codemo, was a classmate of mine in aviation machinist mate school at the Norfolk training station, and we used to go on liberty together in San Diego and Tijuana, Mexico. Another close friend was Lloyd Herring, who would be of great assistance to me at a later date.

The Fightron Two planes were Boeing F4B-4s. Fightron Two pilots were mostly enlisted petty officers, with the designation "aviation pilot." They were not commissioned officers, but they were considered on a par with any of the officer pilots. A part of the squadron was called the "Flying Chiefs," and they would go to air shows around the country, giving demonstrations in close-formation flying and aerobatics. The little F4B-4 was perfectly suited for air shows. It was a single-seated biplane with fabric wings and control surfaces, the same as our F3F-1s, but it was more slender and not as sturdy-looking. The F4B-4s were considered to be too obsolete for combat, and it was decided they should be replaced by a larger, sturdier plane. A single-seated fighter by Brewster was chosen as the replacement.

The Brewster was a mid-wing monoplane. The wing was all aluminum, as opposed to the fabric-covered wings of the F4B-4, and the single wing was attached near the vertical center of the fuselage. It had a more powerful engine than the F4B-4, and the fuselage was considerably larger and bulkier.

In January 1939, the *Lexington* was scheduled to join the fleet for a cruise and extensive maneuvers, which would take it through the Panama Canal to the East Coast, and to the World's Fair in New York. However, Fighting Squadron Two was in the process of receiving the new Brewsters at the scheduled time for departure for the maneuvers, and our Fighting Squadron Three airedales, with the Grumman F3F-1s, were chosen to replace them. So we would be leaving on the *Lexington* in their place. My friends in Fighting Squadron Two were very disappointed about missing the trip, but we were thrilled about it. These maneuvers would be the highlight of my tour of duty in the Navy.

The U.S.S. *Lexington* was the sister ship of the U.S.S. *Saratoga*. The *Lexington* had sailed down from Long Beach to Coronado Roads, which was the name of the anchorage area near North Island. We had been tugged out on the lighter, as usual, and climbed on board. This ship was so much like the *Saratoga* in every respect that it was hard to realize we were on a different ship.

On January 4, 1939, we weighed anchor, headed out to sea, pointed into the wind, and began taking on our Fightron Three Grumman F3F-1s. Then, to my surprise, came Scouting Squadron Three, which was also a replacement squadron from the *Saratoga*. Next came Bombing Squadron Two and then Torpedo Squadron Two. The planes were spotted for long-distance cruising instead of for flight operations as we headed south. After a few hours, I noticed that the sun was behind us, which meant we were headed southeast. It was late in the afternoon and I knew that, in the winter, the sun rose in the southeast. I found a map of North America and was amazed to find that Panama is actually directly southeast of the tip of Baja California and almost directly south of Washington, D.C.

Soon after we had boarded the *Lexington*, we learned it would be the flagship for the ComAirBatFor (Commander Aircraft Battle Force). To quote from *The Observer*, a weekly publication of the U.S.S. *Lexington*, dated January 7, 1939:

> Bearing proudly aloft the three-starred flag of Vice Admiral Ernest J. King, U.S. Navy, Commander Aircraft Battle Force, and housing within her cavernous, almost commodious, and always mystifying living spaces what is probably the largest number of officers and enlisted personnel ever to be attached to a single man-of-war on duty at one time, the *Lexington* sailed from Coronado Roads to take part in Fleet Problem XX on the most impressive voyage in her history.

On the way to Panama, at times we were close enough to Mexico to see the coastline, but most of the time we were in open sea, and all we could see was the sea. We saw porpoises and a few flying fish. As we got farther south, it got balmier and we could sunbathe, if we could find a suitable, unoccupied spot near the superstructure on the flight deck, or in one of the gangways below decks. Many times, the enlisted personnel would be told, "You can't stay here, sailors," when they were swabbing the decks or doing a "clean sweep down, all decks." Later, we learned the reason we seemed to be tripping over each other was that, with the four squadrons aboard, with their supporting personnel, plus the ComAirBatFor, with all of his entourage, the *Lexington* was setting a record for the most people on active duty on a naval vessel ever! There were well over twenty-two hundred naval personnel, Marines, and some Army brass, to observe the flight operations.

Another effect of the overcrowding was felt in the shower room, where a Marine was stationed to prevent wasting of the now overtaxed water supply. We were allowed to turn on the water just long enough to get our bodies wet, then soap down, and then turn it on long enough to rinse off. We were also allowed a bucket of saltwater and saltwater soap for scrubbing our skivvies and socks.

In the large toilet room, or "head," instead of toilet bowls and urinals, there were two long steel channels, back to back, with a wooden board covering each channel, and a common back between the two. Into the seat boards were cut out toilet holes spaced about three feet apart. It reminded me of a pair of outhouse toilet seats about twenty feet long. The two seat boards were hinged, to allow them to be raised for cleaning. A continuous stream of seawater was pumped in and passed below the seat in the steel channel.

We reached the Canal Zone in about three or four days. Getting the *Lexington* through the locks was a tight squeeze. The chambers of the locks were 1,000 feet long and 110 feet wide. The *Lexington* was over 900 feet long and a little over 110 feet wide at the level of the flight deck. The flight deck was a little above the sides of the lock chamber. So there was barely room to fit before the lock was closed behind the ship and the lock doors at the bow of the ship opened to allow the ship to be slowly raised to the level of the water in the second lock chamber. In the first lock chamber, some of the railing along the edge of the chamber was knocked over, and some of the scuppers on the *Lexington* were bent a little, but there was no serious damage.

I was intrigued by the way this huge carrier was towed into the lock chambers by electric locomotive tow vessels on each side of the locks. Going through three locks on the Pacific side of the canal raised the ship to the height of Gatun Lake, and then the three Gatun locks lowered us eighty-five feet, to the level of the Atlantic Ocean. It took about eight hours to cross the whole isthmus, a little more than fifty miles in all. We were amused to see we had gone from the Pacific Ocean to the Atlantic Ocean by going in a northwesterly direction, because the Isthmus of Panama is shaped like an S. It could be called an "essmus."

After getting through the Canal, we were given shore leave in Colon. I remember walking through the seedy part of town with two or three of my friends. I was disgusted with the vulgar exhibitions of body parts by hookers, which attracted a crowd of sailors, on a small stage that was visible from the street. We spent several days in the area of Colon, which I thought was a strange name for a city at the south end of the Northern Hemisphere, until I was informed it is pronounced Colón, the same as cologne, which sounded a little more dignified. Some sailor comic who didn't enjoy his liberty in Colón thought that, since the Isthmus of Panama is shaped like an S, maybe the town should be named Sigmoid Colon.

We sailed for a rendezvous with more of the fleet at Guantanamo Bay, Cuba, a distance of 850 nautical miles. We could see Cuba from a distance, but didn't anchor there. Instead, after picking up our two destroyers for escort, we headed east-southeast toward the British colonial island of Barbados, over 1,000 nautical miles away. During the first day of this three-day trip, the squadrons took off and were gone for about two hours, and then returned, landed, and were gassed up and respotted for takeoff. Then after lunch they took off again, and returned about an hour and a half later. We seldom saw any other aircraft carriers except the *Ranger* with its two escort destroyers. I saw no battleships or cruisers. No one ever discussed what kind of battle games were taking place, but we knew we were involved in Fleet Problem XX.

There were two more days of the flight operations, and then we anchored offshore at Bridgetown, Barbados, where we were given shore leave for two or three days, returning to the ship overnight. This island is twenty-one miles long and fourteen miles wide. There wasn't much to do on liberty. It was just a nice feeling to be back on solid ground. I think I did go to the beach once, to get my swimming trunks wet, and for a picture to prove to myself that I had actually gone swimming in the Caribbean Sea. Actually, Barbados is just outside the chain of islands named Lesser Antilles, so I was really swimming in the Atlantic Ocean. While in Barbados, I tried eating flying fish for the first time, and also pepper pot with rice. These dishes were recommended by people who seemed to know Barbados was famous for the way they prepared them. We were also told that Barbados was well known for its rum, so we had to try that too.

While we were anchored at Bridgetown, Barbados, we learned that we were part of a massive training exercise. The value of this training cannot be overestimated, in view of what lay ahead for these naval personnel and their warships and planes.

After about three or four days of liberty at Barbados Island, we steamed to the Virgin Islands and anchored. At some of the ports where we stopped, we must have been taking on fuel, supplies, and water. Then we headed east into the Atlantic for more extensive maneuvers. According to the records, we were informed, the planes of the four carriers involved in the exercise made a total of over five thousand takeoffs and landings. The flying experience gained by the pilots and crewmembers during this Fleet Problem XX in the Atlantic, and in other maneuvers during the next two years, was to play a large part in turning defeat into victory in the Pacific.

Each plane of Fighting Squadron Three had the name of the pilot stenciled on the edge of the sliding canopy of the cockpit. For most of the time while I was plane captain of 3-F-18, the pilot was Ens. Lamplough. He was a tall, fairly handsome, apparently fun-loving, friendly young man who seemed to be prone to minor mishaps, such as getting a flat tire on the landing gear, or touching wingtips with another plane while taxiing. And rumor had it that he may have belly-landed once with his landing gear retracted. I had heard him referred to, jokingly, as Ace Lamplough, because he had brought down five airplanes, but all of them were ours. The mechanics would kid around between ourselves about whose plane had the best pilot. I knew Mr. Lamplough

was a very good pilot, and I argued that he was the best at gunnery and
dive-bombing. The plane captains had no social contact with the pilots,
who were all officers. We would never say more than "Good morning,
sir" or "Aye, aye, sir." I don't remember ever saluting a pilot unless he was
the squadron commander. We usually wore dungarees or blue denim
clothing and didn't look or feel very military.

Other names I remember on the cockpit canopies of our fighters
were Lt. Com. Cooper in 3-F-1, Lt. Quinn in 3-F-10, and Ens. or
Lt. Jg. J. Thach. I don't remember which plane Thach was flying at that
time, but I remember the name. He was to become the Squadron
Commander of VF-3, and the outstanding Navy fighter pilot of the
Battle of Midway and other action in the Pacific.

After the long-distance exercises in the Atlantic, which took the
fleet in a large, triangular pattern, the *Lexington* headed for Haiti,
where we anchored near the city of Gonaives. Other ships anchored at
Port-au-Prince, the capitol of Haiti. The only thing I can recall about
Gonaives is the extreme poverty of the people, which was evident
everywhere. I walked a few streets, bought postcards, had lunch, and
took the liberty launch back to the ship. After a day or so, we headed
north toward Hampton Roads and Norfolk, Virginia. I could see Cuba
at a distance the first day, and then I don't remember seeing Florida or
any of the East Coast of the U.S. until we passed Cape Hatteras, and
then we could see the Virginia coast. As we approached Hampton
Roads, the four carriers were lined up, with the *Lexington* leading the
way, followed by the *Ranger*, the *Yorktown*, and the *Enterprise*. I have a
photograph of the four ships that was taken by a Navy photographer
from an airplane. I can see the squadrons spotted on the flight deck of
the *Lexington*, and can picture about where my 3-F-18 is tied down.
Every time I look at the picture, I realize I was somewhere on that carrier at that time, sixty-one years ago.

When the fleet anchored at Hampton Roads, it marked the end of
the greatest naval maneuvers to date. At times, the activities on the
Lexington flight deck became hectic, but exciting. It was my responsi-
bility to keep 3-F-18 clean and protected from the salt-water spray, but
most important was the fine-tuning of the engine, to ensure easy starting and smooth running for long periods of time over the open sea,
many miles from the safety of the carrier. We also were continuously

inspecting control surfaces for signs of worn hinges, frayed cables, and so forth. The safety of the pilot was our main concern. During my time in the squadron, seeing thousands of takeoffs and landings, I never heard of any pilot experiencing a problem with his engine, other than maybe burning too much oil.

The great success of the *Lexington* in its role in Fleet Problem XX was a result of the teamwork and the close collaboration of the flight operations officer with the pilots, mechanics, plane handlers, and the whole ship's company. I felt like an important little cog in the whole massive operation. In spite of the overcrowding on the ship, or maybe partly because of it, I felt proud to have been aboard the *Lexington* for this cruise.

Now that the war games were over, we were anticipating the trip to the World's Fair in New York, but then came the announcement that shocked everyone. We would be leaving as soon as possible to return to the Pacific. We never were given the exact reason for this disappointing development, but it was rumored that something had happened concerning the relationship between the United States and Japan, and most of our fleet was in the Atlantic, including almost all of our carriers.

It would take about two weeks for the trip back to San Diego, and I was due for two weeks' leave. Since the planes wouldn't be taking off again until the ship reached San Diego, I decided to leave the ship and take the bus to Louisville, to visit sister Bettye and brother George, and then go cross-country by bus to meet the squadron at North Island. It had been about two years since I had seen Bettye or any of my family, so it was a good break for me, and helped me feel better about missing the World's Fair.

The bus ride across country to San Diego was long and lonely, and I made it nonstop, sleeping on the bus and eating at bus stops. Back at the hangar on North Island, everything seemed normal. The *Lexington* had made it back in record time, without stopping for shore leave. Their logs indicated the entire round trip to the East Coast and back, including all the side-trips for war games and flight operations, covered 19,182 nautical miles, and the squadrons made nearly five thousand landings.

After being aboard the *Lexington* for several months, Fighting Squadron Three was settling back down to normal at North Island. Sometime later in 1939, the squadron was back aboard the *Saratoga*, and we steamed up to San Francisco for the Golden Gate International Exposition. We were told we would have liberty in San Francisco, but, for some reason, we just sat outside the Golden Gate Bridge, which had been completed two years earlier, in 1937. The planes did not take off, and we couldn't go ashore. The next day we left for San Diego, and the planes returned to North Island. I never did learn why we hadn't gone under the bridge, but it may have been because of the size and the draft of the ship, or it may have had something to do with war nerves. As enlisted personnel, we weren't privy to the decisions of the high brass.

A new pilot was assigned to my 3-F-18. He was an Ensign Anderson. He seemed awfully young, but, apparently, he was an excellent pilot and he had a pleasant personality.

One of the most exciting, but nerve-wracking, experiences was the "night qualification" exercises for all new pilots. The flight deck was well lit and the planes had landing-lights. All hands seemed to come up from below decks to the flight deck, to watch from a safe distance as each plane landed. There were several close calls, but I remember only one mishap. I had gone below-decks to go to the head, and on the way back to the flight deck, I looked up and saw a plane leaning, almost upside-down, across the hatch opening, with the pilot almost head-down, still supported by his seatbelt. The plane-handlers quickly righted the plane and freed the unharmed, but embarrassed pilot. This was the only accident I ever saw in my two and a half years in the squadron. However, I heard many stories about planes ditching into the drink and pilots being rescued by the escort destroyers. Once a whole squadron became disoriented and couldn't locate the carrier. One by one the planes ran out of gas and ditched.

We had a Commander Sinton on the *Saratoga*, who was operations officer, I believe. He was referred to as "Sweet-shit Sinton." He had been the commander of the squadron that ditched. The story goes that he had radio contact with the *Saratoga*, which had him on the loudspeaker as he described the ditching of each plane as it went down into the sea. The loudspeaker blared the message loud and clear. He would say, "Well, there goes number four. Oh-oh, there goes number eleven. There goes number six." Then when his engine, on number one, started to sputter, he shouted loudly, "Sweet shit, here I go." All the pilots were rescued, but the planes were lost.

I had several close friends among the mechanics. The plane captains, who were all aviation machinist mate second class, included F. A. Warren, Peterson, and Waltz. Other mechanic friends were Randall Snow, Brems, Bill Boatman, and, of course, Johnny Hann. I don't recall many first names, but I remember the personalities well. I used to kid Warren about being so tall and skinny and not being able to fill out the seat of his pants. I called him "Flat-Ass Warren." He kidded me about always "bitching" about my inconveniences, such as standing in lines for what seemed like hours after hurrying frantically to get there. (We called it "hurry up and wait.") He called my complaints "beating my gums" or "chipping my molars." Everyone called me Settle or J. W. I was short and stocky, and he called me "J. Wide-Bottom Molar Chipper."

In December 1939, I was going to be eligible for the rating of aviation machinist mate first class, AMM 1/c, since I had been AMM 2/c for the required one year. I also had completed and passed the examinations for first class and chief petty officer while I was in aviation mechanic school, and this information was in my records. I had always dreamed of being a pilot in the Army Air Corps, rather than the Navy, and I thought I would have a better chance of being a test pilot if I were in the Army and ashore. This was two years or more before Chuck Yeager trained as an enlisted pilot in the Army. I didn't realize Navy and Marine pilots were also test pilots, but I had made up my mind to be an Army pilot and applied for the flying cadet program of the Army Air Corps.

❧ Flying Cadet ❧

The Air Corps flying cadet program had been in existence for several years. To be eligible for the program, the applicant must have completed two years of college with satisfactory grades before applying, and must pass an extensive physical examination. Originally, the instructors for the primary training were Army pilots, and the training took place at Randolph Field in Texas. As the program grew with the expansion of the Air Corps, more schools were opened. There were at least three primary training schools in California. I know there was one at Hemit, California, and another one somewhere else in Southern California, maybe Oxnard. I was assigned to the one located at the Ryan School of Aeronautics facilities at Lindbergh Field, San Diego, California. To enlist in the Army Air Corps while my four-year hitch in the Navy still had three months left to go, I was required to get a special order discharge from the Bureau of Navigation of the Navy Department. It was urgent that this be done at this time because I was twenty-six years old, and that was the age limit for being commissioned a second lieutenant, which would be my rank after completing advanced training.

December 27, 1939, was the date of my enlistment as a flying cadet in the Army Air Corps. Before my enlistment, I took the Army physical exam and passed, and then I received the special order discharge from the Navy on December 22, 1939. After reporting to the Ryan School of Aeronautics, I was interviewed by another doctor, who asked me why I wanted to be a pilot. I answered that I thought I would make a good pilot. He rechecked my vision, my hearing, and my reflexes. I then met a Captain Horton, who was the commanding officer of the Air Corps primary training school. A Lieutenant Hopwood was second in command. I was issued a flying cadet uniform, which consisted of a light blue-gray shirt and trousers, a matching cap, and a black tie. We also were issued a flying jacket with a fur collar, a helmet with earphones and goggles, and, of course, a long, white scarf.

The sleeping accommodations at the training facility resembled a long row of motel rooms, each with two double-decker bunk beds. There were four cadets assigned to each room. My roommates were Kellor, George, and Peter Packard. Also included in the facility were a dining room, a kitchen, a small office, and a classroom. On a Monday after breakfast, the new class of flying cadets reported to the hangar area of the Ryan School, where we met our assigned instructors. I believe there were about twelve new cadets, and about the same number of cadets who had completed some of the training and were considered our superiors. I was surprised to learn that all the instructors were civilian pilots who were hired by the Army for the primary phase of training.

My instructor was a man in his late thirties or early forties, who didn't seem very friendly, and seemed to feel I was too old to be just beginning to learn to fly. I also got the feeling that he resented my getting free flying instruction while he had sacrificed much to get the same training. I thought there might be a personality problem, but I didn't realize that I could have requested a different instructor, as others had done. I was still on the timid side and was not pushy enough.

The plane used here at Ryan School for primary training was the Ryan ST. This was a sleek little low-winged monoplane, with a long, slender, polished aluminum fuselage with two open cockpits. The wings and control surfaces were fabric-covered. The engine of the earlier Ryan ST model was a Menasco six-cylinder inverted design that turned a two-bladed wooden propeller. The Ryan ST was manufactured at Ryan Aeronautical Company. Their factory was just across the Lindbergh Field runway, right there near the Ryan School of Aeronautics. This small Ryan factory had been even smaller just twelve years earlier, when it built Lindbergh's *Spirit of Saint Louis*. The custom-built plane cost Lindbergh fifteen thousand dollars, not including the engine.

For our flight training, we wore a flight jacket with a sheepskin collar, helmet, goggles, and a long, white scarf. This was in January, and the weather was chilly even in San Diego, so we had to dress warmly.

The Ryan ST plane was given the Air Corps designation of PT, for Primary Trainer, and a number for each plane. I have pictures of the instructor and me taking off in PT 33. The only instruction I was given was that I should follow through the instructor's movement of the stick and rudder pedals while we took off, climbed, and banked to leave Lindbergh and fly over an area just inland from the coast. The instructors had microphones and the students' leather helmets had built-in earphones. When we had climbed to about twenty-two hundred feet, we were over a straight stretch of road, and the instructor said, "Follow me on the controls as I do a few S's over the road." We started with the plane crossing the road at right angles and flying straight ahead for two or three seconds. Then we banked smoothly to the left for a 180-degree turn, then back across the road at right angles, then in two or three seconds, a bank to the right 180 degrees, and across the road again at right angles. This formed an S pattern, and the maneuvers were repeated time after time. Usually there was a crosswind at an off-angle across the road, and in order to have evenly proportioned halves of the S's, the number of seconds before banking varied with the direction and velocity of the wind. After several S's over the road, we flew to an auxiliary field, which was just a flat area in the countryside north of San Diego.

We flew a landing pattern at four hundred feet altitude and shot three or four landings, stopping after each one, and taxiing back to take off again. Then we climbed back to altitude and flew back to Lindbergh Field to land and taxi back to the flight line, near the hangar. We climbed out of the plane, and the instructor just walked away, without saying anything about how I was doing, or giving any advice or suggestions about anything. I presumed this was the way flying was taught. Then I noticed other instructors talking to their students in a friendly manner, and demonstrating, with hand motions, the attitude of the plane during maneuvers. All the other cadets I talked to admitted they already had flying experience, and some had soloed before joining the Army. The next day went almost exactly like the first day. I wasn't told how I had done the day before, and assumed I was doing all right. While being closely monitored, I was allowed to make the landings and takeoffs at the auxiliary field.

During the next several days we went through some aerobatics, such as chandelles and a power-off stall, after which we put the plane into a 720-degree right spin, and pulled out of the spin at the precise heading at which the stall was initiated. We never did do a plain loop, slow roll, or snap roll. Some days, if the weather was too bad for flying, we would have classes in navigation, mechanics, and Morse code. We also had a few sessions of close-order drill. I was already an experienced airplane mechanic and I knew Morse code from the Boy Scout training at Ormsby Village. I had studied simple navigation problems while in the Navy and had marching experience from marching in the band at Ormsby Village, at KMI, in the National Guard, and in boot training in the Navy. So I had no problem with the ground school classes, and was made drill sergeant for the class in simple marching practice.

❧ Flying Cadet Dining Room ❧

During the evening meal in the cadet dining room, we sat four at a small, square table. Some of the cadets were a little more advanced in the primary training program than we newer students. There was at least one advanced cadet at each table. As a form of mild hazing, they required us to memorize several definitions of words unrelated to flying, and the pedantic wording of the definitions was intended to amuse the upperclassmen. This harmless little activity was a tradition passed down from one class to the next, and helped students get acquainted with each other.

At our first evening meal, we were told it would be a square meal, and we should eat it accordingly. We would take food on a fork or spoon, lift it vertically to the height of the mouth, and then to the mouth. If I seemed not to make the required angle, I would be ordered, "Bail out, Mr. Settle." This meant I was to jump out of my chair, land in the aisle at a half-squat while looking skyward, and reach up to hold onto the parachute shrouds, and maybe pretend to be trying to untangle them. The more realistic I could make it appear, the more "points" I might make with my "superior." At times, there would be three or four cadets bailing out at once. It was all a lot of fun and helped us relax a little.

We never knew when we might be asked to recite one of the definitions that we were given to memorize. A week or so after the first dinner meal, we were just finishing another dinner when an advanced student looked at me and asked, "Mr. Settle, are you full?" My answer had to be the memorized definition of being full, so I replied, "Sir, my gastronomic satiety admonishes me that I have reached the limit of deglutition consistent with dietetic integrity."

At another meal one of us might be asked, "Mr. Packard, what is leather?" And Pete would reply, "Sir, if the fresh skin of an animal be cleaned and divested of all hair, fat, and all other extraneous material, and be immersed in a dilute solution of tannic acid, a chemical combination ensues. The gelatinous tissue is converted into a non-putrescible substance impervious to and entirely insoluble in water. That, sir, is leather."

At another dinner, another roommate of mine might be asked, "Mr. Kellor, what is a dodo?" Kellor would be expected to reply, "Sir, a dodo is the amoeba of the Army flier, to be properly christened and subdued by an intricate course of predetermined and idealistically integrated formulae for the purpose of impressing upon the unused convolutions of his cerebrum the correct and proper duties, functions, and the instantaneous assimilation of that compound and aggregate wisdom of those previously initiated intelligentsia in direct control of his movements. That, sir, is a dodo." These ridiculous definitions must be delivered verbatim and with a straight face, or it was, "Bail out, Mister."

The flying instruction continued with several more days of takeoff and landing practice with the instructor on board. I learned that almost all the other cadets had soloed and were taking off and landing at Lindbergh Field. I also learned that several of the other cadets had requested a change of instructors and had been given a fresh start. I didn't realize I could have done the same thing: I could have dumped this character, who had no intention of letting me solo and progress to the next step.

The Army officer in charge of the school, Captain Horton, gave me a progress check flight and had me do a couple of chandelles. He then had me land and take off with him at the auxiliary field. After the second landing, he got out and told me to take it around solo. I couldn't believe what I was hearing. His whole demeanor was completely different from that of the so-called instructor I had been stuck with, and I felt that, at last, I was free to perform on my own. When the nose of the plane lifted off the ground and I was looking at the empty cockpit in front of me, I felt a sensation of being in control for the first time. I would now be able to show that I had the right stuff to be a military pilot, and maybe later, a test pilot. I made three takeoffs and landings, stopping after each landing to talk to Captain Horton and get his comments. After the third landing, he got back in the front cockpit, and we flew back to Lindbergh.

The day after my solo, I had a new instructor, a Mr. Larsen. He was a friendly, slow-talking Scandinavian with a thick accent. The first day with Mr. Larsen, we couldn't use the auxiliary field for landings because of strong crosswinds, and it had rained the night before. The dirt field was too soft to land on, so we practiced the S's over the road and steep turns. Then it rained some more and flooded the auxiliary field. There was a strict rule that no cadet could solo from Lindbergh Field until he had completed three days of solo flights from the auxiliary field. Part of the landing pattern at Lindbergh extended over the city of San Diego, and there was concern about the safety of the people living or working near the airport if student pilots were allowed to fly over them, especially while practicing takeoffs and landings.

My class had been training for almost six weeks and I couldn't solo from Lindbergh to complete all the required solo training, and time ran out on me. I was too far behind to catch up. Also, there was not yet the urgency for pilots in the military that there would be in two more years. The flight schools usually cut two or three out of each class to prevent having more pilots than were needed in the next phase, basic training. I received condolences and my Army Air Corps discharge on February 25, 1940. I have always felt I was washed out of flight school by the rain, and by an instructor who didn't instruct.

I inquired of the military officers at the flight school about the possibility of my going to the Air Corps navigation school or the gunnery school, which I believe were in Colorado. They reminded me that it was too late for me to enroll in one of those classes because, by the time I had completed their six months' course, I would be twenty-seven years old, and the maximum age for a second lieutenant was twenty-six. If I had been a month later in applying for the flying cadet program, I wouldn't have been eligible.

PART IV

A Civilian in the Air

The War Years

❧ The Outcast ❧

So I was cast out, away from my newfound friends, into a depressed society, with no job to support myself. The economic depression had eased up slightly in some areas of the country because of Roosevelt's New Deal programs, such as the Civilian Conservation Corps (CCC), the WPA, and many others. I was devastated to think I had failed to do something I had always dreamed of doing. The only other two failures I could recall were not passing the English major requirement, "The Novel," because of my slow reading ability, and, just once, failing to crank-start 3-F-18 without help during flight operations on the *Saratoga*. The depressed feeling I had because I had failed to accomplish a goal I had set for myself was partially offset as I rationalized that maybe "someone up there" wanted me to try for a different goal. But the important thing for me to do, at once, was to get employment.

I was an aircraft mechanic with considerable experience, and was sure there were lots of job opportunities for me out there somewhere. I applied at the Consolidated Aircraft Corporation, right there next to Ryan School of Aeronautics at Lindbergh Field. I was surprised when I was told there were no openings for aircraft mechanics, but they would hire me to buck rivets, in the B-24 bomber wing assembly department, at a starting rate of forty-five cents an hour. I could even make fifty cents an hour if I worked the night shift. This was a disappointment, but I needed an income and took the job. At first, I considered rejoining the Navy and trying to get back in Fighting Squadron Three. I don't know if it was the possible embarrassment of admitting I had washed out of flight school, or what, but I decided to give civilian life a try.

On my first day at Consolidated, when I walked into the large wing-assembly department, I was met by a foreman and taken up the stairs of a wooden framework that surrounded a B-24 wing, laid lengthwise, with the leading edge down toward the floor. There were several walkways along both sides of the wing, which fit closely near the cambered upper surface and the flat lower surface. I was told to go to the tool crib nearest to my assigned work area. I was given some metal tabs with my assigned number on them. When you checked out an item, you left your numbered tab in its place. I checked out an air riveting gun and a bucking bar. I don't remember much about what my job was, but I felt I was a real beginner, and had to ask where I should be and what I was supposed to be doing. I may have been there long enough to get one week's paycheck, for eighteen dollars. I don't remember if there was any withholding tax, but there wasn't much to withhold from.

During my after-hours from the Consolidated job, I visited the Ryan School hangar and learned of an acquaintance from the Navy, Ray Beckelman, who was in charge of servicing the Ryan STs used by the Air Corps—the same planes I had just been training in. When he saw me, he asked what I had been doing, and when I told him I had been bucking rivets at Consolidated, he offered me a job as airplane mechanic. They were paying fifty cents an hour and fifty-five cents for the night shift.

I was delighted to be back working on planes that were being flown, and servicing the little Menasco engines. By now, some of the Ryans used for training were equipped with five-cylinder radial engines by Kinner. The Air Corps was also using some Stearman trainers that we serviced. I felt right at home servicing the Stearman radial engine, because it reminded me of the radial engines I had serviced in the Navy. I worked on the night shift because it paid a nickel more an hour, and there was more servicing to do after the cadets finished flying for the day.

While I was working at Ryan, I studied for the Department of Commerce aircraft engine license, took the exam at Lindbergh Field, and passed. I received a certificate, or E license, which would allow me to examine aircraft engines and certify them for flight, if I was satisfied they were safe and functioning properly, and if any mechanical work done passed my inspection. I never had occasion to use the license, but it could give me an advantage if I were to apply for a mechanic's job in the future. I planned to get the A license later; then I would be an A&E licensed mechanic. A&E is the abbreviation for aircraft and engine.

This was the year 1940. I was twenty-seven years old. A few of my friends from North Island came to visit me at my little, low-rent apartment in San Diego. One of them, Randy Snow, was married to a student nurse. Through them, I met, and a short time later, married another young student nurse.

❀ Curtiss-Wright Technical Institute Instructor ❀

I worked for several months at Ryan before I heard that a friend of mine, Waltz, from Fighting Squadron Three, had a position at Curtiss-Wright Technical Institute up at Glendale, California. He had been a highly regarded plane captain of 3-F-10, the plane of the second-in-command of Fighting Squadron Three, Lt. Quinn. Waltz was in charge of the aircraft engine test stands, and taught mechanic students how to start engines and fine-tune their operation. I learned from Waltz there was an opening in the aircraft engine overhaul section of the school. I applied, and with my Navy experience in aviation plus my E license, I was hired at $150 per month. My title was Instructor, Aircraft Engine Overhaul.

The name of the new job sounded impressive, and made me feel I was going to make it, after all, in the civilian world. I have a photograph of me wearing a shirt, necktie, and nametag, standing by a large, radial, eighteen-cylinder Wright Twin-Cyclone engine. My job was to teach students to disassemble, repair, and reassemble large radial aircraft engines. The job was interesting for a few months, but I did a lot of standing around and occasionally answering questions. There weren't many students interested in large engines because all the jobs in aviation were concerned with small private aircraft. The users of large aircraft engines were the airlines, which were small companies back then, and the military, which hadn't yet been jolted into increasing their demand for planes and trained mechanics. I attended a night school in Glendale and took a course in welding, which emphasized welding aluminum tubing. This was one of the requirements for passing an examination for the A license. After passing the examination, I was now an A&E licensed mechanic.

While I was an instructor at Curtiss-Wright Tech, I missed being around flying aircraft and using my hands more. I also missed getting dirty oil and grease under my fingernails and on my forearms and elbows. I longed to start up an engine and listen to it purr thankfully in response to my care, and I thought of the old cliché, "Those who can't do, teach." At the risk of being thought of as someone who couldn't hold a job, I inquired about a job opportunity I had heard of at Lockheed Aircraft in Burbank, near Glendale. I found there was an opening for an A&E mechanic on the P-38 fighter plane flight line.

❧ Crew Chief—Lockheed P-38 Fighter ❧

I resigned the instructor job and was hired at Lockheed, at a pay rate of eighty-five cents an hour. My job was to be a crew chief, with several other mechanics working under my supervision. Our job was to receive a P-38 fighter on the flight line after it was rolled out from the factory and pulled to the flight line by a tractor.

I had seen the P-38 fighter in flight on several occasions, and was impressed by its speed and sleek appearance. Its unusual design featured two in-line engines, one on each side of a short fuselage, which contained the cockpit and the armament. The short fuselage also contained the wheel well for the retractable nose-wheel component. Behind each engine, a long boom extended to the tail section, and the two booms were supported and joined together by a wide horizontal stabilizer. Each boom had its vertical fin and rudder, but there was only one wide elevator.

The P-38 was fitted with two Allison twelve-cylinder in-line, Prestone-cooled, supercharged engines. The two Prestone coolers were installed in the booms, just behind the wing. This was a mid-wing monoplane. The engines turned three-bladed Hamilton Standard constant-speed propellers.

The job of the ground crew was to degrease the engines, install the propellers, and start and run up the engines. Then we would make all necessary adjustments, check the operation of the flight control surfaces, and generally make the plane ready for check flight and subsequent delivery to the military.

After a plane left the flight line, and before another plane came out of the factory, sometimes we would just wait around, and there often were two or three crews with no plane to work on. I remember two occasions when the idle mechanics were loaded into a company bus and taken to a nearby field, out of sight of the Lockheed plant, where we could read or walk around to kill time until the end of the shift. We were told there were some high officials visiting the plant, and the foreman wanted everyone on the flight line to look busy. We didn't mind getting paid for loafing. While killing time, we could watch P-38s being flown by test pilots. One pilot would dive steeply downward at high speed and then pull out of the dive and go straight up, corkscrewing at the top of the climb. Then he would go into another dive and repeat the maneuver. I felt pretty useless just sitting there out of sight, being paid eighty-five cents an hour for loafing, when I could have someday qualified to be the pilot in that P-38. Then I told myself, "That guy is just a glorified throttle jockey who was lucky enough to learn how to fly from a competent instructor, and, if the truth be known, he probably couldn't overhaul a magneto, or safety-wire a pushrod-housing packing nut, so there!"

I started working at Lockheed in the summer of 1941. The only person I can remember who worked there was Jim Bishop, who was in charge of the crew chiefs on the flight line. He was highly respected for his knowledge of the P-38 and was always ready to give advice when asked. One day I asked him if he knew why I was being paid only eighty-five cents an hour, when all the other crew chiefs were getting a dollar twenty-five. He seemed shocked to hear it, and said it was a mistake and he would have it corrected. I had worked for about five months for forty cents an hour less than I should have received.

❧ World War II ❧

It was December 1941, and on Sunday the seventh, the shocking news was broadcast that the Japanese had bombed Pearl Harbor. It was hard to believe that it wasn't a hoax. Then I wondered if any of my friends in the Navy were there when it happened. There was no way of finding out what ships were damaged or if any carriers were involved.

On Monday, the day after Pearl Harbor, at the Lockheed plant, everything continued as usual. Everyone was listening to radios for more news of what was going on in the islands. We heard that some battleships had been sunk and airplanes destroyed on the ground. In the next week or so, we seemed to be busier, as more planes were coming from the factory to the flight line. I still hadn't received my pay raise, and I heard the shipyards were hiring unskilled workers for two dollars an hour. During a weekend, I drove to San Diego and visited Lindbergh Field. I found out the Army Air Corps primary training facility had been moved to the north. I also found out my friend Johnny Hann, from Fighting Squadron Three, was chief of inspection for an air transport service the Army had requested Consolidated Aircraft Corporation to organize. It was to be a unit of the Army Air Transport Command. When Johnny learned I was available and had my A&E license, he said he would get me hired as a flight inspector on Consolidated Airways planes. The name of the airline was shortened to Consairway.

❧ B-24 Flight Inspector ❧

When I informed Lockheed I was resigning, and that I had been receiving only eighty-five cents an hour for several months, although I had been promised a dollar twenty-five two or three months earlier, they offered me the raise immediately. They also told me I couldn't change jobs because I was "frozen" to that job, because of the war. I then told them I was going back into the Navy, and they gave me my release. Then I returned to San Diego and was hired by Consairway as a flight inspector, with Johnny Hann as my foreman. I was to be a salaried employee, starting at four hundred dollars a month. Being a salaried employee meant I was now a "company man" and would get no pay for overtime. It also would mean there were no more eight-hour workdays. The extreme urgency of getting pilots, high-ranking officers, munitions, and all kinds of supplies into the war zones put a burden on the young Consairway operation.

Consolidated Aircraft Corporation in San Diego had been producing PBY seaplanes for many years, and they were now seeing war service in many areas. From the factory, Consolidated flight crews had been delivering the PBYs to the East Coast, to Europe, and across the Pacific to places like Suva on Fiji Island, Noumea on New Caledonia, Australia, New Guinea, and the Philippines.

In 1939 and 1940, Consolidated Aircraft Corporation, at the request of General Hap Arnold, developed a strategic bomber with a speed of three hundred miles an hour, a ceiling of thirty thousand feet, and a range of three thousand miles. The company had been testing a Model 31, which had a new thin wing design called the "Davis wing," and a twin tail assembly, which actually consisted of twin vertical fins and rudders connected together by the horizontal stabilizer. The production of the B-24 was in full swing by the end of 1940, and it was to become the most heavily produced four-engine bomber of the war.

By 1941, still before Pearl Harbor, the British used the LB-30s (B-24s) in support of action in North Africa against General Rommel and his German forces. The B-24 or LB-30 was short and stocky-looking, with a low-slung, heavy-set fuselage, with the thin, trim Davis wing, snub nose, and twin tail assembly.

When the Army Air Corps asked Consolidated to start a transport service for the Air Transport Command, they were able to start making flights within a few days, because they were already uniquely prepared to do so. This is a quote from Frank Learman, a high-ranking Consolidated Aircraft official:

In late 1941, Consolidated had fifty-five men delivering PBY sea-planes in the Pacific; Honolulu, Wake, Guam, the Philippines, and Australia. Five were captured by the Japanese and placed in prison camps. These were two Pilots in Command, a Co-Pilot, a Navigator and a Station Manager. They were interned in Santo Tomas Internment Camp on January 8, 1942, transferred to Los Banos, Philippines Internment Camp in May 1943 and liberated in February 23, 1945. The Air Force flew these men to Biak, where a Consairway crew picked them up and brought them home. There were thirty-two consolidated PBY delivery crewmen waiting in Manila for some way back to San Diego, when the Japanese attacked December 8, 1941. Five of these were the ones who had been captured and one was killed. The other twenty-six escaped by being shuttled a few at a time, in a small single-engine plane to Iloilo where they were able to get aboard a freighter bound for Santiago, Chile, then by commercial plane to the U.S.

As I remember, in November, 1941 there were fourteen to sixteen crewmen stranded in Honolulu. We borrowed a British LB-30, Number AL504, put some plank seats in the bomb bay, and Dick McMakin flew to Honolulu from San Diego, refueled, loaded our crews and was back in a little over twenty-four hours. A few weeks later McMakin took off again in AL504, this time to survey a route to Australia and was back in just five days with sixteen more delivery crewmen.

This latter flight attracted the attention of Army Air Force officials, and McMakin was brought to Washington to give a full evaluation of his flight. This was probably the beginning of Consairway. Until this time, land planes had not been used to fly long distances over water. Large flying boats such as the China Clipper were used by Pan American and other airlines for over-water transportation. Consairway was in operation for five months before United Airlines also started flying for the Air Transport Command, using the same route that had been established by Dick McMakin and other Consairway crews. In early 1942, I was proud to be able to join this great group of aviation pioneers, and in a small way, help them to establish many records during the three years and nine months of their existence.

❧ Flight Inspector to Navigator ❧

My duties as a flight inspector of the LB-30s used by Consairway for transport operation were similar to those I had as a plane captain on 3-F-18, except that this was a comparatively huge four-engine converted bomber that had been restored after many bombing missions. Some of our planes had been discarded as being too old for further use, and some had been wrecked in various parts of the world, salvaged by Consairway crews, and flown back to the factory for refurbishing and use for transport flight over thousands of miles of the Pacific Ocean, for the duration of the war.

Consairway started operating as a wartime emergency air transport airline on April 23, 1942. When the operation began, Consairway had only two old LB-30s that had been inherited from the British and had been revamped by removing machine-gun turrets, painting a star on both sides, and installing plank seats in the bomb-bays. As more LB-30s were obtained after being discarded by the British, they were revamped for transport service by removing the bomb-racks, bomb-bay doors, and some bulkheads, and installing a deck that extended from the flight deck to the tail-section. New outer skin was riveted over the bomb-bay section of the plane. The deck was rigged for tying down cargo and for installation of removable passenger seats. Small windows were installed along the sides, one at each seat. Each window had a three-inch hole at the center, which was fitted with a removable plug. This was before planes were pressurized for very high altitudes, and these planes didn't carry oxygen. The usual altitude flown was between eight thousand and thirteen thousand feet. At about fifteen thousand feet, oxygen would have been required.

After the U.S. entered the war effort, they began using thousands of B-24s, and Consairway began getting wrecked B-24s from the Army Air Corps. They were designated B-24A plus their serial number, as in B-24A #02375. Still later, Consolidated built a B-24 especially for transport, which was designated, for example, C-87 #558 or C-87 #706. The last number, or serial number, was stenciled on the outboard side of each vertical fin. Whether the planes were called B-24A, LB-30, or

C-87, they were all B-24s. And they all looked alike, with the thin Davis wing passing through the top of a chubby fuselage, followed by the distinctive twin tail.

My flight inspector job included preparing the LB-30s for the western trip to Australia and back. When I started at Consairway, the route included a stop at Hamilton Field, just north of San Francisco, where Army personnel would load the planes with military personnel, mail, or cargo. Then stops were made at Hickam Field, Oahu, Hawaii, then directly south to Canton Island, then to Nandi on Fiji Island, Plaines des Gaiacs on New Caledonia, and to the western terminal at Amberley Field, near Ipswich, Australia.

When a plane returned from this round trip, it would have logged around eighty hours on the engines, and the landing gear would have been retracted and extended at least a dozen times. The flight engineer, on returning, would sometimes have a list of items that needed to be taken care of before the plane took off on the next trip. The flight inspector was responsible for having a mechanic do all necessary repairs and would put his stamp on all work completed to his satisfaction. The flight engineers were well-trained A&E mechanics with special training on the B-24, and they would make any necessary repairs or adjustments while the plane was on the ground, at the various stops on the way to Australia and back. When the planes returned to the home base at Lindbergh Field, the ground crews there would take over, and the flight inspectors would do a thorough inspection of the entire aircraft: engines, hydraulic systems, arresting gear, etc. Each inspector had a check-off list that included all parts of the aircraft and engines. We each were assigned a number, and were given a rubber stamp with our number on it, with which we would stamp off the items as they passed our inspection. If we found something that needed attention, we would notify a mechanic, show him the problem, and sometimes help him do the repair or adjustment. Sometimes the mechanic would be an inexperienced recent hire, and we would show him how to do the job, and when it was done, stamp it off. It was an interesting job, but the hours were often very long. We were usually on the job for twelve to sixteen hours at a time.

I could see that this was a smooth-running operation. Everyone got along well together, and from the top of the organization on down, everyone was friendly to me. Dick McMakin was head of the Consairway operation, and when he was around the flight line, he would stop and talk to the mechanics and other personnel. He would call me by my first name, and ask how I was getting along. He was actually only five years older than I, and I was amazed when I learned it was he who had pioneered the western route that was now being flown, and he had brought back stranded PBY crewmen he had located in the far western Pacific areas. McMakin, together with another pioneer and chief of Consolidated Aircraft's Flight ANF Service Department, Russ Rogers, organized Consairway, using the prewar PBY delivery crewmen as a nucleus. Dick McMakin was made the head of the new airline, with Richard S. (Dick) Mitchell as his assistant.

My friend Johnny Hann, who got me the flight inspector job, was asked to form and be the head of a new maintenance crew at Amberley Field, in Australia. This was the western terminal of the Consairway operation at that time. He was to collect a crew of mechanics to fly with him on one of the Consairway planes, and they would stay in Australia and perform maintenance, engine changes, etc. on that end of the run. I had been considering taking special training courses on the B-24 in order to become a flight engineer on one of Consairway's flight crews. When Johnny Hann asked me to go to Australia with him as an A&E mechanic, I told him I appreciated the offer, but I wanted to fly as a crewmember.

I had also become friends with the Chief Navigator, Kerry Coughlin. I learned that the navigators on the flight crews were paid more than the flight engineers. The idea of learning navigation and being able to guide a plane to all those little dots on the navigation charts was really intriguing to me. I asked Kerry what I had to do to become eligible to be a navigator. He told me to go to a school that taught navigation, then pass his pre-hire examination, and he would hire me as a navigator; but I would still have to go to his company school for a month.

I enrolled in a navigation course at an adult education night school in San Diego. As I sat in the classroom the first night, it became apparent to me that this course would emphasize the theory of navigation, which was interesting, but I didn't feel that I wanted to wait several months before learning practical navigation, which would enable me to become a flight crewmember. Consairway probably would only be in existence for the duration of the war, so I decided to forget the school's slow pace and plan for myself a course that would concentrate on practical celestial navigation.

Another friend I had known in the Navy was Lloyd Herring, who was now a navigator for Consairway. I learned from Lloyd what books I should study and what I should know to pass Kerry Coughlin's pre-hire test. I borrowed the books from the navigation department and took them home to study. I would study late into the night every day after work.

After Johnny Hann left for Australia, George McIntire became chief flight inspector. At the time there were only three or four of us doing the inspection of the Consairway planes on their return after a trip west. Occasionally we would be asked to inspect a B-24 Army Air Corps bomber that was being delivered from the factory to the Air Corps. This sometimes meant working until late at night. Often, after midnight, I would be starting and running up the four large engines with their three-bladed propellers. The engines were fourteen-cylinder, radial Pratt & Whitneys, with 1200 horsepower each. One at a time, I would run the engines up to 1800 rpm to check the magnetos, the adjustable propellers, and all the pressure gauges for proper readings. This was usually the last thing done to complete checking out the plane for flight. The long hours spent on the flight-line didn't leave me much time to study navigation, but I used what was left of some days and all the time of two weekends.

The most useful book, and one that I practically devoured, was *The American Navigator* by Charles Mattingly, the chief navigation officer for Consolidated-Vultee Aircraft Corporation. The purpose of this great book was to be a learning tool and a reference for navigators making transoceanic flights, with emphasis on celestial navigation. Some Consairway flights were well over two thousand nautical miles over the ocean. Some flights, such as those between California and Hawaii, had no landmarks, and during the war, no radio signals were allowed. Radio communication and navigation aids were practically nonexistent, and weather information was at a minimum. LORAN (Long Range Radio Navigation) would have been helpful, but it wasn't yet available, and then wasn't allowed until the last months of the war, when we practiced using it while approaching the California coast. The distance between bases was much too far to use dead reckoning, so celestial navigation was used almost exclusively.

I studied the world star chart from the *Air Almanac*, which shows all the planets, constellations, and the principal navigable stars. I had learned the names of many of the constellations and the brightest stars, and how to locate them, while studying for the astronomy merit badge back in the Boy Scout troop at Ormsby Village. And I often studied the skies while walking on the flight decks of aircraft carriers in the Navy. It helped pass the time and was a hobby of mine. This previous knowledge was very helpful to me now, and I was pleased to learn that all the stars I had learned to locate were listed as navigable stars in the *Air Almanac*.

I worked problems in dead reckoning, because I knew Kerry's exam would include all types of navigation. I learned about the Earth, the poles, the equator, parallel lines of latitude, and lines of longitude, which converge at each pole, preventing them from being parallel. However, the lines of longitude are made parallel on a Mercator projection chart, which is made by splitting the globe on the lines of longitude and flattening the globe onto a cylinder, which surrounds it and touches it only at the equator. When the cylinder is cut at the Greenwich meridian and flattened out on a table, the lines of longitude are parallel, but distances are distorted everywhere on the chart except at the equator. The farther from the equator the observer gets, the greater the distortion, both in longitude and latitude measurements. For this reason, a great circle line drawn on a Mercator projection is a curved line, but it is actually the shortest distance between the two ends of the line. When navigating across great distances, a straight line is drawn from the starting point to the destination. This line is called a rhumb line. It is not the shortest distance to the destination, but the error is not great, and the advantages of using the Mercator projection are enough to compensate for flying a few extra miles. On the exam, I knew I would have to explain how to make a Mercator projection sea chart, which was the type of chart used by Consairway navigators.

The instruments used in navigation were familiar to me because I had studied about them in aviation mechanic school and checked them out on flights as a flight inspector. I did have to learn how to use the drift meter, and I learned the fundamentals of the octant and how to use it from Lloyd Herring. I learned how to get a position fix from two inter-secting radio bearings and became familiar with radio range beacons.

The most fascinating part of studying navigation was the concept of the celestial sphere, which is described as "a vast globe of infinite radius, the center of which is located at the center of the Earth, and on which the celestial bodies are projected." Thinking of the sky, with all of its heavenly bodies, as a large sphere makes it easier for an observer on Earth to use the concept of vertical circles, which are great circles on the celestial sphere, and which pass through the zenith and the nadir. The zenith is the point on the sphere directly above the observer, and the nadir is the point directly below him.

With my head crammed full of definitions and concepts, and having worked many problems involving the use of the *Air Almanac* and the H.O.214 system, which used a star's altitude and azimuth to get a line of position, I felt ready to ask Kerry Coughlin to give me the pre-hire exam. He agreed to let me take the exam, if I really thought I was up to it. I reasoned that I would at least find out what I was expected to know, even if I failed the test. I passed with a score of ninety-six per-cent, and Kerry seemed happy about it. I was hired as a navigator. This was about three weeks after I had inquired about the possibility of someday joining a flight crew as the navigator. Kerry told me I would be required to study in the navigator office for a month, to learn to use the octant for shooting the sun and moon and plotting lines of position on San Diego. I was also allowed to take the octant on the check flights of Consairway planes, where I could practice shooting the sun and moon through the cockpit windows. A few of the planes had a naviga-tor's dome in the overhead of the flight deck, between the navigator's table and the radioman's table.

The week was spent practicing daytime use of the octant and solving celestial navigation problems, using the charts and figures from previ-ous flights to Australia and back. My second week in Kerry's school was supposed to include allowing me to take an octant home with me for use in shooting the stars and planets at night and plotting fixes on San Diego. I had already practiced some with Lloyd's octant, and was looking forward to using one on my own.

At 2 A.M. on the following Monday, I received a telegram advising me to be down at the flight line at Lindbergh Field, because I was to leave on a plane at 8 A.M., as the navigator on the Australia run. What a shock! I tried to get together some khaki-colored clothing, some brown shoes, and a brown leather jacket, to pass as a flight jacket. We were supposed to look as much as possible like Air Corps personnel, to match the Army Air Transport Command logo on the sides of the plane. When the crew saw my outfit, they snickered a little, but assured me I looked fine.

The usual procedure for checking out a new navigator was to assign him to a crew of which one member was proficient enough at practical navigation to give assistance to the new navigator, if needed. I was assigned to the crew of Captain Bob Jacquot, an experienced old-timer who had logged many hours of flying time. The copilot was J. D. Peters and the flight engineer was R. E. Hasty. The radioman, who was also my check-out navigator, was Henry "Hank" Severin. The whole crew was very friendly, relaxed, but always businesslike and efficient. I realized immediately that each of them knew his job well, and that I would be lucky if I could perform well enough to become a permanent part of such a great crew.

I was given a leather navigator's case with my name and the Consairway logo on it. This satchel was big enough to hold the *American Air Almanac* and several H.O.214 navigation system books, one for each ten degrees of latitude. Each plane in the Consairway fleet was supplied with a padded box containing two chronometers, which were set to the exact twenty-four-hour Greenwich civil time. The chronometers were checked at least once a day by getting a time tick, or signal, from the Naval Observatory in Washington, D.C. The signals were given precisely on the hour and were set up by the radioman, who would inform the navigator when to put on the earphones and watch the second-hand of his chronometers, listening for the tone on the exact second at the beginning of a new hour. Any gain or loss of time by a chronometer was recorded under the instruments in the padded box. A loss or gain of four seconds, if not corrected for, would mean an error of one mile of longitude as measured at the equator. A one-minute error in time would mean a fifteen-mile mistake in determining your location.

As the crew gathered at the flight line, the plane we would be flying,

LB-30 #AL586, was still being prepared by mechanics who had the cowling off engine number three, and were in the process of replacing one of the accessories (I believe it was the starter). When we had been waiting for about an hour, one of the flight operations officials told us the delay in the schedule would mean we couldn't make connections with other flights, and our departure would be delayed until the next morning at 8 A.M. What a relief for me! I would be able to take the octant from the plane and use it that night to shoot stars and plot fixes on San Diego.

Fortunately, I have preserved a record, or logs, of all my flights across the Pacific as a navigator. According to my record, we took off from Lindbergh Field on March 23, 1943, at around 10 A.M. local time, in LB-30 #AL586, for a two-hour-and-twenty-four minute shuttle flight to Hamilton Field, just north of the Golden Gate Bridge. Each Consairway plane would land here at Hamilton Field, designated HO in the logs, for loading with cargo, or passengers, or both. The Army controlled what, or whom, the planes would carry, and they did the loading. The flight crew was given a manifest of the load and also information concerning the amount of weight loaded onto the plane. The pilot and the flight engineer, to avoid overloading, imbalance, and shifting of the load during the flight, always checked the weight and balance figures.

❧ The Navigator ❧

My log indicates we took off seven and a half hours after we landed at Hamilton. It was now about 8 P.M. local time, and it was dark. We circled and climbed as we headed toward the Farallons, a small group of islands just west of San Francisco. I would use these islands as a landmark, because we were at either 8,000 or 10,000 feet cruising altitude, and at our cruising airspeed of 180 knots, by the time we passed over them.

My chart was taped to the top of the navigator's table, which was just behind the pilot's seat. I had drawn a straight course line (rhumb line) from the Farallons to Hickam Field (HZ), Oahu, Hawaii. With my protractor, I determined the compass course by subtracting the 18 degrees easterly variation from the true heading. My compass course would be 227 degrees. This heading would be jotted on a small piece of paper and placed under the compass as an aid to the pilot. After we were leveled off, the pilot, Bob Jacquot, got out of his seat, turned around and smiled at me. Then he stepped down off the flight deck, put his hand on my shoulder and asked, "Well, Jimmie, what course are we going to fly? About 226?" I answered, "Yeah. I figured 227 degrees. How did you know?" He laughed and said, "I always fly 226 to Hickam." Already, I felt more relaxed.

It was difficult for me to realize that within barely a month's time I had studied and learned enough basic facts about navigation, while at the same time putting in long hours on the flight line as an A&E mechanic and flight inspector, that I was now actually the navigator on a four-engined B-24 bomber retread, plotting a route to Australia and back. I'm sure this could only happen in wartime, and it could only happen within an adventurous and imaginative group of pioneers such as Consairway.

Most of the navigators at Consairway that I talked to told me how they would try to get a three-star fix every hour, on the hour, when making extended night flights. I decided to do the same, weather permitting. Having observed the sky every night for a month, I had a good idea which stars would be at a suitable altitude and position relative to the horizon and to each other.

Soon after we had leveled off and were on autopilot, I was looking out the windshield and locating the three stars I would use for getting a fix. This plane didn't have a navigator's dome, but Bob Jacquot, the flight captain, told me if I opened the overhead hatch, I could get an unobstructed view of the sky to locate and shoot the stars. Also, without any curved glass or Plexiglas to sight through, the chance of additional refraction, or bending, of the beam of light from the star would be avoided. The crew was dressed warmly and didn't seem to mind the rush of cold air or the combined noise of the propellers and the air blast coming through the open hatch. The hatch door was two feet square and was hinged to swing down toward the back of the flight deck. When I opened it the first time, I was surprised to see how bright the stars were. It was easy to find three navigable stars, spaced about

120 degrees apart in azimuth, and about 30 to 60 degrees above the horizon. These were ideal conditions for obtaining a good position fix.

Even though the autopilot kept the irregular movements of rolling and pitching of the plane to a minimum, it was still necessary to shoot each star for two minutes in order to get a precise altitude reading. To plot a three-star fix exactly on the hour, at 6 A.M. GCT (or 10 P.M. LCT), I would start shooting the first star at 5:56 and stop at 5:58. Then the average altitude for the two minutes would be calculated for 5:57. The second star was shot from 5:59 to 6:01, and the average altitude plotted to 6:00 A.M. The third star was shot from 6:02 to 6:04 and plotted for 6:03. The line of position for the first star was advanced three minutes along the course line, and the number three line of position was retarded three minutes, from 6:03 to 6:00. This should give a small triangle or, ideally, a pinpoint fix for 6:00 A.M. GCT.

I was a little excited about getting my first nighttime fix while actually flying across the Pacific. Everything went exactly as I had planned. My first position fix was almost a pinpoint, and was a few miles to the right of my course line. The pilot had been watching me with interest, and agreed with me that the compass course should remain the same for another hour. Hank Severin, the check navigator, looked at my fix, grinned, and said nothing. In fact, he was a very quiet person the whole trip. Our only communication was when he would notify me whenever he was getting a time tick on the radio, and he would let me listen with his earphones while I checked my chronometers for accuracy. Also, every hour I was required to give Hank a form on which I had recorded our position, weather information, including wind direction and velocity, cloud type and amount of coverage, and our ETA (estimated time of arrival) at Hickam Field. Hank would use Morse code to telegraph this information to Hickam. This information was considered secret, and I used a special code to enter it onto the form, because this was wartime and we were flying military equipment and personnel. In fact, Consairway planes had often carried weapons, live ammunition, and once even torpedoes for a submarine in the Canton Island area.

Once, on that first flight, I wanted to establish some sort of communication with Hank, who was supposed to be my check navigator. I had been noticing a planet in the northwest sky that I could see through the flight deck windshield and through the small window by Hank's radioman's table. I pointed to the planet and asked Hank, "What planet is that?" He looked out the window at it, shrugged, and said, "I don't know." I hadn't planned to use the planet, but had hoped to break the ice and get more acquainted with him. He seemed to be preoccupied with something he was reading. Anyway, that was the only time on the whole round trip to Australia that I spoke to him concerning navigation. I thought to myself, "This is on-the-job training in its purest form."

My position fixes, on each and every hour, were very small triangles, and our true course remained slightly to the right of the straight rhumb line I had originally drawn on the chart. The great circle route for the flight would have been shown as a slightly curved line to the right of my planned rhumb-line course. So, when we saw the actual course we had flown, we joked that we would cut ten to fifteen miles off the rhumb line route and save four or five minutes flying time.

The stars began to dim as daylight approached, and it was now about two hours before our ETA. I was able to get one more fix, which positioned us 275 nautical miles or one and a half hours from Hickam. After an hour more on the same heading, the islands appeared in the distance, right on schedule. We soon flew past Diamond Head crater on our right, then Waikiki Beach, and a few moments later, after a right-hand approach, we touched down at Hickam Field. We were within four or five minutes of our ETA, and I already felt like an old-timer at this celestial navigation business.

Soon after we landed and checked in at the flight operations office, we were provided transportation across Honolulu to the Moana Hotel at Waikiki Beach. Everything looked about the same as it had five years earlier, when I had used a dressing room near the Moana to change into my swimming trunks while on shore leave from the *Saratoga*. Our rooms at the Moana were very plain. Each of the crew's rooms contained three single beds and a bathroom with one shower-head. Flight crewmembers were assigned three to a room. The hotel charged us nine dollars for the room, three dollars per person. After checking into the room and freshening up a little, we went down to the dining room for lunch. I'll never forget the large glass of iced tea or lemonade, with a huge longitudinal slice of pineapple in it. We ate a small lunch and went back up to the room for a nap. It had been well over twenty-four hours since we had slept, and I was getting a little dopey.

I was awakened at about 8 P.M. by one of the crew, who wondered if I didn't want to eat dinner before the dining room closed. We had a delicious meal, and then I went for a quiet, barefoot walk alone on the balmy Waikiki Beach. It was so peaceful and relaxing, with the surf occasionally lapping at my ankles and the sand squishing between my toes—quite a contrast to the sometimes tense and hectic activity on the flight deck, with its background of steady engine groaning punctuated by the hourly, ten-minute-long routine of opening the hatch and having the air-blast ruffle my hair as I shot my favorite stars.

Here on the beach, I had a clear view of the whole sky, with its many constellations, bright stars, and two or three planets. I wanted to thank my stars for guiding me through the night, across twenty-five hundred miles of water, to this place. While studying with amazement the location of all the heavenly bodies, and the consistency of their positions and movements relative to each other and to the Earth, with its rotation about its sun, I couldn't help recalling that beautifully translated *Rubáiyyat of Omar Khayyám*, by Edward Fitzgerald, in which Omar fatalistically bleats:

> And that inverted bowl they call the sky,
> Whereunder crawling cooped we live and die,
> Lift not your hands to it for help—for it
> As impotently moves as you or I.

I would much prefer the term "infinite celestial sphere" to Omar's "inverted bowl." And I wasn't cooped or crawling, but free and flying; and I lifted my hands, with an octant, to one of its bodies for help, and it gave me an exact circle of position to intersect with two previous circles for a pinpoint fix. My personal belief is that the entire firmament, including you and me, is under the control of an omnipotent Being; such a belief would have been a great help to poor Omar.

Back in the hotel room, I felt completely relaxed. Even though I had taken a nap four hours earlier, I was in bed and asleep by midnight. I must have slept well, because the next thing I heard was the sound of Hawaiian music coming from under the banyan trees in the courtyard of the Moana. It was an unforgettable sound. We were told the Royal Hawaiians had been using the Moana banyan-tree setting for their radio broadcasts every Sunday morning, and I remembered hearing them on the radio in San Diego. Our room windows were open, and the melodious guitar music seemed to be drifting in with the light morning breeze.

Because we never knew for sure when the next Consairway plane would arrive from Stateside, we couldn't go too far from the telephone at the Moana. We lounged around the hotel, on the banyan court, and on Waikiki Beach all day Sunday, and got word we would leave on Monday, around noon. We would be flying on C-87 #029 and our next stop would be Canton Island, on the second leg of our flight to Australia. In advance, I had drawn course lines between our planned stopping points on the charts of the South Sea Islands, and made notes containing the compass headings, distances, and estimated time of flight for all legs of the round trip, in both directions. The compass headings were obtained by subtracting the easterly variation from the true heading. At Hickam, the variation was 11 degrees east. At San Francisco, I had subtracted the 18 degrees easterly variation to arrive at the 227 degrees for the initial compass heading.

We took off from Hickam a little before 1 P.M. local time, headed for Canton Island, which was 1,660 miles southwest of Hickam Field, Oahu. There was a slight overcast, and I hoped I would be able to shoot the sun, and maybe the moon, for lines of position. As long as the surface of the ocean was visible, I would be able to use the drift meter to check the whitecaps and determine the direction of the surface wind. I could also determine the number of degrees we were drifting, right or left, across the surface. The sun was still high in the sky after we had flown for an hour after takeoff, but the moon wasn't visible. I was able to get a sun line, which gave me a fair speed check. An hour later, it was raining. Now I had no way of knowing our position, and I could only wait and pray for a clear sky. Radio silence prevented my getting a bearing on Hickam Field or Canton Island. Then we were shocked by a radio message that directed us to change our course and proceed to Palmyra Island, which was several hundred miles northeast of Canton Island and about a thousand miles directly south of Hawaii.

We understood that it was not safe to land at Canton, because a long-range Japanese bomber had dropped a bomb there, or was detected in the area. It had been generally known that Canton had been bombed once by a single enemy bomber, which was identified as a Big Betty. A PBY parked in the lagoon was slightly damaged by debris. From my dead-reckoning position, I drew a true course line to Palmyra Island, measured the distance, and calculated an ETA, based on our dead-reckoning position and our air speed of 180 knots. It was still raining. What a way to initiate a new navigator. It rained for another two long hours, and I felt helpless. Each hour, I encoded our position, the weather, and our ETA on the trip log and handed it to Hank, who telegraphed it to Palmyra.

Finally, after about three hours of rain, it began to clear a little, and I was able to get a sun line, which showed we were close to our course line, but we had no way of knowing our speed. After six hours of flight, we began scanning the horizon for some sign of land. The next sun line I got was almost parallel to our course line, and I was relieved. I knew we were headed in the right direction. It was half an hour later when we first spotted the low island in the distance. We arrived about twenty minutes after our ETA. The flight lasted a very long and nervous six hours and forty-four minutes. I felt lucky there wasn't a strong cross-wind during the storm, and that the weather cleared in time for us to find the island. That turned out to be one of the two times in almost three years of navigating that I didn't know my position within a few miles.

Palmyra, also called Samarang, was a tiny atoll owned by the United States. The atoll was two miles wide and four miles long, containing fifty sandy islets scattered along a coral perimeter, which enclosed three separate lagoons. The atoll was only six feet above sea level at its highest point. The landing surface was formed on a narrow strip of coral limestone on one side of the lagoon. The South Pacific atolls, which were used as "stepping (lime)stones" on the air route used to supply the armed forces, were actually the tops of volcanic craters, which had been built up over the ages to rise above the ocean's surface. The buildup was composed of layers of limestone produced by the coral growth. This flattened, sandy limestone made a suitable base for a runway.

The low-lying atoll would have been difficult to spot from a great distance, so we felt very lucky that we had been on a course which took us almost directly over it. Later, on other flights, I would often observe what appeared to be islands in the distance, but which were actually shadows from clouds above the area.

The bombing scare at Canton Island disrupted the regular scheduling of the Consairway planes. We were directed to bypass Canton Island, one of the Phoenix Group of atolls, and to fly directly to the Air Transport Command Base at Nadi, in the Fiji Islands. Nadi is pronounced Nandi, so that is the way we spelled it in the logs.

A new course line was drawn from Palmyra to Nandi, and a magnetic heading determined. I measured the distance and estimated a no-wind ETA. We took off at about 7 A.M. local time for another daytime flight. The weather was clear, and in a couple of hours I should be able to get a sun line. I estimated a flight of between ten and twelve hours, depending on the wind direction and velocity. I was able to get sun and moon lines of position most of the day, and after ten and a half hours, we spotted a mountain ahead on our course line. This was the island of Viti Levu, the Fiji Island on which Nandi is located. We landed after eleven hours and ten minutes of daylight flight. Nandi is on the western side of the large island, toward the northern end. The capital of the Fiji Islands is Suva, on the southwest corner of Viti Levu. The British governor of the islands lives at Suva. There are 250 islands in the group, mostly volcanic. Consolidated Aircraft delivery crews, most of them now Consairway crewmembers, were familiar with this area because they delivered PBYs to the British air base at Suva before World War II.

The next stop on the route to Australia was on New Caledonia, a very large island with fairly high mountains, which made it a comparatively easy target. It was only about 750 miles from the Fiji Islands. Nouméa, the chief port of New Caledonia, was another point of delivery of PBYs to the French by Consolidated crews. The Army Air Transport Command base was at Plaines des Gaiacs, PDG for short. Usually, the stop at PDG was for just an hour or so, to unload mail or personnel and reload. Then we would take on fuel and leave for Amberley Field, Australia, our western terminal. PDG was almost exactly in the middle of a straight line from east to west between Nandi, Fiji Islands, and Amberley Field, near Ipswich, Australia.

I was looking forward to seeing Johnny Hann at Amberley Field.

Johnny was my old friend from Fighting Squadron Three, on the aircraft carrier *Saratoga* and the East Coast cruise on the *Lexington*. He was also the chief flight inspector on the flight line for Consairway who got me a job there, and wanted me to go with him to Australia as an A&E mechanic. He was now the supervisor of maintenance here at the western terminal.

Because of the disruption of the regular schedule caused by our bypassing Canton Island, we had flown the same plane all the way from Hawaii. Ordinarily, after a long flight between islands, the schedule called for the crew to leave that plane to a waiting crew, and wait to relieve the crew on the next plane. The planes would be unloaded, reloaded, serviced, gassed up, and off the ground within an hour or two, with the waiting replacement crew. At PDG we were on the ground only for one hour and nine minutes, so from the Fiji Islands to Amberley Field, Brisbane, Australia, our total elapsed time, including the stop at New Caledonia, was ten hours and eighteen minutes.

When I sighted the Australian coast, I was filled with pride. During this fabulous trip, from the time of my first three-star fix, several times I wondered if it was all just a dream. Could this really be happening to me? Guiding this big, beautiful, dependable, multiengined war veteran over thousands of miles of ocean, when only a month earlier, it had been truly just a dream.

Our captain, Bob Jacquot, had been slowly descending from eight thousand feet to about two thousand feet, and we crossed the coastline near the city of Brisbane. Twenty miles inland was Ipswich, and we were soon lined up on the final approach to Amberley Field. I assembled my navigation books, my personal chronometer and charts, and was the last person off the plane. Standing near the plane's exit was none other than the already legendary Dick McMakin, who had pioneered the route we had just completed and was now the head of the Consairway operation. What an unexpected surprise when he gave me a big grin and said, "Well, Jimmie, I see you got them here." I said, "Yessir, but it wasn't easy." I think he was concerned about the diversion caused at Canton Island, but was also aware that this was my first trip as a navigator, and wanted me to feel that I was welcome as one of this great group of aviators. Before being transported to the Ipswich rooming house used by Consairway crews, I found Johnny Hann, just to say hello, and the crew was yelling for me to get on the carryall so we could get to Ipswich.

If we were expecting to have a hot shower and maybe a nap, we were in for a big disappointment. As yet, there was no hot water at the rooming house, called Clifton House. Not only was there no hot water, but also the beds were barely six feet long and three feet wide. The mattress was hard and rounded on top, much like the top of a loaf of bread. Unless one was quite heavy, his weight wouldn't depress the center of the mattress enough to prevent the cold air from blowing in from around the edges of the bed. I was told by one of the old-timers that later in the year, when it was summertime in California, it would be winter in Australia, and it was common practice for small crew members, like myself, to bring their winter flying jacket and boots, both heavily lined with sheepskin, to the Clifton House to sleep in. I later was to take their advice and I slept like a lamb, in sheep's clothing.

Later in the war, Dick Mitchell, assistant to McMakin, replaced the beds with seven-footers, installed mirrors wall-to-wall in the bathrooms, put in a water heater, and replaced the slick toilet paper with some that was more effective. However, there wasn't much he could do about the eggs served in mutton fat or the warm beer that was favored by the natives.

There was a small restaurant near the Clifton House that we could smell from three blocks down the street. The odor of mutton grease was almost enough to spoil my appetite. When we entered the restaurant, whose main customers were Consairway personnel, including flight crews and mechanics, we noticed a large pitcher of milk in the center of each table. Their milk was delicious and the waitresses knew it would be the first thing requested. I was warned not to order eggs over easy, but I thought I should try them anyway. By the time they were brought to the table, the mutton grease had solidified into a layer one-eighth-inch thick covering the bottom of the plate. I scraped enough off the eggs to be able to eat them, but the next time, I ordered soft-boiled eggs. The cooks apparently had never heard of watching an egg for three minutes, because no one, I found out later, had ever been able to get a soft-boiled egg, unless they went into the kitchen and watched it in person.

We wouldn't be at Amberley long enough for us to go to Brisbane, which was about twenty-five miles east of Ipswich near the coast and was reached by a narrow-gauge railroad. Phil Thompson was the station manager at Amberley Field. He was very friendly, helpful, and efficient, running the operation at this western terminal. Johnny Hann was in charge of all the maintenance, including repairs and engine changes, when necessary. I sort of regretted not being able to work with him there in Australia, and I told him so. I always tried to contact him on all the following trips to Amberley, and later, when the terminal was moved up to Nadzab on New Guinea, and after that to the Island of Biak, off the northwest end of New Guinea.

We were in Ipswich for about a day and a half. On the return trip east, we stopped at PDG, New Caledonia, then Nandi, Fiji Islands, and this time we were routed to Canton Island, which we had bypassed on the way down. There was no evidence of any damage from the bombing scare. I did notice slit trenches outside the sleeping areas. These were for sliding into in case there was a bombing alert. They were jokingly referred to as "slip trenches," because we were assured that, if a bomb did actually land on the atoll, among us non-combat flyboys, there would be plenty of slippery stuff around all over the place. I didn't know what they meant.

The seventeen-hundred-mile flight from Canton Island to Hickam Field on Oahu took a little over ten hours. The chow on the Army bases wasn't too bad. There was lots of Spam, macaroni with cheese, and of course, beans. The meals at the Ipswich restaurant, which all seemed to be tainted with the odor of mutton fat, were mediocre at best. So the dining room in the Moana Hotel at Waikiki Beach would become a highlight of all future trips. We were to stay here on all trips, both going and coming. I would eventually, during the remainder of the war, stay at the Moana a total of more than eighty times.

When we landed at Hickam, we were told there were supplies and personnel stranded at Christmas Island, which was some twelve hundred nautical miles south of Oahu, and we were directed to take the next incoming plane and make the round trip to Christmas Island and back before we could return to California. After a good sleep and two nice meals, we flew to Christmas Island, and I didn't have any problem with the navigation. I felt like a veteran already. The extra experience I was getting with the unplanned changes in our schedule of flights, and being able to find these dots in the ocean after hundreds of miles of nothing to see but the sea, gave me more confidence with each completed flight.

The return to Hickam, and then to Hamilton Field, California, to unload mostly returning servicemen and mail, and then the shuttle back to San Diego, completed my first trip on the western run as a navigator. And what a trip! The total flying time logged was ninety-six hours and nineteen minutes. Because of the extra flying to Christmas Island, this first trip covered more miles and racked up more flying hours than would happen on any of my subsequent thirty-six trips.

I became good friends with the whole crew, but never was to be assigned to the same crew with any of them on my future trips. I would never forget their kindness and patience, which helped to make it a truly unforgettable experience for me. I'll always remember the quiet, friendly, extremely smooth and efficient pilot, Captain Bob Jacquot, who made me feel I had nothing to worry about when he apparently sensed my anxiety during my first effort to obtain a reliable three-star fix. Copilot J. D. Peters remained a close friend for the duration of the war. Flight engineer Rudy Hasty and I often discussed airplane mechanics, especially concerning the B-24s we were flying. Radioman Hank Severin, my checkout navigator, seemed to be pleased with the job I had done navigating, without any help from him. I concluded he knew from experience that I would learn faster without him looking over my shoulder. Anyway, it was a comfort to know he was never more than two or three feet from me during all the flights.

❧ Bill Keating's Crew ❧

Having successfully completed my checkout trip to Australia and back, with a few side trips thrown in, I was assigned to a regular crew. Sometimes individual crewmembers remained with the same pilot for the duration of the war, but most often they were moved around between different crews as replacements during vacations or sickness, or when the copilot was advanced to flight captain and was assigned a new crew from the list of available crewmen. My assignment was to the crew of Captain W. F. (Bill) Keating. His copilot was Carlos Mathias, the radioman was H. Jacobson, and the flight engineer was Carl Hall. This was to be the crew I would fly with on the next six trips to the west. The route to Australia would be the same one used on my first trip, except for the surprise change from Canton Island to Palmyra Island and the extra round trip to Christmas Island.

After shuttling from Lindbergh Field, San Diego, to Hamilton Field, and having dinner while the Army loaded the B-24, we were ready to head out over the Farallons toward the balmy Hawaiian Islands. When we boarded the plane, I noticed our copilot, Carlos, was carrying a shiny brown leather briefcase. He carefully put it between his copilot's seat and the bulkhead by his window. At Hickam Field, he carried it off the plane, and after we loaded our B-4 bags into a carryall for transport to the Moana, he sat with it between his feet until we unloaded. I didn't see the satchel again until we were boarding for take-off for Canton Island. When we landed at Canton, checked in, and carried our gear to the hut where we would sleep, Carlos had his little briefcase in hand and set it on his bunk bed or cot. I assumed there must be some very important papers or information that had been entrusted to his care, and he was protecting it with his life.

When all five of us were in the shack, he opened the case and removed a fifth of Canadian Scotch, which was very rare in those times. There were four more fifths in there, all in a row. He got five Dixie cups, poured each one full of Scotch, and passed one to each of us. We were still a little dopey from the long flight, and this looked like just what we needed. I never really liked the taste of Scotch, and I had found that trying to mask the taste by mixing it with something only made it taste worse. Also, there was nothing here in the shack to mix it with, no water, and definitely no ice. So we started sipping it, and the more we sipped, the better it tasted. The sips soon became gulps, and I quickly learned to love the taste of Scotch. The one full cup of straight Scotch had, within thirty minutes, transformed us from being hot and fatigued to being full of life, as we pitched horseshoes in the coral-sand pits outside our hut.

From Canton Island to Amberley Field, Australia, we flew the regular route, stopping at Nandi, Fiji, and Plaines des Gaiacs, New

Caledonia. On our way back from Australia, we bypassed Nandi and flew directly from PDG, New Caledonia, to Canton Island. This made it another long flight and called for another Scotch appetizer from good old Carlos before dinner. After dinner we usually went to bed, since there wasn't much else to do, except maybe take a walk along the edge of the lagoon, enjoying the balmy weather "down where the trade winds play." Canton Island is in the Phoenix Group of islands and is about two degrees below the equator. The weather was hot the year round, but there was almost always a balmy breeze, which made it a little more bearable. There was often a Consolidated Aircraft PBY bomber-observer seaplane tied up in the lagoon, near the headquarters and mess-hall building. Sometimes we were told that an enemy plane had been detected in the area, and we heard that a PBY had been slightly damaged once by a near-miss from a Japanese long-range flying boat. The island would have been a difficult target, because it was an atoll, which is a circular strip of coral limestone encircling a large lagoon. I never saw any evidence of damage from bombs, but each sleeping shelter had its slit trench, just in case.

Our uniform looked similar to the Air Corps uniform, but we had different insignia. We were still civilians, and at the Army bases, we were charged forty-five cents for the cots in the sleeping hut, and forty-five cents for each meal. We were paid a subsistence allowance of ten dollars a day, so it was easy to save most of that. We could even stay within the allowance at the Moana Hotel, where we were charged three dollars a day for the room and ate very good meals in their large dining room.

The flight from Canton Island to Hickam lasted nine hours and thirty minutes, and Hickam to Hamilton Field, in California, took twelve hours and thirty-one minutes. This first trip with my new crew took a total of only seventy-eight hours and seven minutes, compared to my checkout flight of ninety-six hours and nineteen minutes. The next four trips to Australia as navigator with Bill Keating's crew covered exactly the same route as my second trip.

❧ A Leader Is Lost ❧

Just five days after my second trip, on May 10, 1943, a new
Consolidated Aircraft superbomber, model XB-32, was taking off
from its factory at Lindbergh Field. The test pilot was none other than
Dick McMakin, the pioneer of Consairway's Pacific routes, and the
airline's first general manager. He and his assistant manager, Dick
Mitchell, were responsible for the very smooth and efficient operation
of Consairway. Both men were in their early to mid-thirties and both,
despite their youth, were already veteran transoceanic seaplane pilots.
They were now operating an airline using B-24 bomber-type land-
planes to crisscross the Pacific Ocean, as their contribution to the war
effort.

Even though McMakin was running Consairway, he and all
Consairway personnel were considered Consolidated Aircraft
Company employees. He was still available as a company test pilot.
When the superbomber prototype McMakin was piloting neared the
end of the runway, it lifted off, but for some unknown reason it failed
to gain altitude and flew into the Marine barracks, past the end of the
runway. Dick McMakin died at age thirty-four, doing what he loved to
do. He was posthumously awarded the U.S. Air Medal.

Everyone was shocked and saddened by this event. Dick Mitchell
was named general manager of Consairway, and, at age thirty-three,
was the youngest airline chief ever. Under his leadership, Consairway
was able to go on and set many records for ton-miles delivered, passenger miles, and aircraft utilization.

On my seventh trip, I was still with Captain Bill Keating and his
crew, and several changes in the route had been introduced.
Consairway's assignment during the war was to deliver anything and
everything required by our armed forces in the Pacific arena. As some
of the islands were retaken from the Japanese after decisive victories in
the Coral Sea and in the battle to hold Midway, the Navy Sea-Bees
and the Construction Battalion of the U.S. Army built new landing
strips. The Army Air Corps and Consairway, and later on, United
Airlines, worked together in the effort to provide whatever was
needed, and wherever, as quickly as possible.

My seventh trip on Bill Keating's crew took us from Hickam Field to Canton Island, and from Canton Island we were shuttled by another crew to Christmas Island, where we became the crew of the plane that was waiting there, LB-30 #AL586. We were to continue on a new route that had just been added to Consairway's assignment of flights. Every fifth plane would take this change of route on its way to our base in Australia.

From Christmas Island, I laid out our course to what for me was just another pinpoint in the blue water of the South Pacific. Our destination was the small island of Tutuila, in the American Samoan island group, near Pago Pago—pronounced Pango Pango. We were on the ground at Tutuila a little more than an hour, then took off for Nandi, Fiji.

During the flight from Christmas to Tutuila, we had crossed the equator. And from Tutuila to Nandi, Fiji, we had crossed the international date line. Since we had crossed both of these imaginary lines during the same day, we were qualified to join an exclusive fellowship. The membership card states, "To All Denizens of the Sea, Land and Air, Greetings. Know Ye that, by virtue of his crossing both the Equator and the International Date Line on this 2nd day of March, 1943, James W. Settle (Navigator) has become a fully-fledged Fellow of the Inter-Stellar Order of Consairway Charioteers." Signed, W. L. Keating, Flight Captain. I still have the membership card and showed it to Bill Keating fifty-seven years later, at the last reunion of Consairway personnel at Travis Air Force Base at Fairfield, California. This base was our ultimate home base until the end of the war in 1945. At that time, it was named Fairfield-Suisun Army Airfield. When I showed the card to Bill, we reminisced about this first trip to Tutuila, and I've dreamed of the brief times I spent "down where the trade winds play, down where you lose a day."

The international date line, at 180 degrees longitude, is where you lose a day, flying west. It's the same time tomorrow when you cross it. But when you cross it coming back east, it's yesterday again. Fortunately, this had no effect on celestial navigation, since Greenwich civil time is used for all calculations of positions of heavenly bodies, relative to our position on the Earth's surface.

This variation in the route to Australia via Tutuila, every fifth trip in the Consairway schedule, was only assigned to me one more time, when Earl Popp was the flight captain. The return flight to Hickam was by the same route. This allowed me to be able to say that I had crossed the equator and the international date line on the same day, on four different occasions.

On the more distant Polynesian Islands such as Tutuila, where the weather is balmy throughout the year, the natives wear very little clothing. The women were usually barefooted and bare-breasted, but modestly covered elsewhere. One of the Consairway crewmembers struck up a slight acquaintance with one of the young women who was selling seashell products to visitors to the island. He was somewhat embarrassed by her natural and unabashed display of her adequate dimensions, and he decided she might appreciate a gift of a nice brassiere. So, on his next trip to the island, he presented her with one, and she seemed pleased with it. On the following trip to the island, he was eager to see her wearing the bra. When he spotted her, she was wearing it, but as a fanny pack, to hold her shells and the money she earned from their sale.

❧ Christmas to Christmas—21 Minutes ❧

Toward the end of this seventh flight with Bill Keating, when we took off from Christmas Island in the dark of night, headed for Hawaii, everything seemed normal as Bill lifted the nose of the plane off the coral limestone runway. We banked to the left and continued climbing as we headed almost due north toward our destination at Hickam Field, Oahu. About ten minutes had elapsed since takeoff when the odor of raw gasoline, strong enough to make your eyes water, filled the flight deck. Bill leveled off and made a 180-degree turn to take us back to the island. He ordered all electrical switches turned off, and anything that could cause a spark, such as the telegraph key, could not be used. Carl Hall, the flight engineer, opened the overhead hatch and flashed signals with the Aldis lamp, hoping someone on the island base would see it. After our takeoff, moments earlier, the runway lights had been turned off, and the generators would need to run a short time before the lights could come on.

There were no lights of any kind visible to us from the island, but we could make out its shape and were lined up with what Bill thought was one edge of the runway. We were on final approach and getting close to what looked like the end of the runway. It was important to get the plane on the ground because the gas fumes were almost choking us, and the danger of explosion was real. We were aware that some B-24s of this type flown by the Army Air Corps had exploded and crashed shortly after takeoff. Knowing this increased our anxiety, to put it politely. This was "white-knuckle time," and the "pucker factor" was at its maximum.

I was standing behind Bill, looking over his shoulder. As we were about to land, the runway lights came on, showing us to be just off the side of the runway, and ready to land in the rough coral, which could have been disastrous. With a very skillful and smooth maneuver, Bill had us over the runway and safely on the ground, with a perfect touchdown. I noticed the back of his shirt was soaking wet. Sighing deeply after bringing the big bird to a stop, he said, "Let's go to bed."

I don't recall what we were carrying on the plane that night, but we all were thankful to be back on the ground and safe. My flight log lists the flight as: "Christmas to Christmas—twenty-one minutes." It seemed much longer. The flight engineer, Carl Hall, determined that one or more of the fuel caps on the top of the wings must not have sealed completely because of a defective cork seal. If the fuel tanks are completely filled, then during the climb, when the wing is slightly tipped with the leading edge higher, the fuel caps are below the top level of the fuel. This, together with the negative pressure caused by the camber of the top surface of the wing, would suck the fuel out past the defective caps. Then it would run toward the trailing edge of the wing, through the flap openings, and into the wall of the fuselage. The problem apparently was solved, and we took off the next morning for Hawaii, then to Hamilton Field and on to San Diego. I had completed six trips with Bill Keating's crew. Bill was a wonderful pilot. When I see him at Consairway reunions, we recall the exciting flights we had, and we remember Carlos Mathias, his little leather briefcase, and the Dixie cups of Scotch on Canton Island.

Recently, while examining the Pacific Ocean chart, which shows all the routes taken to the many island bases by Consairway planes, I observed that, on my first trip as a navigator—when we were rerouted to bypass Canton Island, landed at Palmyra Island, and the next day flew from Palmyra to the Fiji Islands—we had crossed the equator and then the international date line on that same flight. My main interest, at the time, was to find the Fiji Islands, and I didn't realize we had crossed both of the lines on the same flight, or I would have brought it to the attention of Capt. Bob Jacquot. We could have celebrated this event on my very first trip, instead of six trips later.

One of the captains I flew with would, on some occasions, when I would casually mention that we were flying over the imaginary equator line, disconnect the autopilot and manually cause the plane to dip slightly. If anyone asked what the bump was, he would say, "That was the equator"—anything to break the monotony of the long flights.

❦ Finding Venus ❦

One day, I heard one of the more experienced navigators saying he sometimes used the planet Venus, during broad daylight, to plot a line of position. He mentioned it was hard to find unless its approximate position in the sky was known. By observing Venus in its apparent path across the sky each night, I was able to estimate which times during the year it would be at the proper altitude above the horizon during daylight hours—ideally from forty to seventy degrees. By using the *Air Almanac* and H.O.214 together with my dead-reckoning position, and calculating in reverse, I could find the approximate altitude and azimuth of Venus. Then I would use my three-foot-long roll of charts to reduce the glare of surrounding light, as I sighted through it at the approximate area where I had calculated the planet to be. Once its position was visually located, the octant could be used to get a true line of position.

On one flight, I was fortunate enough to have the sun, the moon, and Venus so ideally located in the sky that I was able to get "three-star fixes" for three consecutive hours. Actually, what I had was one star, which was the sun; a planet of that star, Venus; and the moon of another planet, Earth. My chart, with the three consecutive "three-star fixes" obtained in broad daylight, was something to behold. We were required to return all of our flight charts to the navigation office after all trips. If I had that chart now, I would have it framed and hanging on the wall.

❧ The PBY-5 ❧

My next assignment was with Captain Johnny Moore and his crew: Copilot George Rivers, Flight Engineer Warren Capach, Radioman Ray Jacobs, and Navigator Jim Settle. We were to deliver a PBY-5, an amphibian plane made by Consolidated Aircraft Corporation, to the Naval Seaplane Base at Kaneohe Bay, on Oahu, Hawaii. It was a patrol plane with two engines and retractable landing gear. We took it for a one-hour check flight off San Diego Bay, and Captain Moore was satisfied with its performance. Then the gas tanks were topped off, and two or three naval officers came aboard as passengers for the flight to the islands. The full load of gas, plus the passengers with luggage, added enough weight to the plane to make it difficult to get airborne from the choppy water of the bay. We had to make three attempts to lift off before we finally cleared the surface of the water and headed toward Hawaii. Our route was to be straight from San Diego Bay to Kaneohe Bay. We took off at around 5 P.M. local time, and by the time we had climbed to cruising altitude and leveled off, the sun was too low to shoot for a speed line of position, and it would be another two or three hours before the stars were visible. So I just had to dead-reckon and hope we didn't drift too much before I could get my first three-star fix. I realized the plane was much slower than the B-24s, but I didn't know how much slower.

After four hours, I was able to shoot three stars, including Polaris, for a latitude check, and the three-star fix showed we were right on course, but we had only traveled three hundred fifty nautical miles. We were flying directly into a twenty-five-knot-per-hour head wind, with a ground speed of ninety miles per hour. An hour later, I plotted another fix that indicated we were still on course, but had traveled only one hundred miles. Because of our slow ground speed, my fixes were only one and a half inches apart on the chart, so I decided to get a fix every two hours instead of every hour. This allowed me to take a nap between fixes. One of the naval officers aboard was a new navigator and seemed very interested in my technique. He apparently regarded me as an old-timer and asked a lot of questions. I didn't tell him I had only been navigating about seven months and still considered myself a beginner. The small navigator table was located on the flight deck at a spot that positioned my head next to the thin aluminum skin of the bulkhead, only a few inches from the tips of the propeller blades of the port engine, and if the speed of the engines wasn't synchronized, the throbbing sound was quite nerve-wracking. The naps that I was able to squeeze in between fixes were taken on a bunk, just aft of the flight deck.

We flew through the whole night and into the next day, when I was able to shoot the sun and the moon once more before we finally sighted the islands, and made our way to Oahu and Kaneohe Bay. It had been eighteen hours since we had taken off from San Diego Bay. Johnny Moore made a smooth landing and seemed to be familiar with the bay. He had delivered PBYs for Consolidated before the war, to the U.S. Navy and to the military forces of other countries.

❧ Captain Weatherhead's Crew ❧

After delivery of the PBY-5 to the Navy, I was taken off Captain Moore's crew and shuttled, or dead-headed, from Hickam Air Base to Canton Island on a C-87 flown by Captain Dutch Schiller and his crew. At Canton, I joined my new crew, that of Captain Lee Weatherhead. Jack Freeman was the copilot, Bob Keefer was flight engineer, and Red Morrison, the radio operator. I would be the navigator on this crew for almost all my remaining trips, until the end of the war. Lee Weatherhead, the flight captain, was twenty-four or twenty-five years old; Jack Freeman, the copilot, was twenty-three; Red Morrison was about twenty-two, and Bob Keefer was eighteen or nineteen. I was now thirty years old. To this young crew, I was soon to be known as the "little old man."

During long flights from island to island at 180 nautical miles per hour, I would spend fifteen minutes of each hour pinpointing our position on the course line and encoding our position and weather information for the radioman to telegraph to our Army Air Base destination. The other forty-five minutes were spent chatting with the other crewmembers, playing chess or cribbage, and, oftentimes, just catnapping. I was taking a correspondence course in Spanish from the University of California at Berkeley, and I spent much of the spare time completing the assigned lessons. Studying the Spanish language was an enjoyable hobby.

Often, when carrying only cargo aboard, Flight Captain Lee Weatherhead would allow me to sit in the pilot seat, disconnect the automatic pilot control, and "dry-fly the big bucket of bolts." I would pull the bill of my cap down to shield my eyes from the horizon and practice keeping the plane in straight and level flight, by watching the gyrocompass and the artificial horizon. Lee also let me take off a couple of times, when only the crewmembers were on board. He felt it was important for all the crewmembers to be able to take over the controls in case both the pilots became disabled.

Lee was a very skilled pilot. He also improved his skill as a navigator by taking turns with me, shooting the stars and plotting lines of position for a fix. One of us would use the octant to get the elevation of the heavenly body, and the other would determine the line of position by using the *Air Almanac* and the proper H.O.214 volume. Then we would reverse the roles. Doing the navigation in this manner speeded up the procedure, and helped me to avoid the monotony of the same old routine. The complete cooperation of the entire crew during our long hours of confinement on a small flight deck, one trip after another, produced an efficiency that would be impossible to duplicate in a military unit. The Consairway unit of the Air Transport Command set unimaginable records in aircraft utilization—almost sixteen hours out of every twenty-four were spent in actual flight.

Quoting from a book named *Consairway—An Airman's Airline*:

When the Air Transport Command announced in April 1942, that a cargo service would be established to support the war effort in the Pacific Theater, the San Diego based Consolidated

Aircraft Corporation, which would later become Consolidated Vultee Aircraft Corporation and eventually General Dynamics Convair division—rose to the challenge. They immediately established Consairway Division as the contracted airline to provide military transport services between the mainland and Hawaii, Australia, and the south Pacific.

Consairway was unique: a private corporation had never before operated an airline for the military. It was original: in the beginning, the Consairway fleet consisted of two LB-30 Liberators repossessed from the British, but by 1945 had grown to include seventeen LB-30s, B-24s, and C-87s in service, flying an average fifteen hours, seventeen minutes a day. It was an adventure: Consairway pilots flew their missions efficiently in minimum time, doing with land-based aircraft what had only been done previously with water-based aircraft. They set records: the airline flew a total of 300 million passenger miles and transported 100 million ton-miles of cargo.

During the war in the Pacific arena, I would make a total of thirty-seven trips to Australia, New Guinea, and finally the Philippines, by way of many small islands and atolls, to which I was responsible for guiding our planes. I had the good fortune to be included in Lee Weatherhead's crew for eighteen of these trips.

As more American victories were achieved in the air and on the surface by crews and pilots of aircraft carriers, and by big guns, gunners, and crews of the many surface ships, the biggest heroes were the Marines and infantry soldiers, who were taken in close to the well-fortified, enemy-held beaches and ordered to wade through the surf in the face of heavy rifle and machine-gun fire. Wave after wave was sent until, by sheer numbers, our men overwhelmed the resistance. Many units were involved in more than one such invasion. On Guadalcanal, we were told of some veteran Marines who had survived one or two invasions and were promised they would get leave to go home after each one. When they were told they must do just one more invasion, some committed suicide by climbing a coconut tree and diving, head down.

More than once I heard it rumored that the Air Transport Command was for "flyboys" who had connections that helped them avoid actual military engagement, and that the initials ATC stood for "Allergic To Combat." Usually it was some drunken military noncombatant ground personnel, who resented our more lofty and desirable assignment. I, personally, had tried to be an Air Corps pilot, bombardier, or navigator. I had not been eligible for the Air Corps bombardier school or navigator school because, at age twenty-seven, I was too old to be commissioned a second lieutenant.

Some of our trips took us over parts of the Coral Sea. As we droned over the vast, blue-green expanse of this area, I would sit and stare down at where I estimated the Battle of the Coral Sea had taken place. I tried to imagine the two gigantic sea armadas exchanging cannon fire, and the hundreds of torpedo planes, dive-bombers and fighter planes going after the enemy. The American fighter pilots were so successful in downing the enemy planes that they referred to the air fights as a turkey shoot. The loss of ships on both sides was great. I recall seeing newsreel coverage of the old U.S.S. *Lexington*, during its last moments, turning on its side as sailors jumped off, and sliding at an angle to the bottom of the ocean. The old *Lexington* was my home for about five months in 1939, when I was in Fighting Squadron Three and we were on maneuvers in the Atlantic. That was two years before the war. Now, looking at the spot where I imagined the *Lexington* might have gone down, I wondered if any of my friends had been aboard when it sank. How many escaped? And who might still be down there? I felt a little guilty to be flying safely above it all, and yet, I knew I was doing what I could to help in this massive demonstration of teamwork against a fanatical enemy.

I recently became aware that after the *Lexington* had been severely damaged, but while it remained afloat and seemed to be responding to damage control efforts, a fire started below decks, fed by the carrier's own fuel. The captain realized the ship could not be saved and ordered all hands to abandon ship. No lives were lost during the abandonment. Then one of our destroyers, the U.S.S. *Phelps*, was ordered to fire two torpedoes into her side, which caused her to explode and slide beneath the waves.

Apparently, I was destined to live through all this belligerent behavior. Had I completed flight training in the Army Air Corps in 1940, I could have been a pilot on a B-17 or B-24 in the early days of America's involvement in the war, flying over Germany or Poland without fighter escort protection. Thousands of good pilots were sacrificed to the guns of the Messerschmitts and ack-ack (anti-aircraft) fire by higher brass who, apparently, considered them to be invincible, if not expendable.

On the other hand, if I had chosen to be a naval aviation pilot, after completion of the aviation mechanics school in 1937, I could have been with classmate Bob Miles or Lt. Commander Jimmy Thach at the Battle of Midway, where Miles' TBD squadron was wiped out, and Jimmy Thach became the war's greatest naval ace in the Pacific, while leading his Fighting Squadron Three "airedales." Or, if I had re-enlisted in the Navy, I could still have been the plane captain on 3-F-18, in Lt. Com. Thach's Fighting Squadron Three. (But the Grumman F3F-1 would have been replaced by the F4F-4 Wildcat; and the single .50-caliber and .30-caliber machine-guns would have become six .50-caliber guns. The two fabric-covered wings were replaced by one all-metal mid-wing. Their increased speed, maneuverability, and fire-power made the F4F-4 Wildcats more than a match for the Japanese Zeroes, and helped turn sea-battle defeats into final victory.)

During this time period, on July 6, 1944, my son Jimmy was born.

❧ A Friend Is Lost ❧

On March 22, 1945, while preparing to start another flight to the western Consairway base on the island of Biak, off the north-western corner of New Guinea, I received the heartbreaking news that my very close friend and fellow Consairway navigator, Lloyd Herring, had been killed on Biak, by a Japanese anti-personnel, daisy-cutter-type bomb. We were told he was standing with other members of his flight crew in line in the mess-hall shack, waiting for an evening meal of pancakes and coffee, when a Japanese biplane with floats flew over the base at an altitude of one hundred feet and dropped ten bombs, two at a time. Before dropping the bombs, the pilot had strafed the control tower. Then he dropped two of the daisy-cutters on the edge of the runway and burned out two or three aircraft. One other bomb hit a few feet from the side of the mess hall and blew away one side of it. A piece of shrapnel hit Lloyd in the head and took off most of his face. He died instantly.

According to Don Chandler, a flight engineer who was on his check-out trip to become a navigator, Lloyd was Captain Hank Erdman's navigator and was checking out Don. Don was standing next to Lloyd when the plane approached and everyone in the mess hall dove for the deck. After Lloyd was hit, Dave Fowler, the crew's flight engineer, who was standing on the other side of Lloyd, was heard to moan and say, "I've been hit. My face is covered with blood." Then someone discovered Lloyd and yelled, "Oh, my God! They've killed him." Dave Fowler's face had been peppered with what appeared to be bone fragments from Lloyd's face and probably coral dust blown up by the bomb. The bombing attack also killed eighty-five military personnel.

This sad event pointed up the fact that my job wasn't completely without risk. Actually, during almost four years of operation, Consairway lost four aircraft: three crashed into hilly or mountainous terrain, killing all aboard, and one crashed into the surf, after running out of fuel because those responsible forgot to fill the gas tanks. This last-mentioned plane was on a routine flight from Hickam Field, Oahu, to the Fairfield-Suisun Army Air Base in California. This one loss was completely avoidable. The other three resulted from bad visibility or dangerous terrain.

It is remarkable there were no losses caused by mechanical failure. These planes, most of them old, wrecked, or discarded LB-30s or B-24s, and each with four overhauled engines, flew over water during almost four years of continuous operation, with each plane averaging sixteen hours of flight out of every twenty-four. I alone logged almost three thousand hours over water with the crews to which I was assigned. And there were eighty full flight crews when the war ended. Full credit for the smooth mechanical operation of our planes must be given to the flight engineers, mechanics, and inspection personnel at the foreign bases and at home.

❧ The Short-Snorter ❧

One of the few souvenirs I have to remind me of my flights with Consairway is a faded collection of paper currency, taped end-to-end and folded into a flat roll. Each bill has a collection of signatures of the crewmembers with whom I flew, as well as of interesting people I met during the flights or on the bases after landing. We called it a "short-snorter" list. The first bill is a one-dollar bill, and when it was full of signatures on both sides, we would tape another bill to it, usually a foreign bill. When the second bill was full of names, another bill was added.

I can still make out many of the names of my fellow crewmembers, from when we flew with Flight Captains Bob Jacquot, Bill Keating, Lee Weatherhead, Tommy Lee, and Earl Popp. The name of actor Randolph Scott is still visible. Scott was one of the many people of the entertainment industry who flew into the war zones with USO groups, to help raise the morale of the service personnel. He was a passenger on our plane from Hamilton Field, California, to Hickam Field, Oahu. We met him in the mess hall at Hamilton during a meal, while waiting to take off. After climbing to cruising altitude and leveling off near the Farallon Islands, I was sitting at the navigator's table, taping the chart to the tabletop. When I happened to glance back through the little window in the flight deck door to the passenger compartment, I could see Randolph Scott in the front seat at the right of the aisle, looking in my direction. I grinned at him, and he grinned back and waved his forefinger at me. I asked Lee Weatherhead if we shouldn't invite Scott to the flight deck, and of course he thought it was a great idea. Bob Keefer, our flight engineer, opened the door and asked Scott if he would like to come up and see the flight deck, and he seemed delighted to be asked. He stopped, looked at my chart, and asked a few questions about the flight. Then Lee offered him the copilot's seat, where he sat for the whole flight, until we were ready to start the letdown at Hawaii. Most of the time, he sat sideways in the seat and kept us intrigued with many lively stories of his experiences in movie-making. He told lots of jokes we hadn't heard, and it was a really unique and unforgettable flight for us all. Now, when I see him in an old Western on Turner Classic Movies, it brings back pleasant memories of that one flight.

Another signature on my old short-snorter list is that of Mary Elliott. She was a beautiful movie starlet who was returning with a USO group from the Far Pacific bases. They boarded our plane at Canton Island for a flight to Hawaii. Shortly after we had leveled off, Bob Keefer spotted her in the passenger compartment. These wartime, makeshift seats on our planes weren't the most comfortable things to be sitting on for the ten-to-twelve-hour flight ahead of us. Bob went back and gallantly invited her to sit on the flight deck with the crew. Here she could walk in the aisle between the navigator's and radioman's tables, or she could sit in one of the pilots' seats. She seemed to be very intelligent, asked questions about our duties on the plane, and really brightened up the flight deck. She gladly signed everyone's short-snorter. In Hawaii, Bob and I ran into Miss Elliott on Waikiki Beach. We were all in our swimming outfits. Her group was staying at the Royal Hawaiian Hotel, and we were at the Moana, as usual. She allowed someone to take a picture of her with Keefer on one side and me on the other. When our crew was about to board our plane at Hickam for the flight back to California, she was there with her USO group, and she gave each of the crew a peck on the cheek. What a fond memory. Shortly after that, we heard she had married actor Bob Cummings. We heard they eventually had five or six children. I still have the picture of the three of us, after fifty-six years.

As the war progressed toward the north and west and more Japanese bases were taken, Consairway's western terminal was moved—first, in August 1944, to Nadzab, New Guinea, which is about twenty-five miles inland, up the Markham River from Lae. Then, in November 1944, I went to Mokerang Field on Biak Island, off the northwest coast of New Guinea. The landing field at Nadzab was in a jungle area, at an altitude of two to three thousand feet. My friend Johnny Hann, from old Fighting Squadron Three, was still maintenance chief at this new location. There were still pockets of enemy stragglers in the jungles of New Guinea and a few on Biak Island. Some were even found, poorly disguised in GI clothing that didn't fit, waiting in the chow line. The bases on which we landed where there was the most remaining evidence that our forces had fought, and thousands had died or been badly injured, were Guadalcanal, Tarawa, and Kwajalein. Most of the palm trees near the coast had been denuded and some wrecked landing vehicles were rusting on the beach.

After General MacArthur was moved back to the Philippines, our delivery flights went from Hickam to Kwajalein, to Guam, and back home. Then our route was modified to include an occasional delivery from Guam to Manila, Philippines. I consider myself to be very fortunate to have been able to successfully navigate our planes to these remote areas through all sorts of good and bad weather, including severe thunderstorms, and I thank the Lord and His celestial sphere for guiding me.

Most veterans of World War II talk very little about their contribution to the war effort. I was surprised to learn just recently that my brother-in-law, Earl Stephan, was with the 188 First Engineer Aviation Battalion, which built the steel mat runways at Tacloban Airfield near Leyte Gulf, Philippines, at Nadzab and Hollandia on New Guinea, and at other island bases where we landed our B-24s. I have known Earl for about fifty years, and now I find our paths might have crossed while I was much younger, and he was practically just a kid.

On September 2, 1945, Japan signed surrender documents on board the battleship U.S.S. *Missouri*, in Manila Bay, Philippines. One week later, I was headed to Manila on the B-24 (LB-30) #AL637, as a navigator in the crew of Capt. Boyd O'Donnell. Our transpacific route now included the stop at Hickam Field, Oahu, then a long twelve-hour flight to Kwajalein in the Marshall Island group, where we laid over for twenty-four hours. Next was an eight-hour flight to Guam, where we spent another twenty-four hours. From Guam to Manila took seven hours and thirty minutes. We had heard so much about the loss of the Philippines to superior Japanese forces, and about Bataan and Corregidor. We had also heard about Gen. MacArthur's temporary relocation to Australia, then his move to New Guinea, and finally, his mostly symbolic return to Luzon, in late 1944. Some of Consairway's planes and crews were assigned to fly some of his staff and a large load of wicker furniture and other household items from his Hollandia base in New Guinea. The crews were a little upset. In fact, they were quite flabbergasted by the thought of risking their lives flying over enemy territory, just to carry MacArthur's furniture back to the Philippines. But we carried whatever the Army brass ordered us to, whether it was live torpedoes and ammunition, Officers' Club slot machines, or exhaust mufflers for a Cadillac in Australia.

We were relieved when our crew missed the furniture detail. Consairway planes had no armament on them. When the first plane carrying MacArthur's furniture approached the Tacloban Airfield near Leyte Gulf, they flew through some flack from guns on the ground. The field had been under enemy attack just before they arrived, and they were promised P-38 fighter protection, which didn't show up. After landing and being quickly unloaded and refueled, they took off, and were accompanied by three P-38s until they were able to climb up through a cloud layer and head back to Biak.

Toward the end of our flight between Guam and Manila, we flew along the curved coastline of Luzon Island, the most populous part of the Philippines. Manila is on the southwest coast of Luzon, at the edge of a large lake. Our orders directed us to fly straight to Clark Field and land. The field was a few miles north of Manila. Security had been relaxed somewhat around Manila, but the military didn't want planes flying toward, or over, the city. Capt. O'Donnell and the rest of our crew wanted to get a look at Manila from the air, and this might be our last chance. One of the crew had a small movie camera hidden in his luggage, and another crewmember had a snapshot camera. The plan was to get close enough to the city and the bay to sneak a few shots of damaged buildings or ship wreckage. When we were about five minutes from Clark, the captain called the control tower for landing instructions, but when he was instructed to make a straight-in approach, he somehow lost radio contact and was forced to make a very large circle around the field that took us over the edge of Manila, near the harbor. Then, suddenly, radio contact was reestablished and we were able to land.

We remained at Clark Field for only five hours. This gave us time for a couple of snacks and a little relaxation, while Army personnel unloaded and reloaded the plane and filled the gas tanks. Our load consisted entirely of military personnel returning to the States, with some ambulatory wounded. Also on board were the usual bags of mail. During these last few days, we had flown the same LB-30, AL637, from Guam to Manila, and now we would fly it seven and a half hours back to Guam, eight hours to Kwajalein, twelve and a half hours to Hickam, and twelve and a half hours to FSAAB at Fairfield, California.

Toward the end of the war, we still weren't allowed to carry cameras, but at least one member of the crew always managed to have one. On one trip with the Weatherhead crew, flight engineer Bob Keefer had a small movie camera on one trip, and got some comical action shots on the flight deck. He also had a short movie of a fishing trip our crew got to take while we were laying over at Canton Island. It shows me carrying a barracuda I had just caught. I still have a video copy of Bob's film, but after fifty-seven years, the quality of the film is poor.

The flight to Manila was my next-to-last trip as a navigator for Consairway. My last trip, the thirty-seventh, was with the crew of Capt. E. W. Brown, and was a series of three round trips between Fairfield and Hickam. The six flights lasted from eleven to thirteen hours each, depending on wind direction and velocity.

During the last weeks of the war, I realized the Consairway operation would no doubt be discontinued. I had heard that the Army would terminate the contract in January 1946. I had begun considering possible options for my future, and decided to train myself in a profession that would allow me to be my own boss. I had met a young premedical student in Berkeley who told me what subjects I should brush up on, if I expected to be accepted in a premed course at the University of California at Berkeley. He had a chemistry book that he had used in Chemistry 1A, and he let me borrow it. During my final two or three trips for Consairway, I studied the chemistry book and completed all the exercises at the end of each chapter, completing about half the thick book by the end of my last trip, on October 7, 1945. It had been about a month since the end of the war.

Boot Training—Norfolk, Virginia 1936

Boot Training Chief J. Zoilkewicz C.G.M.

Bill Brennenstuhl & Jim Settle on leave

Bill Brennenstuhl, Gantz & Settle with Bill's mother, Mrs. Brennenstuhl

Sailing instruction in the lagoon

Sea-bag inspection at boot training

Machinist's Mate School 1936

Jim Settle at Machinist Mate's School

Instructor Schweneke ("Ski") M.A. Unit J

Hurricane at Ocean Beach, Virginia, September 1936

Unit J Barracks, December 1936

Ocean Beach boardwalk, August 1936

Aviation Machinist's Mate School 1937

J. Settle, AMM 3/c, on leave in Virginia

Weekend leave at Virginia Beach

Left: Gaines in the "Uniform of the Day"

Right: Jim Settle at Ocean View Beach

Unit J, Aviation Machinist Mate's School, 1937. J. Settle is second from right, squatting.

Minton washing skivvies

At Ocean View Beach

Graduating Class 18-36, Group III Service Schools, Naval Training School, Norfolk, Virginia. C. P. Heitkam C.M.M., Chief Instructor

Graduating Class B-11   Aviation Mechanics School, November 26, 1937

Going to Sea

U.S.S. Ranger launching aircraft

U.S.S. Saratoga as seen from U.S.S. Ranger

U.S.S. Saratoga and U.S.S. Lexington followed by U.S.S. Ranger

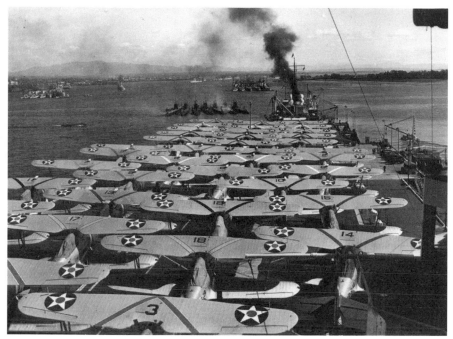

Fighter planes tied down on the bow of U.S.S. Ranger flight deck

U.S.S. Lexington launching fighter planes

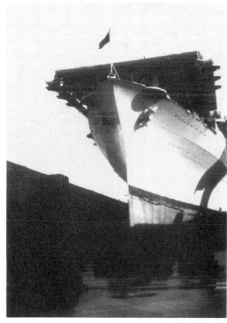

U.S.S. Ranger in dry-dock

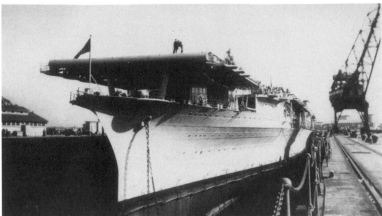
U.S.S. Ranger at the dock

Saratoga, Lexington & Ranger anchored off Waikiki Beach

Sailors returning to U.S.S. Ranger

Carriers off Waikiki Beach

Left: Fleet anchored at Lahaina Roads, Maui 1938

Below: U.S.S. Saratoga, showing the distinctive vertical stripe on the stack to distinguish it from its sister ship, the U.S.S. Lexington

Left: View of Diamond Head and Waikiki Beach Hotels in 1938

Below left: Hawaiian entertainers on rear elevator of aircraft carrier

Below right: View from carrier hungar deck

Grumman F3F–1. Fighter Squadron Three, U.S.S. Saratoga. Pilot, Cadet Anderson; Plane Captain, Jim Settle, AMM 2/c 1937–39.

The Saratoga at sunset, 1938

*Left: Harger and Settle at
Waikiki Beach. Moana
Hotel and Diamond Head
in background*

*Below: Liberty in
Honolulu, 1938*

F3F-1 planes tied down on the Saratoga, 1937

The Season's Greetings
and Best Wishes
from
Fighting Squadron Three
U.S.S. Saratoga

Christmas card from Saratoga crew, 1937

NEWS OF THE MONTH
APRIL, 1938

Pictures, Inc.

ANCHORS AWEIGH
Sailors rush to load Pratt & Whitney engines and other aeronautical equipment on the U. S. S. Ranger before the big aircraft carrier sailed for the Naval maneuvers now being conducted in the Pacific. More than 160 vessels and 500 airplanes are taking part in the maneuvers, said to be the most extensive in Naval history.

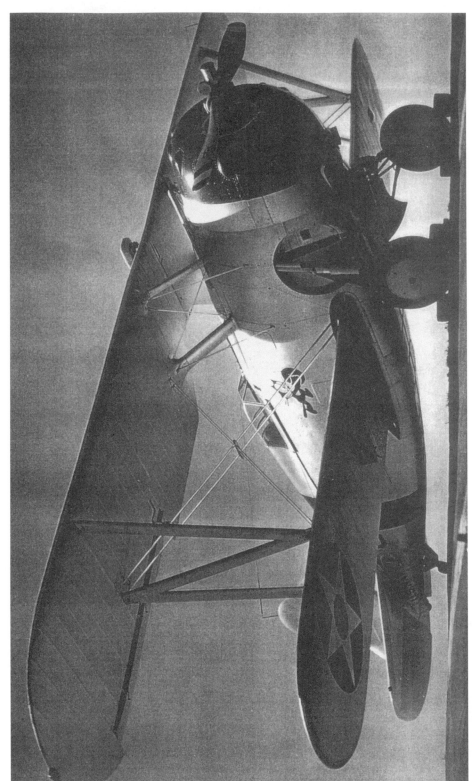

Squadron Commander's Grumman F3F-1—3-F-1

Ryan Aeronautical School 1939

Left: Flying Cadet Jim Settle

Top right: Cadet Settle in rear seat

Bottom right: Cadet Settle standing by in full gear

Civilian Aircraft Mechanic

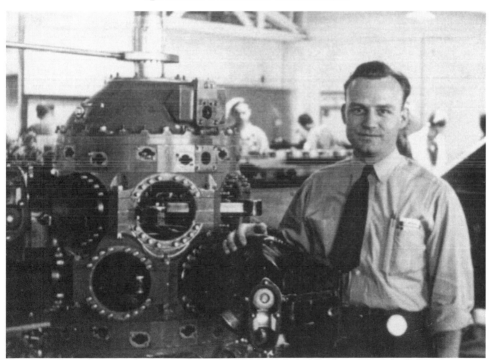

Instructor, large aircraft engine overhaul, Curtiss-Wright Technical Institute, Glendale, California

Consairway

The leaders of Consolidated Airways.

Left: Richard A. McMakin

Right: Richard S. Mitchell

The planes of Consairway.

Top left: The B-24 Liberator

Bottom left: The C-87 (B-24) cargo plane

1998 Consairway reunion: Phil Thompson, Bill Keating, Phil Sullivan

Travis Air Force Base museum. Eleanor Roosevelt (in white blouse in photo on left) used a Consairway plane to visit troops on Pacific island bases.

Left to right: Tom Stanley, Engineer; Rod Jackson, Captain; Ross Peacock, Captain; D. M. McPeak, Radioman; Lloyd Herring, Navigator

Learning Navigation

Shooting a star through navigator's dome

Using drift meter in dead reckoning to determine wind's effect on aircraft's flight path

Top left: Pioneer Aircraft Octant

Bottom left: Optical system of Pioneer Bubble Octant

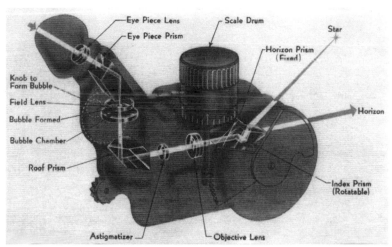

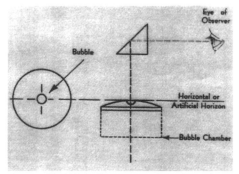

Centered bubble indicates octant is horizontal.

Octant's field of vision when star is centered with bubble octant indicates its altitude above horizon.

Navigating with Consairway

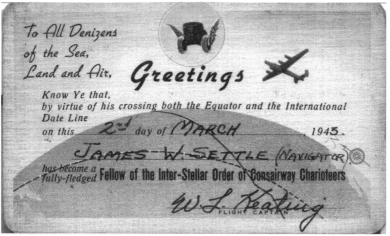

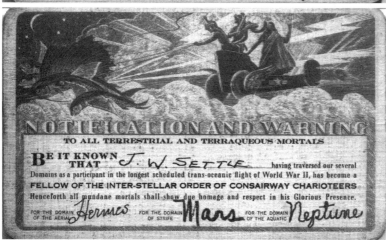

Copilot Hills, Pilot Lee Weatherhead, Station Manager, Navigator Jim Settle

Left: Consairway crew in Fiji, 1943. Jim Settle, Jack Freeman, Lee Weatherhead, Phil Sullivan, Bob Keefer

Below left: John Hann, head of maintenance, and Phil Sullivan, station manager, at Biak

Below right: Jim Settle, Mary Elliott, and Bob Keefer on Waikiki Beach, 1944

Crater left by enemy bombing at Biak in which Lloyd Herring was killed

Nearly 3000 hours logged navigating across Pacific Ocean for Air Transport Command

PART V

Doctor of Dental Surgery

Settling Down After the War

❧ University of California at Berkeley ❧

The University of California at that time was still offering three
semesters a year. A new semester was to start in November 1945,
and another in March 1946. I had a transcript of my collegiate record
sent from the University of Louisville to UC Berkeley. Because I had
taken a Liberal Arts course at U of L, I would be required to take nothing but science courses to complete the premed requirements. Because
of my mechanical background, I decided to try to qualify for a course in
dentistry instead of medicine. The physical science courses required for
a predental program were the same as for premedicine: Chemistry 1A,
1B; Physics 1A, 1B; Biology 1A, 1B (Zoology, Botany); and Organic
Chemistry.

Because of my advanced years, age thirty-two, I set a goal of qualify-
ing for the dental class which would begin in September 1946 at the
UC Dental School in San Francisco. With two semesters remaining
before June 1946, I would be able to complete all the required courses
except Organic Chemistry. During my schooling at U of L, ten years
earlier, I had earned five units in Botany with a grade of B. Otherwise,
I barely had a C average, so it was necessary for me to make all A's and
B's to be considered for acceptance at UC School of Dentistry. During
the ten years since leaving U of L, I had attended service schools in the
Navy, had studied navigation, and had taken a correspondence course
in Spanish from UC. I had learned that, by reading slowly, I was able to
comprehend and remember what I had read.

I enrolled at UC Berkeley for the November semester, which meant
I would have to give up my job of navigator for Consairway. When I
informed Dick Mitchell, Chief of Consairway Operations, that I was

planning to enter UC in November, he seemed very happy for me. I shall never forget his genuine expression of appreciation for my efforts as part of the Consairway team. Dick was a wonderful person, and I have never forgotten him, nor his predecessor, Dick McMakin. These two men were real patriots, and I was lucky to have been a part of their organization. It was also a great privilege for me to have been associated with the many crew members with whom I spent hundreds of hours on the flight decks of the old B-24, LB-30 war birds.

As I drove out of the gate at the Fairfield-Suisun Army Air Field, I realized I was closing another chapter of my life. But the new goal I had set for myself, and the heavy load of scientific subjects I was planning to carry, didn't allow me much time to reminisce about the past— or have any second thoughts about my decision to become a dentist.

❧ Back to the Books ❧

Most of the students at UC Berkeley were receiving some sort of government assistance, but the tuition was small. My greatest expense was the laboratory fees for chemistry, physics, and zoology. They were all five-unit courses, with three units of lecture and two units of laboratory. I was able to buy secondhand books, and for five dollars, I purchased Phi-Bate notes for Chemistry 1A and 1B. These were verbatim transcripts of ten-year-old chemistry lectures, which were now given by the same professor, who was repeating the same lectures word for word, even down to the same old corny jokes. I attended two or three of these lectures to check out the Phi-Bate notes and be sure nothing had been added or subtracted. The professor parroted every word, and I realized I could miss all the remaining lectures and study to memorize the lecture notes at my own pace. The chemistry exams were based entirely on the lectures, so I was able to get A's in Chemistry 1A, 1B.

Biology 1A (Zoology) was my favorite subject. In the lab, using a dissecting microscope, we dissected earthworms (*lumbricus terrestris*), frogs, and parasites from a termite's stomach. I still have some of the colored drawings I made of what I saw in the microscope. The young zoology professor gave very up-to-date, interesting lectures, and I learned to make accurate and complete notes and memorize all significant numbers and names. The scientific nomenclature I learned in Zoology 1A helped make the later study of human anatomy a breeze for me.

Someone informed me that with my previous mechanical experience and schooling, I might be able to receive college credit for Physics 1B, which dealt with the laws of motion, leverage, friction, and so forth. I made a list of all the experience and schooling I had received during the ten years since I attended U of L. Then I made an appointment with the head of the Physics Department and showed him my résumé. He seemed impressed and asked me two or three questions. He asked me if I knew what the capital G meant in an equation. I just happened to remember that G represented the acceleration of a freefalling body due to the force of gravity, which was thirty-two feet per second per second. Then he asked me if I was familiar with the coefficient of friction. I was flabbergasted! This was one of the few definitions I had memorized for use as an inane, pedantic display of erudition. So I recited that the coefficient of friction was "a ratio between the frictional resistance to the motion of an object and the perpendicular pressure between the two surfaces in contact." I was relieved when he didn't ask me any more questions and very grateful when he gave me credit for Physics 1B.

Not having to spend time in three hours of lecture and two hours of lab each week in Physics 1B gave me more time to concentrate on Chemistry 1B in the second semester and start studying organic chemistry in preparation for taking it for credit. My good luck continued when I learned that organic chemistry would be offered in a concentrated six-week course during the summer of 1946. By intensive concentration on organic chemistry for the six-week course, I was able to finish with a high grade, and now I could apply for admittance to the fall class at UC College of Dentistry, at San Francisco. The dean, Willard Flemming, was impressed with my grades, and commented that if I could get A's in chemistry at UC Berkeley, I shouldn't have any problem with classes in the dental school.

At age thirty-three, I started my freshman year at UCSF in dentistry. In spite of all my military experience—ROTC at KMI, three years in the National Guard, a hitch in the U.S. Navy, and three years as a navigator flying in the Pacific war zones—I was one of only three members of my freshman class who were not qualified for the GI benefits of living allowance and completely free dental education. On the technicality that I was a civilian during the war years, I was denied any GI benefits. Prices in the student store for dental instruments, equipment, and supplies doubled when it was learned the government was paying for everything the GI Bill students needed. Several items which were put on the list for students to have were things we never had use for, but I was required to pay cash for them, and at the inflated prices. The tuition, equipment, and supplies put me deeply into debt by the end of the four years of lectures and clinical, hands-on training.

Having committed myself to obtaining a DDS degree from UCSF, I was determined not to risk failing any written exams or laboratory projects. I had learned many techniques for taking time-limited examinations. By closely observing a lecturer, analyzing his presentation, and recording his every thought in my notes, and then memorizing everything I had recorded, including numbers and definitions, I was able to anticipate almost all the exam questions.

Fortunately, secondhand books were available from third- and fourth-year students. I bought a used medical dictionary, which I rarely used, a biochemistry book, a book called *Complete Dentures*, and a human anatomy book by Morris and Shaeffer. No other textbooks were necessary because we were given mimeographed outlines covering most lectures, on the day of the lecture. I found that every item considered important by the lecturer was mentioned in his lectures, which I tried to commit to memory. Each year, we were given a list of books to buy, but I learned to avoid that unnecessary expense.

One book that was extremely necessary was Morris and Shaeffer's *Human Anatomy*. It was at least three inches thick, and the pages were thin. With my slow reading habit, it would have taken four years to read through it, and then only if I did nothing else. In predentistry at UC Berkeley, in the Zoology 1A course, which I had cooled, I learned the scientific nomenclature of all the parts, organs, and systems of the animal being dissected. I learned to study a picture of a dissected animal or organ, and then to reproduce it in a drawing, showing and naming all the important parts, and describing in writing their locations relative to each other, e.g. superior-inferior, medial-distal, capital-caudal, etc.

When I enrolled in dental school at UCSF, I heard of three dental fraternities from some upperclassmen who were members of those fraternities. One of my classmates in the freshman dental class had been in my organic chemistry class at Berkeley. We had studied together and become friends. When he decided to join the Delta Sigma Delta fraternity, I joined it too. We had been told belonging to a professional fraternity would give us the chance to associate and form friendships with other members and with upperclassmen, who could advise us and help us with our lab projects.

There was a small dental lab in the basement of the "Delt" House where we could do projects, such as waxing up and casting inlays, crowns, bridges, and the framework for removable partial dentures.

I had now been married seven years, and my wife informed me that she was having an affair with an insurance salesman. We filed for divorce, she married her new friend, and they took Jimmy to live with them for a few years. Thus I was free to move into the Delt House.

There were several dormitory-type rooms on the second floor of the Delt House and a common bathroom at the end of a hall. There was a full-time cook, who served three meals a day. One of the students served as house manager. Shortly after I joined the Delt fraternity, the house manager dropped out of school, and I was given the job, which meant I could live there without paying for my room. This helped me to stretch my meager savings account a little farther.

Many close friendships were formed between members of the Delt fraternity as we helped each other with our studies. We would spend long hours in the lab room down in the basement of the Delt House, or in our upstairs rooms going over lecture notes. About once a month, on a Saturday night, we would go downtown to a Basque family-style restaurant where, for one dollar, we could join other customers at long tables. Food was placed in the center in large bowls, and everyone took turns ladling out adequate portions of wholesome food into his bowl or plate. There were lots of noodles, fried chicken, potatoes, and French bread. A large pitcher of red wine was always within easy reach. Then we often topped off the evening at the old Sinaloa Night Club, where we nursed one beer all evening, as we watched one floor show after another until the place closed. The club employees knew we were poor students and enjoyed, or at least tolerated, our frugal presence.

Almost all members of my freshman class in dental school were older than the usual age of twenty or twenty-one years. This was the first post-World War II class and ages ranged, mostly, from twenty-four to thirty-four years. Two or three students were twenty or twenty-one and were not war veterans. All the older students were veterans. My mechanical background gave me a big advantage in the required laboratory and clinical procedures. Sitting at lab benches, we were required to carve small rectangular blocks of hard blue wax into predetermined shapes and precise dimensions in millimeters, measured with a Boley gauge. As part of a freshman course in dental morphology, we were required to carve the wax into the exact shape and size of each tooth in the upper and lower dental arches, using average dimensions of adult teeth. We used large plaster models as a guide to reproduce the exact shape of each tooth. Some of the brightest students in the freshman class quit school because they weren't able to use their fingers with sufficient dexterity to get a passing grade on the carvings.

The first two years in dental school are used to prepare the student for the clinic, where he will spend the junior and senior years treating patients from the public, who know they will receive the best of dental care.

On Memorial Day weekend in 1948, I met and became infatuated with the girl who would be my wife for the following fifty-four-plus years, and still counting. We were married September 4, 1948. This was the beginning of my junior year in dental school. We would have a rough time making ends meet during the remaining two years of my schooling, but we were blissfully happy, and very nice things happened to help us get by.

My wife, Shirley, had been in the U.S. Navy as a WAVE during and after World War II. WAVES was the acronym for Women Accepted for Voluntary Emergency Service. Shirley was now working for a San Francisco insurance company. Her salary, together with the remains of my small savings account, allowed us to afford a small, fifty-dollar-per-month, makeshift apartment, which was really a made-over storage area at the rear of an apartment house on Eighth Avenue, near Golden Gate Park, a mile or so from the University. Shirley became an expectant mother in April 1949, but continued to work until October. Our first daughter, Bettye, was born January 15, 1950, just five months before my graduation.

During the last year of dental school, our financial problems became greater. My savings were gone, and when Shirley had to quit working, we were forced to start borrowing from my sister Bettye, my brother George, and a small amount from the university, at four percent interest. In my sophomore year I worked part-time for Jack Gilbert, owner of the John Gilbert Dental Laboratory on Mission Street. For this on-the-job training as a "plaster monkey," he generously paid me seventy-five cents an hour. This job involved mixing plaster or stone and pouring dental models, or mixing a special, finely ground compound for investing the wax patterns for crowns, bridges, or the framework of partial dentures. This job was a godsend, not only for the money I received, but because I was allowed to use Jack's equipment and supplies for my training in the laboratory procedures which were required by the dental school. This gave me a head start on the rest of my class. I became expert at trimming models, because I had done it hundreds of times in Jack's lab. When Jack Gilbert heard we were running out of money, he lent us four hundred dollars on two different occasions and said we could pay it back without interest after graduation, when we were able. After our daughter Bettye was born, our landlady at the apartment house, Mrs. Curry, heard we were struggling to survive, and showed up one day at our door with a coffee can full of hundred-dollar bills. She asked Shirley how many she needed, and said we could repay her if and when we were able, again with no interest.

The owners of the local produce market got to know Shirley and her frugal shopping trips to the store, and they would save loose carrots, bananas, ripe tomatoes, etc., and have them in a bag for her when she showed up. It was all good food, and they charged her nothing for it. So many people were helpful, when they learned we needed help.

We ate a lot of Kraft's macaroni & cheese, which was fifteen cents a box or two boxes for a quarter, so it was a special treat when we ate, maybe once a week, at a nearby Chinese restaurant, for under a dollar apiece. Some Saturdays we went to the Basque family-style restaurant, pigged out for a dollar, and left with our pockets stuffed with any food that was lying loose.

❧ Graduation from UCSF ❧

As the four long years of study at UCSF Dental School were nearing the day of graduation, I learned that my grades were among the highest in our class. I was approached by Dr. Robert Rules, the head of the operative dentistry class, who wondered if I would be interested in joining his staff in the operative clinic. I was flattered, but declined, because I knew the salary would be small, and I needed to start a practice to pay off the debt I had accumulated.

Just the thought of being considered for a position on the faculty of this prestigious institution had me confused. During the four years of my dental education, I was never informed of my progress, except that I was receiving a P for Pass in all subjects on my semester report cards, and also on clinical test cases. A grading system was used that indicated the quality of performance by P, LP, or NP, for Pass, Low Pass, or No Pass. My final grades at graduation time were a P for Pass, and I was finally able to relax a little and not worry about flunking out. More than six months after graduation, I was informed I was eligible for membership in the Omicron Kappa Upsilon Dental Scholastic Honorary Society. I don't know why it took so long for me to be notified that I had done so well. It was a long four years of great effort and sacrifice on my part, and I could have used a little encouragement from someone along the way, but I got none. When Dr. Rule offered me a chance to teach, it was shortly before graduation, and I knew then I had a good chance of graduating. At graduation time, the faculty made us feel our class was one of the most studious and disciplined classes they had ever taught. It was a great school, and the training was superb, but I've always felt, with my advanced years and experience at the time, I could have covered the course of studies in about two years instead of four.

The day of graduation from UCSF Dental School was in early June of 1950. The ceremony was held at Edwards Field on the UC Berkeley campus. There were about forty in our dental graduating class. We were a very small part of the total UC graduating ceremony. Both undergraduate and postgraduate degrees from all the colleges were awarded in the ceremonies. Hard folding chairs were placed on the grassy lawn, and we sat for what seemed like hours. There were a total of about thirty-five hundred students waiting for diplomas, but we had to sit and squirm impatiently, following an impressive speech by the famous American internationalist, Ralph Bunche. He was the first African-American to be a division head in the Department of State. Dr. Bunche was awarded the Nobel Peace Prize in 1950, the same year he spoke at our graduation.

When the loudspeakers finally announced the presentation of the degree, Doctor of Dental Surgery, our relatively small group stood and walked in single file across the front of the stage to receive a roll of blank, thin cardboard, tied with a blue-and-gold ribbon. It was worth the wait. The feeling of accomplishment that I had would be hard to describe.

My wife Shirley was in the audience at the graduation, and was happy and relieved that we had finally made it. My oldest daughter, Bettye, had been born in January 1950, at the midpoint of my senior year. Friends at the apartment house in San Francisco babysat Bettye during the graduation.

❦ State Board Exams ❦

Another big obstacle stood in the way of my earning a living and getting out of debt. To practice dentistry legally anywhere in the United States, every dental graduate must be licensed by the state in which he intends to practice. Toward the middle of June, the California State Board of Dental Examiners conducts examinations at USC in Los Angeles, and a week later, at UCSF in San Francisco. Everyone in my graduating class was almost petrified with fear of failing the licensing examination. We had been constantly reminded that the slightest mistake during the clinical test case could mean failure. We were to be completely at the mercy of the examiner, who watched our every move, and examined every step of the mechanical procedure of placing a gold-foil restoration and a class-II amalgam filling in the teeth of real, live patients in the clinic. We had completed more than two years of training in these procedures, and should not have worried about getting a passing grade, but these politically appointed examiners had complete control over our futures and were not famous for show-ing any sympathy, or exhibiting a friendly demeanor. Yet only one in our class failed and was required to wait six months until the next examination would be given.

The state board examination included several written tests covering different subjects related to the field of dentistry. The UC Dental College was considered one of the best in the country, and we had been well prepared to take these examinations. But we still didn't know what kind of questions to expect. Our fraternity had a member who knew a student at USC who was in the same fraternity. He volunteered to go down to USC at the time of the board exams, and ask members of our fraternity there to remember the questions asked and write them down for us. We could concentrate on these questions and hope we would be given the same exam a week later. Fortunately, these exams were almost identical, and we were relieved. As it happened, the questions asked were quite elementary, and we would have had no problem answering all of them correctly. However, this preparation shortened the length of time we needed to complete the exam, and members of our fraternity all walked out of the examining room several minutes before the other students were finished. I suppose we should have felt a little guilty about trying to get an unfair advantage over our classmates, but with so much importance riding on our passing the exams, and the great amount of time and money it would have taken to wait six more months for another exam, we were just "covering our rears."

Now that we had been graduated and were Doctors of Dental Surgery, I was anxious to start a new career and once again become fis-cally solvent. For some reason that is still unexplainable to me, we were forced to wait from June until September, three months, to learn whether we had passed the state board exams and would be allowed to apply for a license to practice. No one dared to finalize arrangements to start a practice, buy equipment, move to another town, or sign a contract until he knew for sure he wouldn't have to wait for the next state board exam, six months later.

A few days after I had taken the board exam, fortune smiled on us when a dental equipment salesman introduced me to Dr. Clinton Gurnee, Sr., who was interested in accepting a new dental graduate into his long-established practice in Watsonville, California. Dr. Gurnee had been ill with hepatitis after a trip to Mexico, and was recuperating in a Berkeley hospital when I first met him. Shirley and I drove down to Watsonville to meet Mrs. Ruth Gurnee, who was very gracious and friendly. We had little five-month-old Bettye with us. Mrs. Gurnee showed us around the town and served us lunch at her home. She made us feel as if we would be happy here, and we decided to move to the Watsonville area while we waited for the state board exam results.

❧ Goodbye to San Francisco ❧

It was with great nostalgia that we emptied our little apartment on Eighth Avenue in San Francisco, and bid farewell to and got a big hug from Mrs. Curry, our helpful landlady. We loaded up our '41 Chevy five-passenger coupe and a small, attached trailer, plus brother George's car, with the entire extent of our worldly possessions, and took the coast route down to Santa Cruz. George followed closely to check on our trailer. It was loaded rather precariously with two huge laundry tubs, a washing machine with wringer, and a crib mattress, all of which Shirley got from St. Vincent de Paul's for eighteen dollars. They donated the crib mattress because she paid cash for the tubs and washing machine. Also on the trailer was the crib, which had been given to us by a friend named Callahan, who was a dental lab technician at John Gilbert Dental Laboratory where I had worked.

We found a cheap place to stay in Santa Cruz. It was an old house near the beach, where Shirley, little Bettye, and I, together with George and his wife Evelyn, stayed for about two weeks. George paid the rent and bought the food because we were completely broke. Shirley did all the cooking, and we ate better than we had for months. We occupied the whole top floor of the house. There was one huge room with two double beds. We all slept in this room, and Bettye's crib occupied a large closet, with the doors propped open at night.

We wanted to move closer to Watsonville, but couldn't find anything closer than Rio del Mar, where we rented a small house for seventy-five dollars a month. George and Evelyn lived with us again. Or, I should say, we lived with them, because they still paid for everything. It rained almost every day and night, causing the ground to become saturated. This resulted in the overflowing of the septic tank and supplementary parallel drainage channels onto part of the yard and driveway. We were not at all comfortable there, and when one of the rusted burners on the stove fell through into the oven, we started looking more closely in Watsonville. We found a house in Resetar Court, off West Lake Avenue, which rented for fifty dollars a month. We made a hasty departure from Rio del Mar, with the same load of stuff we had hauled from San Francisco.

George and Evelyn found an apartment two blocks from us. George went to work for a local painting contractor. A short time later he got his own contractor's license. Evelyn went to work at the Watsonville Laundry. We enjoyed having them near us, and we visited each other often. They would take Bettye to the beach occasionally and would babysit when we asked.

At about the same time as our move to Watsonville, I was notified I had passed the state board exam and began my dental practice with Dr. Gurnee, on East Lake Avenue. I used one of his three dental units, and he referred some of his patients to me. We shared his one dental assistant, and I was kept busy from the first day on. During the year I practiced with Dr. Gurnee, I was able to pay back all the money we had borrowed, replace our old Chevy with a slightly newer one, and start saving for a down payment on a tract home.

On October 20, 1951, our second daughter, Marilyn Marie, was born at Watsonville Community Hospital. Our family physician and friend, Dr. Avery Wood, delivered her. Shirley named her Marilyn, after her best friend, Marilyn Heeth, and Marie, after my sister Marie. We were still living on Resetar Court, and I was just getting my own practice started. We were quite comfortable in our little cottage just off West Lake Avenue. The reasonable rent of fifty dollars a month allowed us to repaint the inside and fix it up into a very nice home.

Dr. Gurnee and I used the same operatories in the front section of his office building. The large building also contained office spaces for an optometrist and a physician, another dental complex, and a small dental laboratory at the rear. By agreement with Dr. Gurnee, at the end of my first year of practice, I began establishing a private practice of my own. He offered his office location in the front of the building and remodeled an extra room in the back area into two additional operatories. This was to be a temporary arrangement, because he was planning to build new office spaces a short distance away on the same street.

Dr. Gurnee very generously gave me one of his chairs and a dental unit, and I bought new equipment for my front operatory, including a new X-ray unit. Shirley and I felt greatly indebted to Dr. Gurnee and his wife Ruth for all their kindness in helping us get settled into our new home, and helping me to establish a dental practice here in Watsonville. Dr. Gurnee's advice and guidance during the early months were invaluable to me. We'll never forget these wonderful people.

At the beginning of my own private practice, I hired Lois Lyons as my dental assistant. Lois had worked for Dr. Francis Shea, who had recently retired. She later married one of our dental technicians, Emil Gumper. Lois was my faithful assistant for twenty-five years, and she and Emil became good friends of our family. My daughter Judy assisted me for the last ten years of my practice, and my wife Shirley joined us for the final three years. My experiences during those thirty-five years would fill another volume or two. I will never forget the genuine friendships that resulted from my association with thousands of patients.

I found the practice of dentistry could be a very enjoyable and emotionally rewarding experience—or it could be a laborious and stressful effort to accumulate money. Fifty years ago, before there were insurance benefits covering employees, it was often difficult to get patients to pay for their dental treatment. I tended to trust everyone, and if a patient told me ahead of time that he really couldn't pay, and I believed him, I would often treat him as a charity patient. In one case, I agreed to accept one dollar a month for three or four years. I learned that most all emergency, night-time, or weekend toothache patients who were complete strangers to me would never have money to pay, and never did pay. I was still able to make a fair living from those who paid regularly, and I was better off financially than I had ever been. Almost all of my many patients and their families, sometimes three or four generations of the same family, stayed with me until I retired, after thirty-five years of practice. Everyone seemed to appreciate my relaxed and carefree attitude, and many said they even looked forward to coming to my office. They seemed like family to me, and I miss them.

In March 1952, we moved into our new home on Bronson Street.

Our third daughter, Judy, was born in November 1953. Our fourth daughter, Sara, was born in September 1955. We also had custody of my son Jimmy at this time, so Shirley had her hands full.

❦ Drafted Again? ❦

At the same time I was starting my practice of dentistry, after receiving my state license in September 1950, the U.S. Congress enacted Law 775, calling for the induction into military service of dentists, physicians, and veterinarians up to the age of 51 years who had no military service after the year 1940. Because of a shortage of medical personnel in the services during the Korean police action, more doctors were needed to treat dependents of service personnel.

In October 1952, I had been practicing on my own for one year, and had bought all necessary dental equipment to supply two operatories. The selective service draft board had classified me in category III because I was discharged from the U.S. Army Air Corps in February 1940. From 1942 through 1945 I was flying for the Army Air Transport Command into the Pacific war zone, but technically, I was in a special civilian branch of the ATC. In July 1953, at age forty, I received notice to report for a physical exam and induction into one of the services.

With the help of Watsonville City Councilman John Eastman, U.S. Congressman Charles Gubser, and others, we were able to have my case reviewed by the local draft board in Santa Cruz. We pleaded financial hardship, with four small children and another on the way. Also, I was still several thousand dollars in debt for the purchase of dental equipment. I explained that my practice had been gradually growing, and to force me to lose it now, store my equipment, and then try to start all over again several years later, would be grossly unfair to my family and me.

Another thing I tried to explain was how I had applied at age twenty-six for acceptance into the Army Air Corps navigation or gunnery school, and I was told that, by the time of graduation from one of these schools, I would be too old to be a second lieutenant. Now, sixteen years later, by an Act of Congress, I was not too old anymore.

To continue my tear-jerking story, I once again listed my military service record: four years in the National Guard, a hitch in the U.S. Navy in Fighting Squadron Three, two months in the Army Air Corps as a flying cadet, and three years during World War II as a navigator on B-24s, flying in the Pacific war zone for three thousand hours for the Air Transport Command as a civilian. In spite of this service, and because I was technically a civilian after 1940, I had been the only one in my dental class who was refused the GI Bill, and I went deeply into debt for tuition, books, equipment, supplies, and living expenses. After graduation, I was required to spend one year working for another dentist to pay off my debts.

And now that I was almost out of debt, I was to be uprooted again, forced to discontinue my practice, store or try to sell my new equipment that was not paid for, sell or lose our new home, and move my pregnant wife and four children to a military base, where I would be filling the teeth of dependents of service personnel while the police action in Korea was being conducted.

My hard-luck story impressed the local draft board, and they recommended that the Selective Service Agency reclassify me as a hardship case. No luck. In December 1954, I was told I would report for induction in March 1955.

Our U.S. Congressman, Charles Gubser, recommended we try to appeal again and have our physician write a letter to the Selective Service, stressing the emotional effect my induction would have on my wife, Shirley. In March 1955, I received orders to report to Fort Sam Houston in Texas, which is the base for indoctrination of Army medical personnel. I was assured they would try to give me the rank of captain, which would earn me five hundred dollars a month, which should be enough to support my family. We were crushed! But the very next day we received a special delivery letter telling me to disregard the order to report. I had been reclassified, thanks to Shirley.

This is not the end of the fiasco. In 1995, fifty years after World War II, at the age of eighty-two, I received an honorable discharge from the U.S. Air Force, which credited me with having served in the

Air Transport Command during the war. I also received three medals and a Good Conduct lapel button. Shirley is a veteran, having served in the U.S. Navy as a WAVE. She calls the little eagle on the Good Conduct button the "Ruptured Duck." I prefer its less sarcastic name, the "Pleasant Pheasant." The package I received from the Air Force also contained a copy of my service record, which showed the dates of some of my flights into the Pacific zones of conflict. Accompanying this mailing was a letter from the Veteran's Administration informing me that I was eligible for the GI Bill, which I could use to pay for a college education, including money to help pay my living expenses. After fifty years, I am sure these benefits are not retroactive. Nor is a refund likely to be forthcoming, or requested.

During the first part of my dentistry career, we had endured over three years of pressure from the Selective Service Agency, in their attempt to draft me back into the armed services. Now, with the ordeal behind us, we were able to relax a little and get on with our lives. I was now forty-two years old.

PART VI

Flying, Fishing, Traveling, and Tooting

Leisure in Later Years

❦ Alibi Flying Club ❦

Our income from my dental practice was just enough to allow us to spend our many vacations on cross-country trips with our children and grandchildren. These trips fulfilled the need to be together as a family, compensating for the break-up of my family during my infancy and the lonely times spent in the orphanage.

One of our neighbors on Bronson Street was Vernon Samuel Ackerman, an ex-Navy Lt. Commander pilot, who was then manager of the Watsonville Airport. In November 1954, I had joined the new Alibi Flying Club as one of ten members. The club owned a Cessna 140, powered by a 90-horsepower Continental engine, and a Cessna 170, with a 145-horsepower Continental. Early Alibi Club members included Dave Willoughby, Louis Schiavon, Vern Wethy, Pressley Kerns, Dr. Fritz Smith, Nicholson, and myself.

In addition to being airport manager, Ackerman (Ack) also gave flying lessons in his spare time. One day I was telling him about my earlier experience with the Army flying cadet program, and luck smiled on me when he agreed to give me flying instruction to prepare me for obtaining a private pilot's license. We used our Cessna 140 for dual instruction, and it was a thrill for me to be back in the air again. It had been nine years since I completed three thousand hours as a B-24 navigator during the war, but this time, I was in the pilot's seat.

After four hours of dual instruction for familiarization with the 140, Ackerman let me solo. Then came dual and solo cross-country flights of the required duration to various California towns in the Central Valley. In my instruction, he included special emphasis on small field procedures and crosswind landings, with power-on approach and wheel landings.

The written portion of the examination for a private pilot's license was no problem for me because of my previous experience as an airplane mechanic and navigator. Ack, my instructor, was also the licensed examiner for the pilot's license, and I received my private single-engine license in April 1955. After several more dual hours for familiarization with the Cessna 170, I was checked out for soloing it in August 1955.

It was my good fortune to have Ackerman as my instructor. He had been a flying instructor on Consolidated PBY patrol seaplanes in the U.S. Navy, and was flying them in the Pacific when I was with the Air Transport Command on Consolidated B-24s. He was now the commercial pilot for Granite Construction Company, flying their Twin Cessna and later, their private jet, for many years. Ackerman's love of flying, and of all aspects of aviation, was apparent in the efficient way he managed the airport and fought for its improvement. He also spent many hours with his student fliers, on the ground and in the air, for which he charged four dollars an hour, but just for the actual air time. His quiet, easy-going manner made learning to fly a real pleasure. If he had been my instructor in the Army flying cadet program, my life would have followed a completely different direction. Or I might not have lived through the war. Who knows?

After initially paying one-tenth of the value of the planes, for a membership in the Alibi Club each member paid ten dollars per month for hangar rent, maintenance, repairs, etc. For major overhauls or engine and parts replacements, we assessed ourselves any amount necessary to cover it. The charge for flying the 140 was four dollars per hour, including fuel, and for the 170 it was six dollars per hour.

For longer flights, or with more than one passenger, I felt more at ease in the 170. We made trips to Klamath Falls, Oregon, several times to visit my uncle, Willis French Settle, Aunt Sarah, their daughter, my cousin Elizabeth, and her husband, Jimmy Swanson. The Swansons lived in a nice home on Klamath Lake. Their children were Diane, Robert, Marilyn, and Margaret.

Uncle French complained that his dentures didn't fit any more, after many years of use, so I offered to make him a new set. I flew up to Klamath Falls, loaded him and his luggage into the 170, and flew him back down to Watsonville. He stayed with us for eight days, which was sufficient time for me to complete his dentures. It took four appointments to complete my technique, which consisted of two sets of impressions, wax bite rims to reestablish contour and vertical dimension, a chew-in technique to determine centric position, try-in of waxed-up teeth, and delivery of completed dentures. His new dentures caused him to look twenty years younger.

The eight days Uncle French spent with us gave us time to get to know him better. He was one of my father's younger brothers, and he and Aunt Sarah often told me how much they regretted not having been financially able to take my two brothers and two sisters and me to rear after our parents died. I told him I was sorry too, but I thought things probably worked out best for us all, even though we kids grew up never seeing him or his family until many years later. I flew Uncle French back to Oregon, and he later told me he never needed one adjustment as long as he lived. But he was handy with a pocketknife, and I often wondered.

My cousin Betty's husband, Jimmy Swanson, also needed new dentures, so I flew to Oregon and brought him down to our house. He couldn't take enough time away from his barber shop to wait for the final delivery of his dentures, so I mailed them to him, and he said they fit great and looked much better than his old set. He insisted on paying the standard fee, but we finally settled on his paying for an out-of-state Oregon hunting license for me. I have never owned a shotgun, but his family had several. My next flight to Oregon was in duck-hunting season. I took a distant cousin, Don Bowles, with me in the 170, and we brought home twenty-one mallards and pintails. Shirley and a babysitter spent hours pulling off feathers and picking out buckshot. She gave some of the ducks to neighbors and froze the rest.

❧ To Mexico ❧

In February 1956, Shirley and I had the opportunity to fly the Cessna 170 to Mexico on a vacation. Sara was just five months old at the time. With four small girls and me to care for, Shirley hadn't had a vacation for many years, and we grabbed at the opportunity to get away. Our babysitter was Eleanor Richter, a very nice, gentle lady who was well liked by the girls.

Our friend, Lou Foote, and his wife Alla had a shrimp fishing and packing business in Mazatlán, Mexico. They also had acquaintances in Puerto Vallarta. Lou flew to Mexico frequently to check on the shrimp packing plant. He was planning a trip down in his old Howard, and wondered if we would be interested in following them down to Mazatlán, later spending a few days in Puerto Vallarta. We thought it would be a great experience and agreed to go. Dr. Bill Franklin, another dentist in Dr. Gurnee's office building, and his wife Claire were enthusiastic about the chance of accompanying Shirley and me in our Cessna 170. Bill had his pilot's license, but wasn't checked out in the 170; nevertheless, I felt safer having a copilot along.

Lou advised us what his route would be, and we agreed to meet at designated airports on the route. This made us all feel a little safer. It is difficult and tedious to keep another plane in sight on a trip to a prede-termined destination. We could keep in contact by using the Unicom frequency in case of emergency, or to break the monotony. Their plane was slightly faster than ours, so they would arrive first at our fuel stops and wait to be sure of our arrival. We were required to land and go through customs at the Nogales, Arizona, airport as we left the U.S.; then fly across the border and land at the Nogales, Mexico, airport, three or four miles to the south. There in Mexico, we waited in line to go through their customs and have the planes inspected. We learned from Lou Foote that if you just happened to have a couple of bucks vis-ible under your passport and, later, under your private airplane (*avion particular*) registration, it greatly sped up the paperwork, and left more daylight hours for flying. Lou had made many flights into Mexico, and knew all the tricks necessary for a smooth exit-entrance in both directions.

From Nogales, we flew south to Hermosillo Airport, where we had the planes gassed up and parked for the night. The gasoline was pumped out of a fifty-gallon drum into smaller cans, and then strained through chamois skin on a big funnel into our tanks. Then Lou dick-ered with two cab drivers to take us and our overnight bags into town, to an inexpensive hotel. Before we entered the cab (*libro*), he asked, in

Spanish, how far it was and how much we would be charged, and agreed on a price. Lou warned us that if you don't agree on a price ahead of time, the drivers could charge any price they wish, and you must pay.

After a delicious steak dinner and a good night's sleep, we took off and headed south, toward Mazatlán. After flying an hour or so, I decided we might not have enough gas to reach Mazatlán without stretching it. On the chart, I could see that the city of Los Moches was within easy reach, but it was twenty miles to the west of our flight line, on the coast of the Gulf of California. While changing course, I noticed what looked like a landing strip directly below us. There was also a windsock and a large storage building nearby. I was sure they would have gasoline we could buy, so I circled into a landing pattern, and as we approached the end of the runway, we saw pigs and chickens running to clear a path for us. We touched down alongside a fence that bordered the runway. There were a couple of buzzards on the fence-posts, but we weren't concerned about this, because we had been told this was part of the sanitation system south of the border.

When we reached the end of the narrow landing strip and I was taxiing toward the building, which appeared to be a large barn, a native came out and walked toward us. He was very tan and wore dungarees and a short-sleeved white shirt. A large, colorful sombrero shaded his face until he looked up and we saw his handsome features. I didn't stop the engine, but let it idle for a quick getaway, if necessary. He was on the copilot's side of the plane, so Bill opened the window, leaned toward the opening, and asked loudly, "You gottum gasolino?"

The man grinned broadly and replied, "Yeah, Mack. Do you take eighty or ninety octane?" We said we could use either, in a pinch. He said he would check his supply. He returned to the barn and swung open the door. Inside the opening we saw the nose of a beautiful, shiny Twin Beechcraft. He told us he didn't have enough reserve gas for his own requirement. We learned he was the pilot for a big rancher in the area, and had learned to fly in the U.S. during the war. He informed us we could follow the railroad track south to Culiacan, which had an airport and fuel supplies.

The Culiacan airstrip was long enough for commercial transport planes, but was made of cobblestones, and my landing wasn't too smooth. We bought enough gas to get us to Mazatlán. Here, once again, gas was strained through a chamois skin into our tank. We learned to appreciate this extra effort to keep our gas clean. We heard of planes being lost there because of dirty fuel.

Mazatlán is situated on the west coast of Mexico, on the Sea of Cortez, or Gulf of California. We approached it from the north as we flew down the coast. Viewed from the plane, the town appeared to be built on half of a large peninsula, which was divided by a very wide inlet, or stream. Against a background of clear sky and deep blue water, it appeared to be a tropical paradise. As we flew past two small offshore islands and the pointed end of the jetty, I entered a left-hand pattern, following another small plane, and landed.

Mazatlán was a slightly larger town, and had a longer and smoother runway than Hermosillo or Culiacan. Lou and Alla were at the airport waiting for us, and they had arranged for us all to stay at a hotel near the Malecon. This was a street with a walkway along the beachfront, where people could sit and relax in the sun, amble along on foot, or, for a few *pesos*, take a sightseeing ride in an *araña*, the open two-wheeled, horse-drawn buggy-type conveyance that seemed to be always available. I have a color slide of Bill Franklin standing next to the small horse that pulled our *araña*. When we viewed this slide later, on a large screen, everyone noticed that the toe of one of Bill's shoes glistened brightly, from splatter made by the unconcerned animal as he evacuated his bladder. I believe Bill much preferred the picture I took of him, staring proudly at the boatload of fish we caught a few days later.

Deep-sea fishing out of Mazatlán was great. Shirley and I, along with the Franklins, chartered a boat with a three-man crew, and caught many yellowtail tuna and a small shark. There were no limits on the catch of fish, and the crew furnished all fishing gear and bait. The fish we caught would be donated to needy families, we were told. We paid ten dollars each for the day's fishing, with a box of lunch and beer included.

We visited Lou Foote's shrimp operation and were impressed by the size of the plant. There were many workers tending conveyors that carried beautiful shrimp, or prawns, four to five inches long. They were being crated for shipment and placed in huge refrigerated trucks. The plant had its own power generators for electricity. We were told by Lou that the company owned several shrimp trawlers.

After three nights in Mazatlán, we were eagerly anticipating our visit to Puerto Vallarta. Lou had told us it was his favorite spot to relax or fish, and he bragged about the food. We had just visited the open-air food markets in Mazatlán, and seen large cuts of steak meat hanging in the open air. We were told they were curing to make them tender. They looked almost black, and we thought maybe they had cured a little too long. Shirley had been a meat-cutter in the Navy, and she had never seen uncooked black meat before. As we walked closer to the meat cuts, we could see they were completely covered with flies. Apparently, this wasn't considered a problem there. I will admit that the steaks we ate in Mexico were the tenderest and tastiest I have ever eaten, and extremely inexpensive.

After Lou Foote's Howard was airborne, we took off, and I pointed the nose of the 170 toward the south—down the coast, toward Puerto Vallarta. The balmy weather and clear, bright sky tended to make us a little drowsy. Shirley always slept from just after takeoff until the final approach for landing at our destination. Just watching the ground go past gets monotonous for passengers. Lou had told us to watch for a round island, a little inland from the coast, at about the halfway point of the flight to Puerto Vallarta. We could use it as a reference point, and it gave us something to do besides watching the horizon and waiting. I had spent about three thousand hours in B-24s looking at horizons and ocean surfaces during the war, and this aspect of flying was a little tedious to me now. But I couldn't sleep, even with a copilot, knowing I was responsible for four lives while we were in the air.

Near the midpoint of this leg of the flight, we were straining our eyes, looking into the sun, trying to locate Round Island. Shirley awoke from a nap, and when we told her we hadn't seen the island, she looked out her window, almost straight down under the plane, pointed, and asked, "Is that it?" She was sitting behind me. I looked at where she was pointing, and there it was, in plain view. I banked and circled it for a couple of pictures. It was a complete town on a perfectly round little island, with streets laid out in a circular pattern, completely surrounded by water. We could see boats around its circumference, but there were no houses on any of the land surrounding the island, which made it even more isolated and a real curiosity. Shirley would remind me for the next few years that she was the one who found the island, even though she was half asleep at the time.

Puerto Vallarta, at this time, was a small coastal town between Mazatlán and Acapulco. Its airport had a small building and a wind-sock to help us identify it, and its airstrip was short, consisting of packed dirt and some gravel. When our plane rolled to a stop, Lou was there and showed us where we could park it, in an open field beside his. We were assured no one would bother our planes during our stay.

Lou and Alla stayed with friends of theirs, but the Franklins and we found rooms in a small hotel that was still being built. We were in rooms on the second floor, and the third floor had two rooms which were still under construction, but almost complete. The other rooms were just a framework. Our quarters had a double bed in one room, a partition, and a doorway without a door. The bathroom consisted of a sink, a showerhead on one wall with a drain hole in the floor, and a toilet without a seat. The water was piped in from a large water tank on the roof. The tank was fully exposed to the hot sun all day long, and this provided a warm evening shower, but only to the first person using it; after that it was cool. So much for early solar energy. The bedroom was provided with two kerosene lamps that we could use at night, in case of a shortage of electricity. When we checked into the hotel, we were shown two cans which had been provided for us. We were told we should fill the five-gallon cans with water for use in case an electricity shortage prevented the pump from keeping the storage tank on the roof filled. Once this tank contained water, the rooms could be supplied by gravity. We probably had more fun in these comparatively primitive conditions than we would have had in a more fancy hotel. And the price was right. We were charged $6.85 per day, per couple, for the room, and this included two nice meals and a box lunch.

Bill and I rented a boat, fishing equipment, and crew for twenty dollars for a full day's fishing. We caught roosterfish, cabrilla, mahi mahi (dolphin fish), and tuna until our hands were sore, but the fishing crew kept baiting our hooks and seemed to enjoy watching our excitement with each catch. Most of the fish we caught were in the vicinity of a rocky point called Piedra Blanca ("white stone"). It was easily located from a distance because of its white top. It was a favorite spot for birds to sit while they waited for fish to appear in the water. Their droppings (*guano*) over the years made the rock surface white.

We had fun using our limited knowledge of Spanish to joke and sing with the boat crew. They were experts at fishing and handling the boat. They told of how they watched and followed the sea birds as an aid in finding the fish. The Gulf of California (Sea of Cortez) is referred to as the biggest fish trap in the world, and the size of our catch proved it.

As we chugged back toward land with our boatload of fish, we could see a bunch of people gathering near the spot where we would anchor. Bill and I wanted a picture of us standing next to our catch, so someone found a ten-foot-long tree limb, and the fish were strung along its length. Many of the natives gathered around us, and it made a great picture.

During the days we weren't fishing, we walked around the little town, visiting the unfinished church and the marketplace, and there was a tiny beach area a short walk from town. On the way to and from the beach, we crossed a bridge over a slow-running creek, where natives bathed and washed their clothing. They helped conceal and shade themselves with long reeds and palm branches, piled in the pointed, conical shape of an Indian teepee. When we arrived at the beach, we found we were the only ones there. Alla had told us it wasn't much of a beach, but there was a shaded area where we could sit in our swimming trunks and bask for a few minutes in the tropical sun.

The nights were balmy, and we would sit at the hotel and have a margarita or bottle of Dos Equis Beer before going to bed. Some nights, in the wee hours of the morning, we would hear mariachi musicians, still playing and singing loudly on their way home, obviously feeling no pain. I remember hearing, "*No vale nada la vida,*" from *Camino de Guanajuato.* Then, at what seemed to be about 4 A.M., the church bells would start chiming. We were confused, and asked, "Why so early?" Everyone laughed and told us the church had an ulterior motive. They reasoned that if the natives are awakened from a sound sleep, they might have trouble going back to sleep. Some might even be inclined to make love and possibly increase the church population.

We still have the slides of the entire trip to the Mexican west coast. We view the slides occasionally and enjoy reliving the experience and recalling the fun we had south of the border, down Mexico way, forty-five years ago.

At the time of our visit, Puerto Vallarta was a quaint, isolated, and unspoiled little village on the coast, and we were lucky to have visited it as early as we did. Within a few years, Pan Am built a huge runway and terminal. Then the movie, *Night of the Iguana*, transformed the place into a tourist trap for Gringos.

We were able to talk the airport attendant at Puerto Vallarta out of enough gasoline to get us to Culiacan, on our return flight. Our next stop was Hermosillo and then to the border at Nogales, and the routine of getting us and our plane out of the country, with four one-gallon jugs of good, cheap red wine. One gallon each was the limit allowed. When an inspector came to check out the plane for illegal contraband, we showed him the wine and slipped him a couple of dollars, and he signed our papers without looking in the baggage compartment. This saved us a little time and we were able to go through customs on both sides of the border, and get on our way back to California and home. This had been an unforgettable experience for us, but we were very glad to be back, and couldn't wait to see our kids again.

We learned that little Sara had gotten sick almost as soon as we had left, and Eleanor had placed her in the hospital in the care of our physician, Dr. Avery Wood. We learned that shortly after we took off on the vacation to Mexico, the babysitter had trouble getting Sara to nurse on a bottle. It was painful for her and she developed a slightly elevated temperature. The condition was diagnosed as Coffey's disease, an inflammation of the membrane lining of the jaws. The pressure of drawing in on a nipple caused pain. She was released from the hospital on our return, and Shirley continued the original plan of baby aspirin one-half-hour before feeding. Sara outgrew the condition during the next few weeks.

The girls got along well with Eleanor, but seemed very happy to see us when we got home. They, and our home, looked wonderful to us. We still had the weekend off, and then it was "back to the grind," as I used to jokingly refer to the preparation of teeth for restorations. Some witty patient would always counter with, "It must be very *boring* work." Not to be upstaged, I couldn't resist offering, "I get tired of being *down in the mouth* all day."

The old-fashioned way of doing dentistry was in a standing position, leaning sideways and to the right over the patient. After thirty-seven years of this unnatural position, my right shoulder appears to be two inches lower than the left, and my navel is a full three inches to the right of the midline of my abdomen. Today's dentists, who sit on a stool and bend their heads downward, tend to complain of pains in the neck and hemorrhoids. I'll take my misplaced belly button.

❦ The State of Alaska ❧

In 1957 we joined the Santa Cruz County Airmen's Association, and in 1958, five small planes took off for Alaska to help them celebrate becoming one of the United States. We had become acquainted with Everett Mollenhauer and his wife, Doris, who were in the Airmen's Association. Everett owned a Stinson "Flying Station Wagon," which was a four-place, high-wing monoplane. He asked if we wanted to fly with them on the trip to Alaska. He offered to let me sit in the pilot's seat and fly every other leg of the trip, if I wanted to. We accepted the invitation, made all the preparations for time off, and arranged for a babysitter for the month we would be gone. The girls were getting older, and we thought this would be the last trip we would want to take without them.

We studied the regulations governing private plane travel across Canada, and learned we would have to go through customs, going both into and out of the country. We also were required to carry equipment and supplies for survival, in case of an emergency landing. And we were warned that if we strayed more than five miles from the Al-Can Highway, we would not be searched for if we went down.

We loaded our emergency food supply and equipment, including a first-aid kit, fishing gear, a hunting knife, a rope, a tent, four sleeping bags, and a rifle. It was necessary to restrict the weight of our luggage to avoid overloading the plane. To make room for the equipment and our luggage, Everett removed two rear seats, and Shirley and Doris traveled the almost forty hours of flight sitting on our rolled-up sleeping bags, which they claimed were more comfortable than the seats would have been. The seat belts were attached to the deck of the plane.

We boarded the bright red Stinson at the Watsonville Airport and took off on July 3, 1958. We decided we would stop for gas every two to three hundred miles. I have a beautiful color slide of Crater Lake, taken as we flew across Oregon. On our stop at Wenatchee, Washington, we spent the nights of July 3 and 4 with relatives of Everett, who lived nearby. They owned a large farming area and were in the process of harvesting peas for the Jolly Green Giant. A large machine would literally clear the field by pulling up the entire plants and feeding them into another noisy machine, and peas would fall into a big bin. When we asked how the machine removed the peas from the plants, our hosts seemed to be anticipating our question, and gave their stock answer: "It beats the pea out of them!"

On July 5, we headed across the Canadian border toward Pintictin, the Port of Entry, about 120 miles north of the border. Here, all five planes of our flying group were together for the first time. There were four Cessnas and our pretty little Stinson Flying Station Wagon. After clearing customs and having lunch, we headed toward Williams Lake, our next gas stop. I flew this leg of the trip, which took two hours and twenty minutes, and covered 290 miles. On the landing at Williams Lake, I noticed that, after touching down, the plane tended to roll to the right, even without a crosswind from that direction. I used left rudder and brake, and we still skimmed the right edge of the runway. That's when Everett informed me it was a strange characteristic of the plane, for which he always compensated ahead of time. He had flown this plane for years and knew it well. I wondered how many other aberrations this plane might have, and decided I would have a more relaxing trip if I insisted Everett do all the flying. I'm sure he was a little relieved, too, and I was free to do the navigating and photography. The next leg of the trip took us to Prince George for a gas stop, and then to Fort St. Johns, where we got hotel rooms, ate a great dinner, and spent the warm evening walking around the town and reminiscing about the Gold Rush days.

Our flight so far had taken us over beautiful forests and alongside spectacular mountain peaks. Occasionally, we would spot another plane of our group and wave our wings at them. They were a fun group of people to fly with.

On July 6, we flew to Ft. Nelson, Watson Lake, and then to White Horse for our third overnight stay. Flying over White Horse, I got a great color slide picture of five old steam riverboats, resting side-by-side in a neat group on the shore of the Yukon River. Apparently, this was to be their final resting place. Their steam whistles and calliopes would be heard no more. After we secured our hotel rooms here and had dinner, we walked down to the river and got a closer look at the sad-looking retired fleet from a more splendid past. The sun was still well above the horizon, so I was able to get a close-up picture of them, even though it was 10:30 P.M.

From White Horse to Northway was 320 air miles, and took two hours and thirty-eight minutes flying time. Northway is just a few miles across the Canadian border into Alaska. After taking on more gas, we flew another 250 miles to Fairbanks. I had heard of Fairbanks, Alaska, since I was a kid at Ormsby Village, and expected to see a much larger city. By the time we landed, the other four planes in our group were already there. We got hotel rooms and went for refreshments and dinner at a recommended bar-restaurant. I remember most of the group and have color slides of them, all lined up at the railing of the bar, and later at the dining table. Lou Foote's passengers in his Cessna 182 were another pilot and math teacher, Jean Pogue, head of the math department at Watsonville High School; and another high school teacher, Jeanette Koebel. Then there was a Santa Cruz dental lab owner, Roy Sherrill, who was accompanied by Watsonville pharmacist Murray Nixon.

The group decided to fly toward Mt. McKinley, to the southwest of Fairbanks, and take some pictures of the 20,320-foot-high, snow-covered peak and the surrounding glaciers. We spotted some Dall sheep on one of the mountain slopes. After getting some spectacular pictures, we landed at a small strip at the Mt. McKinley National Park. We had lunch at the park and were given dogsled demonstrations, with teams of huskies pulling a sled with driver around a dirt track. There was no snow on the ground at this low elevation in July. The dogs were beautiful and well disciplined. We spent the night at the hotel in the park. Earlier, back in Watsonville, when we planned the Alaska trip, we had talked about the possibility of landing some place above the Arctic Circle, since we would be near it in Fairbanks. Our navigation chart showed an airport at Fort Yukon, which was almost exactly on, but a mile or so north of, the Arctic Circle. So the next day, all five planes took off, flew back to Fairbanks, and gassed up near an airport hangar. A native lady in the hangar office was wearing a beautiful sheepskin-lined jacket with a wolverine-lined hood. The front of the jacket and the waistband had different animal outlines worked into the leather. We were so impressed with it that she took it off and let Shirley and me put it on, for a picture of each of us, standing by the red Stinson. In the color slide, we look like genuine Arctic explorers.

An hour and thirty-five minutes north of Fairbanks, we were setting down at Fort Yukon, and we had just crossed the Arctic Circle. We now decided to go to another recommended place called Cheena Hot Springs, so after finding it on the chart, we took off and flew southeast. I believe it was about seventy-five miles from Fort Yukon, and required flying into a sort of secluded ravine. When we approached the hilly area, the weather became threatening. We had been warned not to fly near the hills if the good weather deteriorated and clouds formed. We had been told many small planes were lost in Alaska every year, and we did see the remains of a few of them during our trip. We decided to land at another small strip, called Circle City.

When I said the strip was small, I didn't realize how small. Everett came in as low as he could, keeping an eye on buildings at the approach end of the runway. We were on the ground and rolling toward the end, braking hard and puckering harder, as a fence approached our nose. By the time we stopped rolling, we had increased the length of the runway by several yards as our propeller chopped tall weeds that hadn't seemed to bother the other fliers in the group. It was late in the day, and we all decided to spend the night in Circle City, which got its name from its proximity to the Arctic Circle. We were told this was as far north in Alaska as one could drive in a car. There wasn't much of a town here at Circle. I remember a sawmill and several trailer houses. Accommodations were scarce. Seven of us were stuck with the last available spots to spend the night. Ten feet from the banks of the Yukon River, there were two small shacks or cabins that resembled oversized outhouses.

They were about eight by ten feet in size. Each had two double-decker bunks at one side of the room, and a wee table and four chairs at the other side. Shirley, Doris, and another lady slept in one cabin, and Everett, Murray Nixon, Roy Sherrill, and I slept in the other.

We were advised to rid the cabin of mosquitoes by smoking them out with a smoldering can of mosquito repellent. One can was provided for each cabin. We were told to close the room tightly and set the can just inside the door. Then we left to eat a snack at a small café. This would allow time for the elimination of all the mosquitoes from the cabin. It was dark when we returned to the cabins, got undressed, and climbed into our bunks. We were all choking and coughing from smoke and complaining about the smell. Doris knocked on our door and asked what the trouble was. Then she opened the door and saw the smoking can. She couldn't believe we didn't know enough to quickly sneak it outside the door before we got into bed. It took years to live that down.

The next day, we flew back to Fort Yukon. Everett had been trying to practice low, short-field approaches. After each landing, he would measure the length of the landing run, from the point of touchdown to the end of the roll. After landing at Fort Yukon, he stepped off less than two hundred feet, and seemed pleased with his accomplishment. We spent some time here sightseeing and talking with some Eskimo children. We visited their little Catholic chapel and then the one-room post office, to mail to ourselves some postal cards stamped with the Fort Yukon postmark. Along the banks of the Yukon, there were several native Indian fish traps and several smoking racks of salmon nearby. We were told it was illegal for the general population to have fish traps.

After several hours, we gassed up and took off from Fort Yukon, crossed the wide Yukon River, and one hour and thirty minutes later, we were back in Fairbanks. After another nice meal and a mosquito-free night in a hotel, we took off for Anchorage, Alaska. I was curious about this city, which had the same name as the Kentucky village that was on the postal address of all mail addressed to my childhood sanctuary, Ormsby Village. Many Ormsby Village kids graduated from Anchorage High School in Kentucky, before the home developed its own high school program.

It was a three-and-a-half-hour flight to Anchorage. As we approached this largest city in Alaska, we could see Elmendorf Air Base and carefully avoided its space. The air view of the Anchorage area was very interesting because of its adjoining bay and lake areas, which were solidly lined with private floatplanes. We were told at that time almost every family in Alaska had a plane, most with floats. After filling our tanks at the Anchorage airport, which, we were told, was the busiest airport in the world, we left on a short one-hour-and-twenty-minute flight down the west coast of the Kenai Peninsula, or the east coast of Cook Inlet, to Kachemak Bay and the little town of Homer. Doris Mollenhauer was eagerly anticipating our arrival at Homer. This was the home of her stepbrother, and he and his family had invited them, and us, to stay with them for a few days.

As we approached Kachemak Bay, we saw a beautiful panorama of rugged snow-capped mountain peaks and many glaciers in the distance. Before we spotted the airport and town of Homer, we were fascinated by a long sliver of land extending into the bay. Doris told us this was called the Homer Spit. I took many pictures of the spit, with the airport and town showing in some, and the glaciered mountains providing the background in the others.

We landed at Homer and were met and warmly greeted by Doris's relatives, the Smiths. We were impressed by their fourteen-year-old son, Arthur, who had already become an experienced hunter and fisherman. They wanted us to do some fishing, and also help them eat the remainder of their bear and moose meat from the freezer. Hunting season for bear was approaching, and they needed the freezer space for the fresh meat. Each licensed hunter is allowed one moose and one bear per year. Arthur had gotten his the year before and was anxious to try again.

The other four planeloads of our flying club members planned to leave Homer after a day or two and begin their return trip to California. We all decided to have one more get-together at a restaurant on the Spit. Before we ate, we went out to the tip of the spit to check out the small building we had seen from the air. It was a cute little bar and museum called the Salty Dawg. There were a few whalebones lying near it and an old lantern hanging by the door. A small, blue Alaskan flag, with white stars forming a Big Dipper and the

North Star, was flying from its roof. We went into the Salty Dawg, where we had a short snort or two and examined their interesting display of flotsam from the beach, including the vertebra of a whale and the pizzle of a walrus.

The restaurant where we ate was famous for its seafood. The menu included a popular delicacy called halibut cheeks, which were exactly that. Everyone decided to try them. They had the appearance of large chunky scallops, only much thicker. They were two inches or more across, and we wondered how large a halibut would have to be to have that much meat in its cheeks. They were the most delicious fish I have ever tasted.

❧ The Shortest Landing ❧

We were enjoying our stay with our hosts, the Smiths. I can't recall their first names, except for their son, Arthur, who became our fishing buddy and instructor on local fishing techniques. We were told of a fishing village across Kachemak Bay, called Seldovia. They told us it was partly built on pilings that extended out from the shoreline. This allowed the fishing boats to unload directly onto docks and into the frozen-storage buildings. When we learned there was an airport at Seldovia, we decided to fly across the bay and land there. We also learned that there was a mail delivery boat that traveled around the edge of the bay to reach Seldovia without crossing the deep water. Storms can develop quickly and the boat wasn't considered very seaworthy. The girls were invited to ride the boat around the bay and meet us in Seldovia, after we landed there. Then, after visiting the town and taking a few pictures, we would all fly back to Homer.

Everett and I waited for about two hours and then took off for Seldovia. It took only a few minutes until we were circling the short Seldovia strip. We checked the windsock on the roof of a small hangar at the south end of the runway. The north end stopped at the edge of the bay. The windsock was hanging limp, so Everett decided to come in from over the bay, because there would be no trees or buildings to worry about avoiding on a low approach. As we turned into the final approach and headed toward the end of the runway and the edge of the bay shoreline, we were approaching low and slow, and I was thinking this would be another of our short landings of which Everett had been so proud.

The next thing I remember was waking from a temporarily shocked condition, sitting close to the gravel on the runway. My right knee was hurting and I felt a knot on my forehead. Then I heard Everett say, "Well, what the hell caused that?" He seemed to be suffering more from embarrassment than from physical injury. In a few moments his upper lip, under his nose, began to swell. He was somewhat taller than I and, whereas the top of my head hit the wheel of the steering column, he hit it just below his nose. Otherwise, he wasn't hurt. My right knee had plowed into a toggle on the control panel, and I walked with a limp for a while.

After just sitting for a few seconds, we quickly unbuckled our safety belts, and I crawled out my doorway on my hands and knees in the gravel. I felt a drop of gasoline on the back of my neck from the wing above. Everett wasted no time crawling out behind me. The pilot's door next to Everett had been jammed shut and he hadn't been able to open it. We were still partly in a state of shock as we stood up and quickly walked away from what had been a beautiful and dependable little plane. When it seemed safe to do so, we went back closer to assess the damage. The door on my side had been ripped off at the hinges and was lying on the ground a few feet away. The main landing gear was completely squashed into the underbelly of the plane. The wooden propeller blades had plowed into the landing surface when the plane tipped forward. The tapered cowling, below the engine and propeller shaft, was smashed flat and had been scraped with gravel and dirt, indicating we had scooted almost onto our nose before the tail settled back down. With the fuel still dripping from the wing, we realized that if we had flipped completely over, we might have exploded. Or, if we had landed a few inches lower, we would have been in the bay.

After retrieving my camera from the cockpit floor and my sunglasses from near the windshield where they had been thrown, we walked, somewhat sheepishly and with slight limps, down the length of the runway to the hangar. Someone there said they had heard a crunching sound and seen the tail of the plane rise up and fall back down. While walking from the airport into town, we were dreading having to face Shirley and Doris and tell them what had happened. They saw us walking toward them and knew something was wrong, by the way we walked and looked. When they saw Everett's puffed-up lip, they kidded that he looked like Andy Gump. The bump on my head was barely noticeable, but I had a definite limp.

After relating to the girls what had happened, we decided to go on with our sightseeing anyway. We visited the wharf area where the fish were stored in large refrigerated rooms. In one room, I remember seeing halibut measuring at least five feet in length and two feet in width, stacked from the floor nearly to the ceiling. Now we knew the source of the large halibut cheeks we had enjoyed so much.

Everett arranged to have a local small-plane owner fly us, two at a time, to Homer. He took Shirley and Doris first, and then returned for us. The Smiths were waiting for us at the Homer airport and took us to their home, where they had prepared a nice dinner, including moose and bear meat. They were very sad Everett had wrecked his plane, and they insisted we stay with them for a week or ten days, while the plane was being retrieved and stored on their property. They were planning to repair it the following summer.

From the Smiths' living room, we were able to see a beautiful view of the snow-capped mountains and glaciers framing Kachemak Bay. And the fireweed was beginning to bloom. It covered the lawns and fields with a red blanket. This was a comfortable home in an ideal setting. We were treated to several fishing trips, to their favorite streams and spots along the bay. At one river where we were fishing for salmon, we would cast out from the bank with a lure, and a big Dolly Varden trout would grab it immediately. We caught a huge number of trout, but no salmon. Arthur seemed disappointed that we couldn't land a big salmon, but we were tickled to be catching so many trout. One of my favorite pictures is of me holding up a long string of trout, smiling, with the sun shining in my face at ten o'clock in the evening.

Our hosts insisted we stay long enough to eat the rest of their moose steaks, moose burgers, chicken-fried moose, and even moose chow mein. We did other things besides fish and eat moose. They were in the process of building a large ramp at the edge of the water for their float-plane to be more easily beached. Everett and I helped carry boards and hammered some of the nails. We were treated to a sightseeing flight in their seaplane.

This had been one of the most relaxing and enjoyable vacations we could have imagined. Then it was time to return to reality. Shirley and I bought tickets for a commercial flight home. Everett and Doris would stay there longer, but we were missing the girls and had to get back to work. We were driven from Homer to Anchorage, where we boarded a TWA Lockheed Constellation, which took us to San Francisco. A smaller plane shuttled us to Monterey, where our babysitter, Eva Marinelli, had our four daughters all dressed up and waiting for us at the airport as we walked from the plane to the gate. What a happy moment for us all! I made a large print of the slide, which shows Shirley holding little Sara, with Judy, Mela, and Bettye standing close to her. Eva is in the picture also. She was a wonderful person and we shall never forget what a big help she was to our family.

When Everett and Doris finally returned from Alaska, and he seemed to have gotten over the shock and embarrassment of wrecking his airplane, I kidded him, from a safe distance, that he had set a world's record for the shortest landing by a conventional aircraft—about fifteen or twenty feet. I recalled it was a shorter distance than that used by the old biplane fighters on the flight decks of the *Saratoga* and *Lexington*—and they had a tail hook and arresting cable to help them stop. He just laughed and seemed to be thankful that neither of us was injured. A short time later, he bought a little Luscomb aircraft, and we made one or two flights with them in that plane. We heard a few years later that the wrecked Stinson had been repaired and fitted with pontoons, and was flying all over Alaska.

❧ Relaxation and Happiness ❧

As I attempt to recount episodes of the past fifty years of my life, I tend to dwell more on the time spent with my family, at home and on our many trips traveling across country together, than on the long hours spent in my practice of dentistry, which made the vacations possible. I learned early on in my practice to present a relaxed and pleasant demeanor, never to appear to be tense or overly concerned during a difficult surgical procedure, or in any potentially stressful situation. I learned to reduce my tendency to get migraine headaches during or after long and demanding operations. By using a technique referred to as "serial relaxation," beginning with the head and neck muscles, I was able to relax my whole body completely, and eliminate the pain, nausea, and peripheral blind spots associated with migraine. To this day, I periodically practice this technique whenever I think of it, and I haven't had a migraine headache for at least twenty-five years.

We also found that taking off from our daily routine helped us to relax and enjoy life more. As the girls became older and started in school, we planned our vacations during their times out of school, at Easter, Christmas, and during the summer months. These were happy and relaxed times. Every summer, we eagerly anticipated a vacation in our station wagon, usually to Klamath Falls, and later, when the girls were older, to Kentucky, Iowa, and Denver, to visit relatives living in those distant places. We tried to plan to leave Watsonville after the Fourth of July. This allowed us to see the annual parade down Main Street, where I was thrilled to see and hear the familiar march music of the Watsonville Band and the Sciots Drill Team, with their precision marching. I recalled the many years I had spent marching and playing in bands at Ormsby Village, KMI, U of L, and in the Kentucky National Guard.

Some years, we would have the station wagon loaded and ready to leave town as soon as the parade was over. Our load usually consisted of seven suitcases tied down toward the back of the roof, covered with a waterproof tarp. Inside the station wagon, we carried ice water in a large thermos jug and an ice chest for snack-type food, such as carrot sticks, sandwiches, and fruit. Shirley would buy a five-pound bag of sunflower seeds from a health food store and boil them in salt water, to give them flavor. Then she would give a small bag of them to each of the children. They would put them in their mouths one at a time, crack them with their teeth, remove the kernel, and spit out the hull neatly into a garbage bag. This was a great help in passing the time, especially at night, when it was dark and the passing scenery couldn't be seen.

When our Rambler Ambassador station wagon was new, we drove it to Denver, a distance of fifteen hundred miles at that time, on the roads then available. We had been invited to visit Shirley's family, who were all still living then. This was to be the longest trip we had driven so far, and as it turned out, we ended up driving it nonstop, one driver. My favorite time to drive was late at night and in the wee hours of the morning, especially when passing through large cities, where I would often have four or five lanes of freeway all to myself, well-lighted and free of traffic. There was plenty of time to read highway signs, choose the proper lane, and avoid taking the wrong off-ramp. Shirley would usually stay awake while we passed through the center of large cities, to point me into the proper lane for leaving town toward our next destination.

I believe I was partly conditioned for nighttime driving by the many times I had navigated all through the night during the war. I often went twenty-four hours or more without sleep. On this first trip to Denver by car, before we made it out of California, we had lost nearly two hours on a wrong road, headed into the high Sierras out of Sacramento. By the time we had crossed Nevada and reached the salt flats of Utah, I stopped for the first time to rest my eyes. After a few minutes, I realized I wasn't sleepy. Everyone in the car was sound asleep, and when I saw daylight approaching, I knew the salt flats would be unbearably hot in a few hours, and we didn't have air-conditioning in the station wagon. In California, we had never needed it. This was July, but the outside air was still cool, and I decided to drive on, at least as far as Salt Lake City. When we arrived there, I still wasn't sleepy, and we didn't want to stay in a motel during the day. We decided to continue driving, and we arrived in Denver in the evening, thirty-one hours after we had left Watsonville. It took us about two days to rest up and get back to normal. The two-week visit with Shirley's parents allowed us to get better acquainted with them and her whole family. We would return to Denver many more times, with our children and our grandchildren.

When our youngest daughter, Sara, was five years old, we decided we should drive to Kentucky to visit my brothers and sisters. Sister Bettye and her husband, Elliott Ashcraft, had been inviting us to come to their comfortable little home at the South Park Country Club at Fairdale, Kentucky, just at the southern outskirts of Louisville. I hadn't visited them for fourteen years, and they had never seen Sara, and were looking forward to seeing all of us. We had written often, and sister

Bettye and brother George had lent us the money to help us when we were in debt, but we hadn't attempted to drive that far with the children.

We decided to go to Kentucky by the shortest route. At that time, this would be by way of Route 66, which we joined at Needles, in Southern California. We had planned ahead of time to stop at several points of interest we had heard about. This route passed near the Grand Canyon, many ancient Indian ruins, a black volcanic crater with acres of lava still visible on the surface of the surrounding landscape, the Petrified Forest, and a huge meteor crater. We visited and took slide pictures of all these famous attractions. Most of the pictures included some or all of us posing, to prove we had been there, like Kilroy.

Back then, forty years ago, the National Park areas were more accessible to visitors. In the Petrified Forest, we were able to get up close to the petrified logs, appropriately named "agate rainbows," and kids were even allowed to walk across the petrified Agate Bridge, at their own risk. We were allowed to observe the ancient Indian petroglyphs from within touching distance. But now, they are fenced off and must be viewed from afar. We now know that these precautions are necessary to preserve these treasures for the future. We are glad, now, that we bothered to record photographically these happy times we spent together. After enjoying these Arizona attractions, we crossed New Mexico, another colorful state, and then the Texas Panhandle.

On one extremely hot day, at a potty stop, we bought everyone a milkshake, which we were to drink as we continued driving. Daughter Bettye's favorite place to ride in the car was close behind me, looking over my shoulder at the road ahead and the scenery. I was sitting very relaxed at the wheel when I had to brake suddenly, and felt something ice-cold on my back, from my neck to my waist. Bettye had lost control of her shake and emptied the entire drink down my back. After the initial refreshing shock, followed by a period of joyous celebration, we used wet washcloths on my neck and back to make the sticky milkshake more wearable, at least until we stopped for the night in Shamrock, Texas.

We left Shamrock and followed Route 66 through Oklahoma to St. Louis, Missouri, then took Highway 50 east through the southern tip of Illinois, into southern Indiana to Vincennes, then southeast on

Highway 150 to the Ohio River and Louisville. The countryside of
Illinois and Indiana was unbelievably lush and green. I had become
accustomed to the brown, parched hills of California in the summertime. We crossed the river to Louisville from the Jeffersonville side just
as it was getting dark. When we arrived at sister Bettye's home at the
South Park Country Club in Fairdale, the Fourth of July fireworks
were just coming to an end. We had driven nonstop from Shamrock,
Texas, to see the fireworks at South Park, and we almost made it. We
were groggy and tired of driving, but the warm greeting we received
made us glad we had made the effort to get there.

Originally, South Park was a small fishing club. There was a nice,
but small clubhouse next to the private lake, which was stocked with
bass and catfish. There was a wharf with some rowboats, but each
homeowner at the lake had his own boat, with a dock and a wooden
stairway up to his house, which was on the elevated side of the lake
opposite the clubhouse. The view of the lake, clubhouse, and surrounding forest area was a perfect picture of Southern comfort. The lake had
a roped-off swimming area and a walkway leading out to a platform
with a high-dive. We adults went swimming and sunbathing once or
twice, but the kids spent almost every day in the water, when we
weren't visiting local tourist attractions, antique stores, or yard sales.

My sister Bettye accompanied us all to the state capital at Frankfort,
where she had friends in the governor's office. We were permitted to
get a slide picture of each daughter sitting in the governor's chair, pretending to sign something important. Eventually, each of us was commissioned a colonel in the Honorable Order of Kentucky Colonels, a
charitable organization which has many other important members
throughout the country. Membership in the organization is especially
sought-after and prized by Kentuckians. As a result of Bettye's many
years of work in the State Senate as a recorder of the minutes, and
through the influence of political friends in high places, she has been
able to get colonel's commissions for all her relatives and a great number of friends over the years.

On this trip to Kentucky, or on the succeeding yearly trips, we
would visit Mammoth Cave, Lincoln's birthplace, Shakertown,
Cumberland Falls, Berea College, the Hillerich and Bradsby bat factory, the Brown and Williamson tobacco factory, Churchill Downs,

Speed Memorial Museum at U of L, the Belle of Louisville paddle-wheel steamboat, relatives in Horse Cave, Bear Wallow, and Glasgow, the flea market at the State Fairgrounds, and most of the antique shops and finest eating places. We all value the memory of these early trips back to the state of my birth, and thank sister Bettye for her generous hospitality.

❧ Los Pajaros ❧

I joined Los Pajaros Flying Club and became the joint owner of a Ryan Navion and a Beechcraft Bonanza. Now, I had five different aircraft to fly. Early every spring, usually before Easter, we would fly to Baja California, Mexico, for deep-sea fishing. We usually flew the Bonanza or the Navion because, with their larger engines and retractable landing gears, they were somewhat faster than the Cessnas.

Our trips to Baja involved landing at Calexico, California, and Mexicali, Mexico, for the exit-entrance routine, in both directions, to satisfy customs personnel that we were just amateur fishermen and not international smugglers. Our most frequent stops in Baja were Bahia de Los Angeles (Bay of the Angels), Mulege, Loreto, La Paz (capital of Baja, Sur), Punta Colorada, near Puenta Pescadores, and Cabo San Lucas.

For flying time in our Bonanza, we charged ourselves ten dollars per hour, which included fuel. When split four ways, this was two-fifty per person per hour. Flying time for the round trip from Watsonville to Cabo was about twenty hours, which meant a cost of fifty dollars per person for transportation. If we flew only to Loreto or Mulege, the cost was even less, and the charges for simple lodging and magnificent meals were unbelievably affordable. If our stay in Baja was to be limited, we usually spent all of our time at Bay of the Angels. Here we slept on the long, open porch of a beach shack. At night there was often a cool breeze, which helped us sleep soundly after we had gorged on turtle-meat cutlets or lobster, with Cervesa Carta Blanca or Dos Equis. The mornings were beautiful and peaceful. I have a color slide that I took at dawn, while lying on my back on the cot. The focus is on my feet, and shows the sun just poking up above the horizon, between my two big toes.

We were never pressured to go fishing in the mornings until we had had a good breakfast. There were plenty of fish in the Sea of Cortez, and they could wait for us. We were there just to relax and forget work. There was always time to relax on the chartered fishing boats, which took us out to the favorite fishing areas of the skilled boat crews. I had fun trying to speak Spanish to the fishermen. If I could get them to slow down a little, and just use words that they had heard me use, we were able to understand each other a little more. If I concentrated on words that pertained to fishing, birds, and directions for steering the boat, I became able to converse with them by the time we were ready to leave and return home.

We never had to wait long before circling birds in the distance told us where the fish were feeding. Under the birds, the water often would be literally churning with fish activity. With each pass of the boat across the spot, with the lures trailing behind, every pole would soon be bending and jerking from the weight of a large fish, usually a tuna, but sometimes a rooster fish or a dolphin fish (mahi mahi).

The fishermen all seemed to know the location of every deep spot where we could catch cabrilla, red snapper, or huge groupers. From Bay of the Angels, we were able to fly home with fillets of various fish, big chunks of grouper, or turtle meat from one of the gigantic *tortugas*, which were caught there and trucked north for sale above the border. We could pack some of our catch in dry ice, which would keep it frozen for the short flight home. Shirley's expertise as a great cook could again be demonstrated by the delicious fish meals she prepared from our Baja catch, and by her surprise presentation of breaded turtle cutlets during the following Christmas vacation, when my whole family happened to be visiting from Kentucky.

During the 1960s, we kept the club airplanes in the air with many trips, together with flying and fishing buddies, to remote hot spots for trout. These were mostly in Canada and Montana. In Canada, Canim Lake was accessible only by air or water; the only road to isolated Chilko Lake was twenty miles from the nearest town, and was navigable only by high-axle, four-wheel-drive vehicles. In Montana, we landed on several occasions at a small strip near Ennis Lake on the

Madison River, and another strip at Henry's Lake, near West Yellowstone. I also remember flying, on two different weekends, to a spot on the upper Sacramento River, near Yuba City, and fishing for shad. After one long day of fishing, I recall hearing a fisherman suggesting we put the fish on a rack outside the cabin to be smoked, and I couldn't resist another feeble attempt to make a pun on three names from the Bible that had been used in a popular song. I must have been extremely tired and getting a little silly when I actually said, "Let's put the fish on a shad rack, by me shack, and to bed we go." I expected, at the very least, a chuckle or two, but all I got was a simple sympathetic smile from one of the guys. However, I survived the letdown.

❧ Montreal's Expo '67 ❧

When we heard the Watsonville Band was going to Montreal for the Expo '67 World's Fair, we planned a summer vacation that would take us across Canada to see the fair. We wanted to be there when the band was performing, and decided to leave about ten days before their scheduled arrival there. From there we planned to go down the East Coast to New York, Washington, D.C., Williamsburg, Virginia, and then to Louisville, Kentucky, for a month of relaxation at sister Bettye's. Next, we would go to Mason City, Iowa, to visit some of Shirley's family, then head back west by I-80 to Salt Lake City, and then home. We considered buying a motor home for the two months of travel, with our four girls and a kitten that had just adopted us.

Louis Schiavon, a flying buddy in the Alibi Club, owned an Aristocrat trailer agency in Freedom. Louie convinced us we wouldn't like a motor home, and talked us into buying a long trailer. We owned a Ford V-8 Country Squire station wagon, which was specially equipped for pulling a trailer. It had an oversized radiator fan, heavy-duty shocks, and a transmission oil cooler. I had never pulled a trailer, and all of our friends were surprised that my first trip pulling a long trailer would take us up to and across Canada, and then on a roundabout return through the States back to the Pacific Coast. The total distance covered was about eight thousand miles. Some of the narrow, winding roads were a little treacherous and exciting, but we survived, I learned a lot about trailer life, and we met many nice, helpful people.

One thing we learned about trailer-traveling for long distances with young children was that we couldn't cover as many miles in a day as we had planned. Since it was illegal for anyone to ride in the trailer when it was being towed, it was necessary to get up early, and get the girls cleaned up, dressed, fed, and into the car before we could start driving. Most days it was 10 A.M. before we could get going. The speed limit for pulling a trailer was forty-five miles per hour, and we didn't feel comfortable driving after dark on the long, sparsely populated Trans-Canada Highway.

Another handicap to our progress on the trip was the fact that the gas stations in the small towns along the highway all closed for the night at sundown. The large load we were pulling decreased the number of miles we could travel on a tank of gas. We tried to stop each night near a gas station because of our fear of running out of gas.

On one occasion, when I tried to stretch our gas supply to reach the next town, we did run out of gas. It was just before sundown. I pulled off the road, put out our emergency signals, and warned Shirley to lock the car doors, while I started to walk back down the highway to where I had seen another car parked. I had walked only a short distance when a Royal Canadian Highway Patrol car approached from the opposite direction. He had seen our car and trailer and noticed me walking away from it. When I told him my problem, he turned his car around, asked me to get in, and headed back in the direction we were traveling. He told me the filling station at the next little town might have a can for the gas and should still be open. We were traveling about ninety miles per hour. As we approached the little town, he saw that the station was dark. He said the next station was about fifteen miles farther, and he was sure they would have gas available, and also a can. He seemed to know the filling station owners, and whether they would have a gas can he could borrow for me temporarily.

We arrived at the slightly larger town in a few more minutes. He pulled the patrol car into a station which was just then turning off its lights. He went around to the back of the station to a small house, where he knew the owner lived, and asked him if he could get some gas for me. The man said he didn't know if his can had been returned by the last borrower. The Canadian Mounty hunted in the back room of the station and finally came out smiling, with a five-gallon can. He operated the pump to fill the can. I paid him less than two dollars for the five gallons. The Mounty put the can of gas in his trunk, and we went streaking back to the trailer at a very high speed. Shirley was relieved to see us return. I took off the gas cap and reached for the can, but the Mounty told me to stand back or I might get gas on my shoes, and he emptied the can into my tank. Then he waited there to be sure I could get the engine started. I offered to reward him for his most unusual assistance, but he laughed and said this was part of his job. Then he said he hoped we would enjoy Canada, and that he would have to go back to return the gas can. It was dark when we reached the next town, where we found a trailer park and settled down for another night. We never ran out of gas again on the whole eight-thousand-mile trip.

We used up the ten days we had allowed for traveling, and arrived in Montreal a day after the Watsonville Band had flown back to California. We were disappointed, but we enjoyed the Expo for three days. Our trailer park was fairly close to a bus line, which took us to the subway (Metro), which hauled the masses of people to the fairgrounds. A very fast Metro delivered us to the Expo in a short time. The buses and the Metro were always crowded, and I don't remember that any of us had a seat for the ride. Everyone who was standing had to hold onto overhead straps. We still remember the hot, sweaty, crowded, poorly ventilated rides on the buses and the subway cars. The body odors were most unpleasant, especially with arms raised over the head for support from the straps. Our oldest daughter, Bettye, was seventeen years old at the time. On one occasion, when we were crammed into a subway car after transferring from another subway, she had her nose almost buried in a strange Canadian armpit, when she practically shouted out, good-naturedly, "Next pit stop!" Everyone who heard her laughed sympathetically.

We enjoyed many such moments of frivolity on this long vacation together. The traveling was tiring for all of us, but when we stopped, we enjoyed seeing things that were new to us and meeting friendly people in the heartland of both Canada and the United States.

While traveling from Montreal down the East Coast, we decided to skip New York City and its crowds and drive straight down to Baltimore, and then to Washington, D.C. We parked the trailer in a recreation vehicle facility just outside the north edge of the loop. The next morning we called our friends, Col. Gerry and Mrs. Jane Borg, who lived there with their four sons. Gerry was on duty in the area, and we had planned to contact them and had their Washington phone number with us when we left home. Jane was the daughter of our family physician, Dr. Avery Wood, who had delivered three of our daughters and was a close family friend. He and his wife, Lois, together with the Gurnees and Shirley and I, often made excursions throughout the state to study and collect rock samples for our hobbies of geology and paleontology.

The Borgs were happy to hear from us and generously offered to have their oldest son, Axel, show us around the capital. We met Axel at a predetermined location, and he seemed delighted to help us. He was just fourteen years old, but he was already quite tall, matured, and had studied Washington as a hobby. He was the perfect guide for us. He spent two days directing us to the main points of interest in the area. This was an experience far exceeding our Expo '67 visit. We were greatly indebted to Axel and his family for their kindness.

Our next stop was Williamsburg, Virginia, near where my ancestors had landed after their migration from England. From Williamsburg, we headed west through the Appalachian Mountains to Ashland, Kentucky, then to Louisville and South Park. Here we would spend three or four weeks with Bettye and her husband, Elliott. Pulling the long trailer along the narrow country roads in the southern suburbs of Louisville was a new experience for me. I had gone down the same little roads many times before in a car, but with an eight-foot wide trailer behind me, the roads looked even narrower and the mail boxes even closer to the edge of the road. When we reached Bettye's house on the elevated Club Hill Drive, we saw a large sign next door, in the Kelleys' parking space. The sign read, "Reserved for the Settles." The Kelleys realized we wouldn't be able to park and level the trailer on Bettye's steeply sloping driveway, and they had the foresight to arrange for our comfort. For the sixty-plus years Bettye has lived on the club property, she and all of her neighbors have been very friendly and helpful to each other. We and our children and grandchildren always look forward to returning there.

After three or four weeks of hot and humid weather, which included visiting interesting landmarks, shopping for antiques, swimming and cat-fishing in the lake, working in brother Garnett's vegetable garden, finishing antiques, working crossword puzzles, eating out, or helping cook for eight to ten people, we had to start heading west to prepare the girls for another school year.

Our plans included visiting Shirley's sister, Fritzie, and her family in Mason City, Iowa. We headed north to Indianapolis, where we hit the worst thunderstorm I have ever driven through. The terrifying bolts of lightning and rumbling thunder were something the girls hadn't experienced in California, at least nothing that spectacular while riding in a car. We kept moving and were soon in calm weather again.

When we got to Fritzie's, she and her husband, Arthur, were glad to see us, and we stayed with them three or four days. They owned a large farm with a very nice old farmhouse. They fed us royally, and we had fun visiting together and playing horseshoes. The girls all got to take turns driving the riding lawnmower. They ran it out of gas twice. The girls also were thrilled to hold and snuggle tiny, pink piglets that had recently arrived. Their thrill was somewhat dampened when one of the piglets pooped down the front of Sara's clothing. Shirley had warned them that might happen, "but, Mother, they're so cute."

Daughter Bettye was a member of the Watsonville High School cheerleader squad, which had signed up to go to a course or seminar on cheerleading in Nevada. We couldn't possibly make it back to Watsonville in time for that, so we made arrangements for her to fly home. A shuttle plane took her to Minneapolis, where she would have to wait on standby for the next available seat to California.

While waiting in the passenger lounge, hoping for a possible cancellation, Bettye must have appeared desperate, because one of the pilots offered her the last seat on the plane to San Francisco, and it was up front in the first class compartment. She still gloats over the first-class treatment, which included being served champagne. She made it back in time to join the cheerleading team, but we missed her from our traveling family group. We hit I-80 West near Des Moines, and it took us across Nebraska, Wyoming, Utah, Nevada, and California, to the San Francisco Bay Area. We arrived home in three or four days. This trip had been a great introduction to trailering, an eight-thousand-mile introduction.

We used the trailer on a few shorter trips in 1968. One was to the Salton Sea in Southern California, the lowest spot in the United States. We went with a group of three or four other trailers. Our next trip was to South Shore, Lake Tahoe, and the Richardson campgrounds on the west shoreline. Here we met other trailer families, including the extremely congenial Steve Komjathy family. He was a highly regarded engineer in the Sacramento area. Steve had been a landed nobleman in one of the Eastern European countries and was forced to flee, penniless, to America after his country was invaded by Germany, or Russia, or both. For several years after that trip to Tahoe, we would visit them in their East Sacramento suburban home.

Before even considering another trip across the country to Kentucky, we informed Louie Schiavon that we still thought a motor home would be better for us, because we could travel more easily at night and could be riding while everyone but the driver was still in bed. Louie told us he knew the owner of another, larger trailer dealership, which also sold Winnebago motor homes. He said he would be able to get us a special dealership discount. And we found out later his brother, Marty, would buy our trailer, and also the Ford station wagon. We went to the Winnebago dealership in San Leandro and agreed on the purchase of the medium-sized model. We added several optional items that seemed attractive to us, such as dual gas tanks, a transmission oil cooler, an Onan generator, an eight-track tape deck with six speakers, and special Mooride shocks for the dual-wheeled rear axle. Total cost, after a two-thousand-dollar discount, was around ten thousand dollars. We saved even more by agreeing to take delivery at the Winnebago factory at Forest City, Iowa, just a few miles from the home of Shirley's relatives in Mason City, where we had just recently visited. The sale of our trailer and car made the purchase price of the motor home a little less traumatic. It was a '69 model, but we were able to purchase it in the summer of 1968.

❧ Watsonville Band ❧

After watching the Fourth of July parade in 1968, I followed the Watsonville Band back to the bandroom at the high school. The band director at that time was Don Pellerin, and the business manager was Jack Lundy. I knew Don and Ed Pio, another band member, from our days in the Lion's Club together. I knew Jack and his wife, Sadie, as well as two of their daughters, Marty and Sandy, all of whom played in the Watsonville Band. Marty used to babysit our girls when she wasn't much older than they were. Once, when they were playing softball in front of the house, Bettye pitched to Marty from about ten feet away, and was struck in the middle of the forehead by the fast-moving hardball from Marty's line drive. Within seconds, a bulge about one-half-inch high rose up on Bettye's forehead, just above her left eyebrow. Marty was scared to death until she saw that Bettye was all right, and soon they were both laughing about it.

When I told Don Pellerin and Ed Pio about my earlier experience playing in several bands, and wondered what it would take for me to get into the Watsonville Band, they told me to get a horn and come on down. I asked if there was a horn I could try to blow to see if I could make a noise on it. It had been thirty-two years since I had last played, at the University of Louisville and in the National Guard. Lundy told me to ask Warren Penniman, who mostly played baritone, but had been known to own a small tuba of some sort. Warren told me it was a very small E-flat tuba. I preferred to try a larger BB-flat Sousaphone, with which I could march more easily. I asked Gene Smith, a tuba player in the band, about finding a horn, and he advised me to go to a music store in San Jose, which often had bargains on musical instruments. Shirley and I drove to San Jose, found the store, and found a brand-new King BB-flat Sousaphone they would let me have for four hundred dollars. It had been ordered by the school system, which was going to pay eight hundred dollars for it, but they rejected it when someone found two tiny dents in it. This was my lucky day! At that price, I was willing to buy it even if I couldn't make any sound on it. It was a beautiful instrument. In a very few days my lip began to vibrate in the mouthpiece, just the way it once did. Two weeks after I bought the horn, I was at band practice on Wednesday night, and have been a member of the great Watsonville Band ever since—for thirty-three years.

It is hard for me to put into words what the Watsonville Band has meant to me. They have always been a close-knit family-oriented group, open to all ages, from teenagers to some members in their late eighties and early nineties. The joy of belonging to this organization and being able to continue playing music, long after playing in school music programs, is evident to all who have seen and heard them perform. Members of the band come from several different counties in the Monterey Bay area, but it is still called the Watsonville Band because it originally started here, many decades ago.

The band is completely self-supporting. No one in the organization receives any remuneration, including the director, business manager, and music librarian. All performances are free to the public, even though the band must pay exorbitant rental fees for use of some of the sites in which the free concerts are performed. Band booster membership fees provide some help, but most of the money needed for uniforms, music, and travel comes from the preparation and sale of artichoke hearts, mushrooms, and zucchini, deep-fried in a special, secret batter. Other food items sold include Icelandic cod, calamari, clam strips, shrimp, French fries, soft drinks, and coffee. The food is prepared in a specially designed trailer, which contains six huge deep fryers, using peanut oil only; a large hot table to keep food ready to serve; and a large mixer for the batter. This trailer is pulled to the location of several events during the year, such as the Antique Airplane Fly-in at the Watsonville Airport, the Monterey and Santa Cruz County Fairs, and the Gilroy Garlic Festival. Band manager Edward Pio also manages the food trailer operation.

Don Pellerin was band director for about eighteen months, and then the regular director, Gonzalo H. Viales, returned to assume the position after taking some time off. "Bert" Viales remained the director for some thirty-five years. I played under his direction for thirty years until he retired from the director's position. I am still a member of Bert's Pacific Brass Band, and still enjoy sitting next to him in the Thirsty Nine German Band and listening to his melodious double-belled euphonium, especially when he ad-libs "over the fence is out" at the end of some of the marches. This is a naughty little deviation from the standard last two measures of a march. It brings back to me fond memories of Mr. Norman, our band director at Ormsby Village, when he would sometimes use the same musical phrase on his cornet, when accompanying the band in the playing of some marches. I felt then that he was just clowning around, trying to lighten up a gloomy situation and have a little fun. I began playing this phrase occasionally, risking his reprimand, but he would just grin and chuckle a little. However, I never dared press my luck and let it slip out during a performance. The first time I heard Bert do it was in the German Band, which is a completely relaxed group, even before the first *"Ein Prosit der Gemütlichkeit"* is sung with raised krugs of beer.

When I joined the Watsonville Band, I sold my memberships in the two flying clubs. I had continued to fly for another ten years following the crash in Alaska. Having made so many long, over-water navigation flights during the war in the Pacific, I didn't feel as "gung ho" about being that far above the earth, especially with only one low-powered engine and a small fan keeping me aloft. Flying now, to me, was just a quick way to get to where the best fishing spots were. But I also got great pleasure from my association with the friendly crews of flying fishermen. Usually, there were three or four planeloads, and we would try to go to Baja every spring before Easter, to avoid extremely hot weather. Dave Willoughby was usually the instigator of the flights and "big daddy" of the group. I usually flew with him, Tony Meidl, Dr. Bill Franklin, or Dr. Tom Ford. We all were pilots and flew the club planes. Merle Weedon and Dr. Harlow Standage each had twin-engine Apaches. These getaways to Baja were a great way to relax and forget work.

After I sold my flying club memberships, Shirley and I were often invited by Tony Meidl to go deep-sea fishing in his small commercial-type boat out of Santa Cruz, in Monterey Bay. Over the years, we caught many tuna in their season, but most of the time we bottom-fished for ling cod and bluefish. We used some of the smaller bluefish for live bait. Shirley still brags about catching the very large ling cod on her tiny bait pole. One day when our total catch for the day was seven ling cod, she had caught five of them on the jigging bait pole, by gently teasing one to the surface while it was still holding onto a bluefish, then having one of us "big pole" fishermen ease a net under it before it let go of the bluefish or jerked it loose from the tiny jig hook. It took Tony and me some time to live that one down.

Playing in the band was also a great way to relieve the stresses of the workplace. Rehearsing or performing on the stage or on the street requires ridding the mind of any thoughts other than how to transform black-and-white notes from the paper page into pleasing tones from the horn. I didn't realize how much I had missed being in a band until I had rejoined one. I was soon playing tuba in the Thirsty Nine German Band and the Dixieland Band as well as the big marching and concert band.

At one time, the Watsonville Band played every year at the California State Fair in Sacramento and at various county fairs, in addition to its regular spring and Christmas concert series. It was about eight years after the Expo '67 trip that the band again started making trips out of the country. Shirley and I have been very fortunate to travel with the band on all of the foreign trips they have made since we joined. An attempt to write about everything worth recalling that happened on these trips would require enough pages to fill a sizable volume. I will condense it to a page or less.

Our first trip was to Honolulu, Hawaii, for the Aloha Festival parade. Three of our daughters, Mela, Judy, and Sara, made the trip with us, and we all had a wonderful time—that is, after I completed an arduous five-mile parade in the boiling-hot sun, carrying and blowing my thirty-six-pound Sousaphone. Next, we went to Mexico City, where we gave a special concert on their national television network, then to the Calgary Stampede in Canada, where the band won six thousand dollars for first place in the marching competition.

Our first European trip, via Iceland, included parades and concerts in Germany, Switzerland, and Vienna, Austria, for five nights, then behind the Iron Curtain to Budapest, Hungary, where we had the thrill of playing "The Stars and Stripes Forever," accompanied by the rhythmic applause of the audience. Next we flew to Auckland, New Zealand, paraded, and gave a concert on a program preceding the world-famous Auckland Brass Band. This trip to Down-under included a shorter flight from Auckland to Brisbane, Australia, where we were to represent the United States at the 1988 World's Fair, then by bus to Sydney for three nights. And finally back home, by way of

Honolulu, or the Fiji Islands, if preferred. Having been to Nadi, Fiji, many times during the war, I opted for Hawaii.

On the next trip, we returned to Europe—this time to London, Paris, Madrid, five nights on the Mediterranean at Costa del Sol; then to Seville, for yet another World's Fair; across the Strait of Gibraltar, for a day in Tangier, Morocco, that I'm still trying to forget; then to Lisbon, Portugal, and the flight home via New York City.

The next trip, our last one so far, was a pleasant surprise to everyone, especially to band manager Ed Pio. He had hoped, after months of great effort on his part, to get us invited to Washington, D.C., to participate in the 1996 Fourth of July parade down Constitution Blvd. Then he dreamed that maybe, through President Clinton's Chief of Staff, Leon Panetta, we might even be invited to play a two-hour concert for a private presidential party of some eight thousand invited guests, plus our band boosters, on the lawn of the White House's West Wing—hopefully, with the president at home. Everything went perfectly as planned. We even had our own cameraman, Pio's son Greg, and our personal video cameraman. The band, about eighty strong, in its colorful uniforms of gold and green with a red cummerbund, when viewed from the front against a background of our five shining Sousaphones, was a sight worth capturing on film, and often reviewing. I was really delighted to be parading in the capital, and I, for one, hadn't believed Pio could pull it off. I think I underestimated the influence of the band's longtime friend, Leon Panetta.

❧ White House Concert ☙

A fter an extensive security check of our identities, credentials, and musical instruments, we were directed to the White House, where we all lined up to use the downstairs bathroom, whether or not we really needed it—any excuse, to be able to tell our descendants we had peed in the White House, just as Lincoln often had.

When we began our pre-fireworks concert, I saw Mr. Panetta in the area between the band and the White House. Then, after a few selections by the band, President Clinton appeared on the second-floor balcony. He greeted the party guests and thanked the Watsonville Band for performing. He got a big laugh from the band when he wondered if Leon Panetta had anything to do with our replacing "his own" Marine Corps Band. We learned we were the first band ever to play for the Fourth of July celebration in their place. We learned Mr. Panetta had requested of Col. John Bourgeois, the Marine Corps Band director, that his home area band be allowed to play the gig, and he graciously agreed, probably thankful for the day off.

At rehearsals just before the concert, we had practiced Bill Clinton's high school song, and when he appeared on the balcony a second time, and was just leaving to go back into the White House, the band started playing his school song. He immediately came down to the band, with Panetta at his side. He was shaking his head and grinning broadly. They went to the front of the band and stayed there, listening to several selections. Bert and others tried to get him to sit and play in the saxophone section, but he bashfully declined. Then Bert asked him to select his favorite Sousa march, and he selected "Thunderer" or "Washington Post," I don't remember which. Bert tried to get him to direct it, but he begged off and acted a little embarrassed. When we played the march, he beat time with his fist through most of it, and really seemed to be enjoying himself. He then complimented the band on our performance and thanked us for the music. Then he put his arm around Bert's shoulder and thanked him personally. I couldn't believe it was really happening, and the following fireworks were the best I have ever seen.

My first trip to the nation's capital was back in 1937, when I was fresh out of the Navy's aviation mechanic school in Norfolk, Virginia. Then thirty years later, I was there with Shirley and our four girls. And now, after another thirty years, we were back again. Over the past sixty years, a few more marbled halls had been added, such as the Pentagon and the Senate Office Building. The Smithsonian exhibits had been added to and made more up-to-date, with some space-travel vehicles and the latest in electronics, but what attracted me most was the display of old tools and machinery. Included was Lindbergh's old Ryan high-winged monoplane that I had seen him land at Bowman Field in Louisville in 1927, the Grumman F3F-1 that, except for its color, was an exact replica of my old 3-F-18 on the *Saratoga* and *Lexington*.

The visit to Arlington made me deeply sad once again, when I could tell that more thousands of heroes had been honored here in the past sixty years. But the same old thrill returned when I saw the Washington Monument and the awe-inspiring statue of Kentucky's Abe Lincoln, sitting and smiling down at me. This very well could have been our last Watsonville Band trip, but it was truly one to remember.

Shirley and I have helped finance our band trips by putting in many hours in the band's food-concession trailer. Without this help, I don't believe we would have been able to go on all of them. They have given us many unforgettable memories of places and people we would have otherwise missed.

When Bert Viales, after thirty-five years, decided to retire from his position as director of the Watsonville Concert and Marching Band, he allowed the band enough time to select a suitable replacement. We were extremely fortunate to have a band member who had a vast amount of musical experience, and who applied for the position. Sylvester "Mac" McElroy had taught band music to high school students for over forty-five years, and had been playing French horn in the Watsonville Band for ten years. He had recently retired from his last position as music director at Monte Vista Christian High School, near Watsonville. When Bert announced his plan to retire, Mac was chosen as our new director.

Within a very short time, Mac has, with a seemingly endless supply of energy and almost fanatical dedication, demonstrated he was the best possible replacement for Maestro Viales. His ability to select the right concert music for a given audience is apparent in the audience's reaction and favorable comments. And Mr. Mac is continually encouraging this bunch of music-loving amateurs, and giving recognition to anyone who excels. I look forward to playing for many more years under his talented baton.

Now I can brag that I have played under the batons of George Gray and C. E. Norman at Ormsby Village, John Philip Sousa and Edwin Franco Goldman in Flint, Michigan, Eddie Wotowa at U of L, Bill Hildebrandt in the Kentucky National Guard Band, Don Pellerin, Bert Viales, and Sylvester McElroy in the Watsonville Band, and most recently, under the direction of Col. John R. Bourgeois, the conductor of the U.S. Marine Band at the White House. He served in this capacity during the tenure of five different presidents. Col. Bourgeois was a guest conductor of the Watsonville Band on April 12, 2002.

❧ Looking for Ancestors ❧

Many years ago, my sister Bettye came into possession of an old violin which, supposedly, had been made by one of our ancestors, in the 1800s. She gave the violin to me to keep it in the family. If our great-grandparents had left us some record of their lives and activities, there would be no doubt concerning the violin's history. Now, we can only wonder.

We do have positive proof that several generations of our family on the Settle side were designers and manufacturers of long rifles, during the early and middle part of the 1800s. These Settle long rifles were famous for their accuracy and were in great demand by early homesteaders during their migrations to Texas, and other states west of the Mississippi, before the Civil War. They were also greatly prized by early game-hunters. We have one of the rifles, with the barely visible name and date of manufacture, "W. F. Settle 1866," stamped into the metal behind the barrel. My father's brother, my uncle, was named Willis French Settle, after one of our ancestors who may have made this rifle; or it may have been made by an earlier W. F. (Felix) Settle.

A few years back, when our daughter, Bettye, and her family were stationed in Baumholder, Germany, as part of a U.S. Army component there, during their second tour of duty in Germany, Shirley and I had the good fortune of accompanying them on a one-week tour of a part of England. We were traveling in their Volkswagen Vanagon—seven of us, with our luggage. There were Bettye and her husband, Randy; their children, James, Charles, and Kathryn; and Shirley and I. It was slightly crowded, but we really were anxious to see England; and in Europe, distances between cities, and even from border to border across countries, are very short, comparatively speaking.

We crossed the English Channel from Brúgge, Belgium, to Dover, England. We chose to bypass London, driving straight across southern

England to Portsmouth, where we recalled the huge buildup of the costly invasion of Normandy. Then on to Plymouth, from where my ancestors are supposed to have set sail for America in the seventeenth and eighteenth centuries.

On our AAA map, we had found a town we had heard of named Settle, up in the northern Yorkshire region. With a very good highway to travel, on the "wrong" side of the road, we were in the town of Settle within a few hours. The town is just across the Ribble River from a sister town named Giggleswick. Someone recently suggested that I just as easily could have been named Jim Giggleswick, and I replied that now I am more giggles than wick.

Settle is a quaint little town, with a colorful Settle Coat of Arms at its entrance and its exit. Many of its stone buildings are several centuries old and are well preserved. We stayed at a bed-and-breakfast farmhouse that was four to five hundred years old. Massive wooden beams still supported the second floor, where we spent two nights. From there we enjoyed two partly-foggy daybreaks, looking out through a window opening that had been twisted out of square because of the sagging, well-worn floorboards. The green fields were sectioned off by fences of precisely piled stones collected from the fields. In the town, most of the old buildings appeared to be the original, block-stone structures. Some doorways have their dates of construction chiseled into the stone across the top, dating back to the sixteenth or seventeenth century. The stones were cleared from the land to make it more tillable and more suitable for herds of sheep. From the center of the town, the streets were inclined towards the outskirts. Slightly elevated above the center of town on the east side, we found a sign which designated that section "Cheap-side Settle." Shirley still laughs about that and tells me she's sure that's where I came from. I don't know what she means.

We collected anything we could find there with the name Settle on it—a book, napkins, programs, thimbles, placemats, etc.—things we would bring back home to give to our other daughters and to our Kentucky relatives. I wanted to say something about how expensive everything was as I calculated the totals in my head, but the thought of being called "Cheap-side Settle" gave me pause.

Now we plan to make a trip to the Jamestown, Virginia, area, in the near future, to follow more leads concerning the Settle, Walton, Carter, and Redford migrations from England, many of which ended up in Kentucky.

Reportedly, some of my ancestors settled in Virginia and owned some property there. Some others came west, apparently through the Cumberland Gap, to Daniel Boone's "Happy Hunting Grounds," and settled in central Kentucky. They may even have encountered some of Abe Lincoln's folks along the way. Who knows? All we know for sure is that William Settle, son of George Settle, built a house at Old Rocky Hill, Kentucky, near Glasgow, in 1803, and designed and made the first Settle long rifles. His sons, Simon and W. F. (Felix) Settle, carried on the rifle-making, and their sons also manufactured fine jewelry. These ancestors didn't leave their memoirs or a record of their lives, but the rifles that remain, long after their passing, have their names and a date to tell us some of their story.

It seems I have heard of some evidence that my siblings and my descendants may be related to a Walton who was the first Methodist minister in America. And I've heard that someone has even connected us to the line of descendants of George Walton, a signer of the Declaration of Independence and an early governor of Georgia. It would be interesting to know for sure. What I do know for sure is where I came from, what I have seen, felt, and tried to accomplish in the past four score and eight years, and I am attempting to record it for our progeny. If more of our ancestors had taken the time to leave us some remembrance of what their lives were like, there wouldn't be so many unanswered questions for our generation and those that follow.

While daughter Bettye and her family were stationed in Germany, we were able to visit there on four different occasions, and spent a total of ten months living on U.S. Army bases and traveling to the Netherlands, Belgium, England, France, Austria, and all over Germany. Counting time spent on these four trips, plus two European trips with the Watsonville Band, and an earlier Rhine River cruise trip, Shirley and I have spent over a year in Europe.

❧ Rock Hunting ❧

Our interest in geology and paleontology resulted from our many family trips to the Central California beaches, where we found agatized pieces of whalebone and smoothly rounded stones imbedded with many types of seashells. Then came car trips with the Gurnees and the Woods into the Coastal Range foothills, to collect fossilized, giant oyster shells, many over twelve inches long, turretella, and shark teeth.

A geology course at Hartnell College and field trips with its professor, Raymond Puck, greatly improved our knowledge of and interest in both rock-hunting and fossil identification. We became great friends with Raymond and he made other trips with us after we completed the geology course. One day we were discussing the upcoming construction of the Glen Canyon Dam at Page, Arizona. The purpose of this dam would be to hold back the Colorado River to form a huge lake, which would be called Lake Powell. This lake would cover up many interesting geological formations, ancient Indian cliff dwellings, and petroglyphs in the Navajo sandstone canyon walls in Utah.

The dam construction had already begun, and someone suggested the possibility of our taking a trip down the Colorado River by boat, to visit and photograph some of the features of the canyon that would be deep under water after the dam's completion. Dr. Wood had heard of a Georgie White who had a river-rafting operation called the Georgie White River Rats. She organized and led white-water rafting trips down the rapids of some rivers in the western part of the country, including parts of the Colorado River. And she just happened to have such a trip planned, from Hite, Utah, all the way down to Page, Arizona, where the bridge was already under construction. We found there was considerable interest shown by others who also wanted to make this rafting trip and see the area before it became flooded.

Avery Wood made reservations for himself, Raymond Puck, and me to be part of the rafting group, which would board inflated rubber rafts in the Colorado River at Hite, Utah, and cast off, to be carried downstream by the current and an outboard motor. The motor was helpful in steering the raft through the rapids, and during the landings and castoffs. We were to spend six nights along the length of the voyage to

Page and the dam site. In order to be able to complete this trip during the eight days of Easter week, I offered to fly the three of us and our luggage to Page, Arizona, where we were to stay in a motel, and then at daybreak on Sunday, we would be ferried by another small plane to Hite, Utah, to board the rafts.

We left Watsonville Airport in our club Bonanza, stopped for gas at Kingman, Arizona, and flew toward Flagstaff, to avoid flying too near the Grand Canyon. At Flagstaff, I planned to turn north and follow the highway to Page. East of Kingman, there were layers of cumulus clouds building up and I had planned to climb up and stay above them in the mountainous area, for better visibility and to avoid flying near the highest peaks. In order to climb, especially with our heavy load, the propeller had to be in high rpm and the throttle fully advanced. Our Bonanza propeller governor was electrically controlled, but for some reason, on this occasion, the governor failed to function, and I was unable to climb. Fortunately, there were still holes in the cloud layer, and through one of the holes, I was still able to see the ground below and a part of the highway. I made a sharp spiral down through a large hole, being very careful not to get into the clouds and lose my orientation. In mountainous country, flying can be treacherous. When we were down in the clear, flying just above Interstate 40 on our way back to Kingman, I gave a big sigh of relief. We landed at Kingman, rented a car, and drove to Page, arriving at the motel just before dark. The trip organizers had been worried when we didn't arrive on schedule, and were relieved when we finally checked in.

We were told that there were so many people signed up for the shuttle flights to Hite that there was no way we three late arrivers could be flown there during daylight hours, so an additional flight was scheduled for us that would take off just before dawn. The shuttle plane was a four-place Cessna, and the four of us, with our gear, would be quite a load. We were disappointed about having to fly mostly in the dark, because we had expected to get some good pictures from the air of Glen Canyon and the surrounding land formations.

The next morning our shuttle plane took off just before the break of dawn, and after about an hour's flight, the small plane suddenly banked steeply to the left, lost altitude rapidly, and leveled off, just before touching down on a flat creek bed that was being used as a makeshift landing strip. Now I realized why we had been advised not to try to fly to the boat-launching area. Also, we needed to have our means of transportation waiting at the end of the trip down the river.

The rubber raft transportation for the large group consisted of three separate units of three rubber boats each. Three large, inflatable boats, about twelve to fifteen feet long and about eight feet wide, were tied together as a unit. Each unit had a motor on the center boat. Georgie White steered the lead unit, and her two assistants steered the other two units. My slide pictures cover the whole trip, including the points of interest where we made landings and hiked, from one to three miles in some spots, to reach ancient petroglyphs, native Indian caves high in the canyon walls, Rainbow Bridge, and "Hole in the Rock," the spot where early Mormons dragged their wagon up a sheer cliff that had an incline approaching the perpendicular. At noon, box lunches were passed out, and water and soft drinks were always available. A few extra stops along the bank of the river were planned to coincide with and accommodate the inopportune physiological necessities of members of the party—then it was "the girls upstream; boys downstream." My ankle-length poncho served me well on such occasions.

When we stopped for the night to set up camp, hot food, mostly from cans, was prepared on campfires for dinner and breakfast. The food was very adequate, considering the fact we were just camping out. There were only a few rough rapids with white water, but they were exciting and we got splashed a few times. Geologist Puck had to hold his poncho over his maps and notebook at times. With his maps and papers, Raymond kept us informed about the names of all the layers of rocks and the ages of each. The weather turned cold and windy and there were even some flurries of snow. We hadn't taken along warm clothing because it was spring and this was supposed to be sort of a desert area, we thought. But I still think about this exciting trip and relive the experience whenever we view the slides.

On one of our nightly stops, we landed early enough to allow time for a long hike down a meandering streambed to reach the Rainbow Bridge, a gigantic arch of Navajo sandstone. We were told we could climb to its top at our own risk, but just a few people wanted to make the attempt. I still don't know how, or why, I did it, but I did. On one steep wall, it was necessary for me to remove my shoes so I could get a toehold in the rock crevices. I had to stuff my shoes and socks in my side pockets because I would need them later for walking on the gravelly flat areas. Once I had reached the top of the arch, I felt it was well worth the effort. The view from the top was spectacular. Avery and Raymond thought I was nuts to do it at my age—about forty-seven at the time—and a little overweight.

Georgie White was a nice-looking, but very rugged, outdoor-type person who ran a well-organized operation. She and her boatmen were quite skilled at handling the rafts, as well as the people being transported on them. Georgie led all the shore-side hikes and climbs and was quite agile. Still, she was congenial and patient with us slow hikers and not-so-agile climbers. We were all thankful for this trip she had organized, which allowed us to see many interesting things that will never be seen again.

The trip back home was uneventful. We drove from Page back to Kingman, stopping on the way at the Grand Canyon for more pictures, and an instructive lecture from Professor Puck. Then we turned in the rental car and loaded into the Bonanza. I started the engine, with the prop set for high rpm, and it seemed to work perfectly, allowing us to take off and climb normally. Back at the Watsonville Airport, I reported the malfunction to our mechanic, and I believe he replaced some parts, but I never did find out why it had to act up on that one critical occasion. Maybe we weren't supposed to be flirting with the mountains in those weather conditions.

When I got home, it was the day before Easter. Shirley and the girls had colored the Easter eggs for the annual hunt in our back yard. I was grateful to be safely back home, and have always been thankful to have a mate like Shirley, who was stuck at home with the children during their Easter holiday week out of school.

About twenty years or so after the Glen Canyon Dam was completed, Shirley and I were invited to accompany Everett and Doris Mollenhauer, our old flying buddies, on their trailer-houseboat for a week on Lake Powell, which was formed by the dam. This was an unforgettable experience. There is a dock near the dam where boats can be launched. Their houseboat was built like a trailer on the inside, but was actually a large boat, sitting on a trailer when on land. The surface of Lake Powell gives a panoramic reflection of the very tops of the hills we had seen earlier, on the River Rat cruise. Almost nothing of what we had seen on the river trip, along the original creek bed, is now visible. The one thing that hasn't changed is Rainbow Bridge. What has changed is its availability. Before the river was dammed and formed Lake Powell, we were required to hike about three miles in canyons, sometimes wading across creeks, in order to reach Rainbow Bridge. But now, there is a docking area a few feet from its base—and no one is allowed to approach too closely to it, let alone climb to its top. But the whole wide lake is beautiful and peaceful. We tried to fish, but got not a bite. Some people who had apparently fished there before advised us not to waste our time. So we just relaxed, enjoying the colorful reflections of the red Navajo sandstone in the glassy surface of the lake.

❧ Paleontology ❧

Most of our rock-hounding was accomplished in one-day trips, on a weekend, to areas fairly close to home. We made several trips to an area near Hollister, to dig for pretty, round crystal formations of selenite, and we had a large collection of them. They were from one-half inch to nine or ten inches in diameter. Then we learned of an area on the western slope of the San Joaquin Valley where some patients of mine had located sections of fossilized jawbones, with teeth still intact. These had once been part of a water-dwelling mammal known to paleontologists, and given the unusual name of *desmostylus*. This creature has been extinct since the Miocene epoch, some twelve million years ago, give or take a couple of long weekends, and the only evidence it ever existed is found in fragmentary pieces of the skull, but most often found are the teeth and jawbones. The crowns of the teeth are mostly circular or tubular in shape, and the molars have the appearance of clusters of two rows of the circular crowns. We have saved an interesting collection of them. The desmostylus is believed by some to have been related to the sea cow, manatee, or dugong. But other fossil findings indicate it probably had short legs, like a hippopotamus. It lived along the edge of the ocean, in the shallow water.

No other creature has been known to have teeth resembling those of the desmostylus, and that's how it got its strange name. The teeth we found are worn flat on the occlusal surface, probably indicating that it crunched seashells for food. No doubt the animal was too sluggish to catch fish.

On some of our trips to Kentucky in the motor home, we would cross the Ohio River and go east to the little town of Madison, Indiana. My brother, Garnett, lived there on the Schirmer farm for many years, and the Schirmers thought of him as one of the family. The farm is just a short drive from Madison, and is located near the Ohio River bank. Garnett had told us of many fossils lying around in the fields, and he would uncover more of them each time he plowed. He had told us some of them were shaped like the end of a cow's horn. When we saw the cone-shaped fossils, we identified them from our fossil book as tetracoral, sometimes called horned coral.

We hauled home boxes and bags of them, together with fossil sponges and other fossils from that area, and from the exposed river bottom at Falls of the Ohio River, near Jeffersonville, Indiana. These fossils supposedly lived in the Paleozoic Era, up until about one-quarter-billion years ago.

For a while, we did collect pretty rocks and had a tumbler to polish them, but we never got into the lapidary aspect of rock-hounding. To me, that was too much like dentistry to be a hobby.

❧ Woodworking ❧

My interest in working with wood was awakened way back in Gilder Grayson's carpenter shop at Ormsby Village. He permitted Boy Scout members to work in the shop under his supervision, and to use some of his large collection of tools to work on projects that could be submitted when applying for the carpentry merit badge. Mr. Grayson would also instruct us in the use of tools, and show us some of the techniques he had used over the years. He had learned the carpenter trade at the old LIS when he and his brother, Erby, were there.

Our residence of forty-five years on Beverly Drive in Watsonville was built and occupied by Cliff Rosenbaum in 1953. He also built and installed all of the cabinetwork for the many homes he had built on Beverly Drive. At the rear of his home, he built a large woodworking shop, and when we purchased the house, the shop was ready-built for us to use for our woodworking projects. Shirley had used it for several years for her Girl Scout troop as their meeting place. During the years, we have purchased all the machinery needed for making most anything with wood. We have built some furniture for the home, but most of our woodworking projects have been things our daughters have needed and requested, mostly bookcases, desks, and stereo cabinets. For our daughter Sara's preschool and day-care business, we made little-people's chairs (twelve so far), three tables, three full-sized bookcases, and a cubbyhole cabinet for fifteen or so of her children to store their things in.

My next project will be making three short storage cabinets for daughter Mela. She needs them as a place for her four-year-old daughter Sarah's toys, to keep them off the floor. Some forty years ago, I started on an oak roll-top desk. It's about two-thirds complete, but I got sidetracked by the need for more useful furniture.

Shirley and I enjoy keeping both physically and mentally active by doing yard work by day, and reading or working crossword puzzles at night, while watching the news or Turner Classic Movies—no cursing. And I try to practice my tuba for one hour each day, concentrating on the music for upcoming concerts of Mac's big Watsonville Band, or Bert's Pacific Brass Band. The Thirsty Nine German Band performs about six or eight times throughout the year, mostly during Oktoberfest.

❧ The Pettit Building Revisited ☙

During our visit to my sister Bettye's home in Fairdale in September and October 2001, we attended the reunion of past Ormsby Village citizens. The only alumnus who attended who had known of me was eighty-one-year-old Hansford Frederick. His daughter, Olivia, is now the chief archivist of Jefferson County, and was kind enough to provide me with many copies of news articles and pictures of Ormsby Village from her holdings.

Dr. William Morison, history professor and Chief of Archives at the University of Louisville, invited Shirley, sister Bettye, and me to visit his archives office, and then invited us all to lunch at the exclusive University Club.

When our daughter Bettye flew in from the coast to join us for the Ormsby Village reunion, she and I revisited Dr. Morison, and he was kind enough to take the time to accompany us on a tour of the U of L campus. He pointed out parts of the old stone wall, which is now about three feet high, and then took us into what remains of the original Pettit Building, in which I was sheltered some eighty years earlier. We used an elevator to reach the third floor, and I could look out the same window from which I remembered seeing the old Ford Motor Company building and its water tank. The building is still there, but has been renamed, as has the Pettit Building. The floors of all the rooms of the Pettit Building were carpeted, so we were not able to see the old wooden floorboards where we kids knelt and scrubbed so many times.

Then we were allowed to climb the original steep stairs to the attic. I was thankful I was allowed to be up there again and to touch the same old rough, heavy, oaken beams that supported the roof of this three-story, brick house, which had given me and many other young boys refuge from the weather and the world outside. This had been my "house of refuge," and it was now difficult for me to conceal my choked-up feelings. Dr. Morison and my daughter Bettye also seemed to thoroughly enjoy this journey into my past.

Long ago, during my two-year stay there, we young inmates had spent much of our spare time playing in the tall, three-story, steel, silo-shaped fire escape outside the back of the original building. Inside this six-feet-in-diameter cylinder was a slick, spiral steel slide, which was our introduction to a sliding-board. I don't remember that this was an approved recreational activity, but anything forbidden, at that age, seemed to be more enjoyable. I'm sorry the fire escape is no longer there. I would have loved to touch it again.

UNIVERSITY OF CALIFORNIA

COLLEGE OF DENTISTRY
UNIVERSITY OF CALIFORNIA MEDICAL CENTER
SAN FRANCISCO 22, CALIFORNIA

December 21, 1950

Dr. James W. Settle
213 E. Lake Ave.
Watsonville, California

Dear Doctor Settle:

We are pleased to inform you that you are eligible to become an
alumni member of the Rho Rho Chapter of Omicron Kappa Upsilon,
the national dental scholastic honor society. Rho Rho Chapter
of Omicron Kappa Upsilon was organized in 1914 to promote scholarship and honorable character among students of dentistry. Former
graduates may be elected to alumni membership provided their standing as students would have made them eligible for membership, such
eligibility, however, being conditional upon an ethical and unblem-
ished record since graduation. As you were one of the highest 12
per cent in your class, you are most cordially invited to join this
society. Your acceptance to this invitation to membership should
be forwarded to the office of the secretary-treasurer prior to
January 15, 1951.

There is a $4.00 initiation fee, $2.00 of which goes to the Supreme
Chapter for the certificate of membership; and it is left to your
choice whether you want ot obtain the OKU key for which an additional $6.00 should be enclosed. Should you accept membership, would you
please advise as to how you wish your name to appear on the certificate of membership. Please make checks payable to Charles W. Craig.

The present officers will be happy to welcome you as a member of this
society which has done so much for dentistry and from which we can
all benefit.

Very sincerely yours,

Edmund V. Street, President

George A. Hughes, Vice-President

Hermann Becks, President-Elect

Charles W. Craig, Secretary-Treasurer

CC/pm

Letter inviting me to join Omicron Kappa Upsilon

SELECTIVE SERVICE SYSTEM

ORDER TO REPORT FOR INDUCTION

LOCAL BOARD NO 59
Santa Cruz County

Civic Auditorium
Santa Cruz, California

(LOCAL BOARD DATE STAMP WITH CODE)

Dec. 29, 1954
(Date of mailing)

The President of the United States,

To ____ James _____ W. _____ Settle _____ 3D | 4 | 59 | 13 | 41

(First name) ____ (Middle name) ____ (Last name) ____ (Selective Service Number)

21 Bronson St.
(Street and number)

Watsonville, Calif.
(City) ____ (State)

GREETING:

Having submitted yourself to a Local Board composed of your neighbors for the purpose of determining your availability for service in the armed forces of the United States, you are hereby ordered to

report to the Local Board named above at **Pacific Greyhound Depot, 702 Front St., Santa Cruz, Calif.**
(Place of reporting)

at ____ 6:55 A.m., on the ____ 30th _____ day of ____ March _____, 19 55, for
(Hour of reporting)
forwarding to an induction station.

This Local Board will furnish transportation to the induction station where you will be examined, and, if accepted for service, you will then be inducted into a branch of the armed forces.

Persons reporting to the induction station in some instances are found to have developed disqualifying defects since being examined and may be rejected for these or other reasons. It is well to keep this in mind in arranging your affairs, to prevent any undue hardship if you are rejected at the induction station. If you are employed, you should advise your employer of this notice and of the possibility that you may not be accepted at the induction station. Your employer can then be prepared to replace you if you are accepted, or to continue your employment if you are rejected.

If you are not accepted, return transportation will be provided.

Willful failure to report promptly to this Local Board at the place specified above and at the hour and on the day named in this notice is a violation of the Selective Service Act of 1948, and subjects the violator to fine and imprisonment.

You must keep this form and bring it with you when you report to the Local Board. Bring with you sufficient clothing for 3 days.

If you are so far removed from your own Local Board that reporting in compliance with this Order will be a serious hardship and you desire to report to a Local Board in the area of which you are now located, go immediately to that Local Board and make written request for transfer of your delivery for induction, taking this Order with you.

Mary Ann Thomas
Member of Local Board.

U. S. GOVERNMENT PRINTING OFFICE: 1948 O—792517

16—18271-1

Letter ordering me to report for induction

6-22-55

Dear Colonel Settle:

We have been informed by our Commander-in-Chief, Governor Lawrence W. Wetherby, that you have been appointed as Aide-de-Camp on his staff with the rank of Colonel.

This appointment made you eligible for membership in the Honorable Order of Kentucky Colonels, an organization started in 1933 for the express purpose of making Kentucky Colonels everywhere proud of their commission and association.

It is our pleasure to enclose your membership card for the current year.

Very truly yours,

Colonel Anna Friedman,
Secretary and Keeper of the Great
Seal,
The Honorable Order of Kentucky
Colonels.

AF:mp

Letter appointing me to the Kentucky Colonels

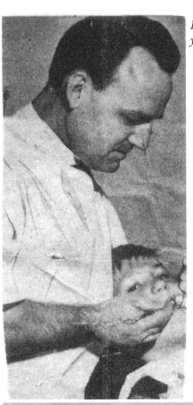
Dr. Settle works on a young patient

Mexico Trips

Round Island

Dr. Franklin and friend at Mazatlán, Mexico

Above: The day's catch at Puerto Vallarta. Below: The day's catch at the Hotel Oasis Loreto in Baja.

Alaska Trip, Summer 1958

James & Shirley by Stinson Flying Station Wagon at Fort Yukon, Alaska, July 1958

Plane's owner, Everett Molenhauer, with Shirley

Shirley wearing sheepskin-lined jacket with wolverine-lined hood, Fairbanks, Alaska, 1958

Above and below: Our "shortest landing" at Seldovia, Alaska, airport. Kachemak Bay in background

Homer Spit, Kachemak Bay, Alaska, 1958

Homecoming: Shirley is greeted by our four daughters

Watsonville Band

Herr Ziesing and the Thirsty Nine, mid-1980s

The Thirsty Nine German Band with Budweiser Clydesdale horses in Stockton, California

Above and below: Feldkirch, Austria, June–July, 1985

Jim Settle on European tour with Watsonville Band, summer 1985

Shirley Settle and Kay Burtness at band concession booth

Jim Settle, Gene Smith & Brian Kane practicing for Watsonville Band parade in Auckland, New Zealand, June 28, 1988—my seventy-fifth birthday. (Photo by Wal Britton, © The Auckland Sun.)

Above and below: Parade down Constitution Avenue

Jim O'Briant, Guy Welty, Brian Kane, Bill Baken & Jim Settle

Two-hour concert at the White House

Chief of staff Leon Panetta, President Bill Clinton, and Maestro Bert Viales discussing performance

Left: Watsonville Band on steps of White House West Wing

Band manager Ed Pio gets a laugh from President Bill Clinton

The White House reflected in the bell of my Sousaphone

Fourth of July Parade, 2000

Still tooting at 87

Tired and still smiling

John Philip Sousa (1854–1932). At age twenty-six, Sousa was appointed Director, U.S. Marine Band, Washington, D.C. He grew the beard to appear older and more dignified.

Col. John R. Bourgeois (guest conductor of the Watsonville Band, April 4 & 5, 2002), Director of "The President's Own" U.S. Marine Band, White House Coordinator (1979–1996), under five different presidents. Col. Bourgeois is holding Sousa's baton.

I am fortunate to have had the privilege and honor of playing under the direction of both of these great band musicians.

Searching for Roots . . . in England

The towns of Settle and Giggleswick as seen from the Castleberg, Yorkshire, England

The Settle coat of arms

. . . and in Kentucky

The floral clock at the state capitol in Frankfort, Kentucky

Nine "Belles of Louisville" on the Ohio River

Sister Bettye's cozy cottage on the lake at South Park Country Club

Taking the girls to the swimming hole across the lake

THE
UNIVERSITY OF
LOUISVILLE

Dwayne D. Cox
and
William J. Morison

For James W. Settle – This land was your home before it became U of L's main campus! Thank you for writing about Sept. Colvin. Best wishes.

– W.J. Morison

Oct. 2, 2000

THE UNIVERSITY PRESS OF KENTUCKY

Inscription in book given to James by University of Louisville archivist William Morison

Left: U of L archivist, Dr. William Morison, listens as Dr. Settle recalls his youth

Left: A touching experience in the attic of the old Pettit Building

View of Ford Building and water tank from Pettit Building window

The clock on the Colgate-Palmolive Building—my view from the Detention Home as a child

Postscript: Looking Back

For the writing of my memoirs, I keep a little tablet by my lounge chair, and jot down things as I visualize them. It has been an exciting experience for me as I recall and relive in my mind all the things I have seen and done. When I project myself back to those simpler days, and recall how I was influenced and directed by those good leaders at Ormsby Village toward a happy and productive life, I realize how fortunate I was that there was such a place, and such people there, for George and me. With the Boy Scout Oath as a guide, we were taught to respect our families, including other children in the home, to show reverence to a Supreme Being, to be helpful to others, and to love our country.

In the years past, I was greatly influenced by the works of the literary giants of English poetry and prose, and have conveniently borrowed tidbits from them, all of which we were required to commit to memory at the orphanage school. I have used some phrases which helped to curb my early anxieties, and others which gave me guidance through a confusing and sometimes lonely youth, and far beyond.

To me, the letters KKK would come to mean Khayyam, Kipling,

and Keats. I had refused to be cooped and crawling under Omar's "inverted bowl they call the sky." From Kipling's poem, "If," I learned to "keep my head when all about me" were successfully starting their engines, while I failed to do so. I also learned to "walk with kings, nor lose the common touch." And I've always tried to "fill the unforgiving minute with sixty seconds' worth of distance run." And, after a lifelong love of music, I'm touched by young Keats' "ere music's golden tongue flattered to tears this ancient man, and poor."

When my old Navy friend, F. A. (Flat Ass) Warren, nicknamed me Molar-Chipper, I never dreamed that my ultimate profession and means of a good livelihood would involve me in the "chipping" of thousands of molars, as well as bicuspids, canines, and incisors.

Maybe because I have always pictured my sad, little mother as an angel, I have always had a deep respect for all womankind. My sister Bettye has told me that the last words spoken by my mother were, "Take care of my children." Some say she died of a broken heart, because she was helpless, and we looked so vulnerable.

For my sister Bettye's whole life, and even now, at age ninety-five, she has looked after the other four of us in every way she could. When George and I were in the orphanage, we always knew she was nearby and she saw us as often as she could. Her little home on the lake at South Park in Fairdale, Kentucky, has always been a place where we all feel welcomed and completely at home. Garnett, Marie, and George and Evelyn all lived with her for many years.

For the past forty years, Shirley and I have returned each year to Kentucky, usually via Denver, to visit Shirley's family, and then on to my sister Bettye's home for a stay of several weeks. We, our daughters, and our grandchildren have always felt welcome there and look forward to each visit. It has now been eighty years since our young mother spoke her last words, and throughout these many years, sister Bettye has done a wonderful job of taking care of our mother's children.

In relating this long story of my life, as I remember it, and as I recall how I dealt with each disappointment and convinced myself that maybe it was for the best whenever I was detoured into a different endeavor, it was not easy for me to forget my early dreams of becoming a test pilot and reaching for the stars. But then, when I finally succeeded in becoming a dentist and resumed playing the tuba, I could tell myself that I had almost made my youthful dreams a reality, because space pioneer John Glenn's father-in-law was a dentist, and Neil Armstrong, first man on the moon, once played the tuba!

Bibliography and Photograph Credits

Note: New materials are constantly available in the library and on the Internet. Please check these resources as well as your local veterans' associations, museums, and docents who may give tours of the historical sights and lectures of the past.

Cox, Wayne D. and William J. Morison. *The University of Louisville.* University Press of Kentucky, 1999. Louisville House of Refuge and Industrial School of Reform pictures.

Fredrickson, Olivia. Jefferson County, Kentucky, Archives. Jefferson County Parental Home and Ormsby Village pictures.

Keefer, Bob, Flight Engineer. Pictures of Capt. Lee Weatherhead's crew.

Kentucky Military Institute 1928–29 Catalog and 1931 Yearbook. KMI pictures and information.

Mattingly, Charles. *American Air Navigator.* Consairway navigation pictures and information.

Ormsby Village. *The Villager,* a school publication of Ormsby Village history 1925–1950. History and photos of the schoolhouse and cottages, including earlier history.

Settle, James W., D.D.S. Personal scrapbooks, photos, and memorabilia, including naval photos.

Sousa, John Philip. *Sousa: The Complete Marches,* record album. Photo of Sousa in band uniform.

Spight, Edwin and Jeanne. *Eagles of the Pacific, Consairways . . . Memoirs of an Air Transport Service during World War II.* Historical Aviation Album, P.O. Box 33, Temple City, CA 91780, 1980.

Thompson, David. *Consairway, an Airman's Airline.* San Diego, CA, May 1994. Consairway personnel, planes, bases, and quotes.

U.S. Naval photographs. Museums and Internet sources. Naval aircraft carriers and planes at sea.

Watsonville Band. Davis Photography, Greg Pio Photography.

Books Available From Robert D. Reed Publishers

Please include payment with orders. Send indicated book/s to:

Name:_____

Address:_____

City:_____ State:_____ Zip:_____

Phone:(_____)_____ E-mail:_____

Titles and Authors	Unit Price
_____ *The Beanery: A Village Called Ormsby* by James W. Settle	$24.95
_____ *Brain Teasers* by Kiran Srinivan	9.95
_____ *Gotta Minute? The ABC's of Successful Living* by Tom Massey, Ph.D., N.D.	9.95
_____ *Gotta Minute? Practical Tips for Abundant Living:* *The ABC's of Total Health* by Tom Massey, Ph.D., N.D.	9.95
_____ *Gotta Minute? How to Look & Feel Great!* by Marcia F. Kamph, M.S., D.C.	11.95
_____ *Gotta Minute? Yoga for Health, Relaxation & Well-being* by Nirvair Singh Khalsa	9.95
_____ *Gotta Minute? Ultimate Guide of One-Minute* *Workouts for Anyone, Anywhere, Anytime!* by Bonnie Nygard, M.Ed. & Bonnie Hopper, M.Ed.	9.95
_____ *A Kid's Herb Book for Children of All Ages* by Lesley Tierra, Acupuncturist and Herbalist	19.95
_____ *House Calls: How we can all heal the world one visit at a time* by Patch Adams, M.D.	11.95

Enclose a copy of this order form with payment for books. Send to the address below. Shipping & handling: $2.50 for first book plus $1.00 for each additional book. California residents add 8.5% sales tax. We offer discounts for large orders.

Please make checks payable to: **Robert D. Reed Publishers.**
Total enclosed: $_____. See our website for more books!

Robert D. Reed Publishers
P.O. Box 1992, Bandon, OR 97411
Phone: 541-347-9882 • Fax: 541-347-9883
Email: 4bobreed@msn.com • www.rdrpublishers.com